D1519895

SOCRATES AND THE IRRATIONAL

SOCRATES AND THE IRRATIONAL

|| JAMES S. HANS

UNIVERSITY OF VIRGINIA PRESS

CHARLOTTESVILLE AND LONDON

University of Virginia Press
Printed in the United States of America on acid-free paper

First published 2006

9 8 7 6 5 4 3 2 1

LIBRARY OF CONGRESS CATALOGING-IN-PUBLICATION DATA

Hans, James S., 1950–
    Socrates and the irrational / James S. Hans.
        p.   cm.
    Includes bibliographical references and index.
    ISBN-13: 978-0-8139-2553-0 (cloth : alk. paper)
    1. Socrates.   2. Plato.   3. Reason.   I. Title.
    B319.H36 2006
    183′.2—dc22

                                 2006004912

IN MEMORY OF MY MOTHER

FOR MY FATHER

.

CONTENTS

ACKNOWLEDGMENTS

THANKS, as always, to Hilma and Heather, to Allen Mandelbaum for his long support of my work and well-being, to Ed Wilson, Dick Martin, and Carola Sautter for their regular encouragement over the years, to Eric Wilson, to Mary Pendergraft for carefully reading the manuscript and offering valuable advice, and to the outside readers of the press for their excellent suggestions. Thanks especially to Cathie Brettschneider at the University of Virginia Press for her expert attention throughout.

I would also like to thank Wake Forest University for a leave that helped me complete the manuscript and for funds that assisted in the preparation of it as well.

SOCRATES AND THE IRRATIONAL

INTRODUCTION

SOCRATIC DIVAGATION/DIVINATION

SOCRATES has long been one of the exemplary figures of Western civilization. As a result, it is not surprising that our idea of him has been susceptible to many interpretations over the millennia, including the various prisms through which he was construed in his own day. If some have believed the Delphic Oracle's declaration that Socrates was the wisest person in Athens, others have seen him as a wily individual who was capable of twisting the rhetoric of any particular discussion to suit his own ends. If he remains one of the original embodiments of the idea of reason, he also possesses irrational inclinations that too often are ignored. Like his protégé Plato, Socrates can be seen as someone who wants to impose a dogmatic ideology on people for the good of the community, but he is fully capable of celebrating the heterogeneity of humanity as well. He acknowledges his own ignorance and demonstrates a willingness to see what comes next. If he has been construed as the essential gadfly of Athenian society, the chief mechanism through which the most important questions are asked, he has also been declared the greatest danger to the city because there is nothing to stop his mad questions, no civilizing impulse that will constrain him when the city is threatened and immediate action must be taken.

When thinking about Socrates, one must invariably ask why he has been so deified and demonized from his own day down to the present. Socrates seems most often remembered as the master of reason. We imagine him as the figure who inaugurated the Western mode of being by insisting that all arguments be examined rationally and coolly without regard for prejudgments or irrational biases. Time and again in Plato's dialogues, we see Socrates in this guise, and he gives reason a good name. His method—*elenchus*—is specifically designed to sort things into carefully delineated categories, thereby determining what is and isn't the case. This kind of analysis can be thought of as a practice of reason, and there are also many cases in the dialogues where Socrates uses specific forms of logic that are demonstrably rational. For the most part, though, his idea of reason is based on simple analysis, on inferring qualities and characteristics from previous evidence and drawing conclusions that lead to further analysis. In this way Socrates systematically manages to strip concepts of the illusions that have been attached to them. We may often end up not understanding very much in particular about truth, justice, or *arete,* but we learn a great deal about what they are not, and this is as important to our understanding as knowing specific definitions. If Socrates had done nothing more than employ analysis so masterfully, he would have been entitled to his place of honor in our history.

At the same time, it is hard to ignore the fact that Socrates' mode of analysis is connected to other characteristics that aren't quite so rational. Socrates is also famous for his irony, so much so that the term *Socratic irony* is an essential part of our vocabulary. As with the idea of reason at the center of Socrates' mode of thought, his irony is various. In some respects, it is a function of his eagerness to lay snares for his interlocutors—often through flattery—that induce them to contradict themselves. In turn this ironic mode is related to Socrates' lifelong profession of ignorance. It is a function of pretending to respect the seeming wisdom of one's interlocutors while showing that they are in fact *savantasses,* individuals who make a vain display of learning but really know very little. Socratic irony, though, goes beyond probing a category mistake to show that specific expertise doesn't lead to general wisdom. The dialogues may in theory be committed to the rational elucidation of the properties of human existence, but their methods are often based on a kind of Odyssean wiliness that is designed to humiliate people as much as it is to get to the bottom of things. Socrates clearly relishes the moments when he catches his interlocutors in a violation of the law of noncontradiction. This is a form of pleasure so common to our species that it is found even—perhaps especially—in the young, who love to show their parents the absurdity of their ways, who enjoy demonstrating their mastery over past thinkers by pointing out their contradictions. To contradict oneself is to be negated.

What is striking about the wiliness that induces Socrates to embarrass his interlocutors is that he is smart enough to realize the harmful effects these public hazings have on his reputation, yet he seems helpless against the impulse to strip individuals of their pretensions. Perhaps his commitment to reason was so strong that nothing else mattered: as long as he could provide rational arguments for his positions and bolster the great power of reason, he achieved his goals. But if he was at the same time undermining those goals by alienating people through his irony, he was diminishing the chances for reasonable discourse rather than enhancing them. Even if one accepts that there are individuals who are so foolish they deserve public exposure, there are many occasions when people could be more convincingly brought to reason by gentler methods than Socrates'. One wonders why he was so little interested in gauging his stratagems to fit the particular audience at hand.

Reason and irony in Socrates easily rub up against another of his characteristics, his wisdom. For all practical purposes, they are inseparable. In some respects, the attribution of wisdom is little more than a nod to Socrates' rational abilities: anyone who can wield the analytic knife as carefully as he can is in some narrow sense wise. One might even go so far as to link his wisdom to his irony, for, again, he instinctively knows how to root out the weaknesses in other people's arguments, which takes a high degree of intelligence. But I think even Socrates would see these attributes as skills rather than wisdom. The practitioner of reason has acquired intricate techniques in order to analyze situations carefully, but he is hardly wise as a result. Irony is similarly based on mastering specific interpersonal skills, and whereas we might admire the individual who has developed the ironic stance, the techniques inherent in the strategy don't apply to the whole of life and therefore don't qualify as wisdom.

However true and simple Socrates' admissions of ignorance are, people today are as susceptible to the weakness Socrates points out as any of the early Greeks were. Those who have expertise in one area too easily generalize what they understand and assume they know much more about other things than they do. This is readily apparent in most academic fields, where people who are praised for their intelligence and learning in specific areas too often assume they know more about the world as a whole than they do. Surely, they think, their extensive knowledge qualifies them to be a spokesperson for a whole range of human behavior. Analysis itself is problematic without both a specific knowledge of the subject matter and the synthetic ability to draw the proper conclusions from one's analysis. Likewise, the ability to memorize certain documents confers no specific benefits beyond the ability to remember the details of the material. It doesn't necessarily translate into anything that can be usefully employed in other domains. Inasmuch as Socrates recognizes what he does and doesn't know, he truly is wise in a way that virtually no one else is.

Having said as much, one must also concede that Socrates' ignorance is a ruse used to snare interlocutors. Even if Socrates only acknowledges that he has no specific form of expertise, he is smart enough to know that such a declaration can induce others to think they have the upper hand. Because they possess some kind of knowledge, they believe they are superior to one who claims none and so are easily led down the wrong track by their mistaken assumption. One of Socrates' salient characteristics is that his behavior is more obviously overdetermined than most other people's. As Nietzsche might put it, so many different capacities inhere in the man that he stands out in contrast to us. This variousness allows Socrates to be sincere in his protestations of ignorance even as he knows that others will mistake him for less than he is as a result, even as he knows this will be a good stratagem to show how people presume more about their knowledge than they should.

It is worth emphasizing that the word *overdetermined* doesn't simply mean *multifarious,* for one can be multifarious without being overdetermined. Having a variety of capacities makes one multifarious, but an overdetermined individual is one whose capacities can't be reduced to a coherent framework. The capacities are at odds with each other, cannot be reconciled, cannot be assumed under the law of noncontradiction. Socrates is sincere in his admission of ignorance, but he is insincere in his use of this admission to lure gullible victims to their humiliation. He is committed to discovering what we know and don't know, but he is also endlessly playful, indifferent to the outcome of his inquiries. Even worse, he uses his inquiries to diminish individuals he doesn't like and to build up his regard with those with whom he wishes to curry favor. He pursues completely disinterested inquiry into the nature of things and hopes to seduce the boy sitting next to him at the same time. These impulses and characteristics cannot be reconciled, and one seems to cancel out the others. But that is not so in everyday life, so Socrates' wisdom is ironic in about five different ways and very unstable as a result. He is not to be trusted.

Socrates' admission that he has no specific forms of knowledge doesn't mean that he lacks wisdom. He may be wise beyond others in spite of the fact that he has no expertise, can lay claim to no body of knowledge, and has had no formal training that would give him bragging rights over anything. Wisdom is not a function of either knowledge or information, and in some respects it is antithetical to both. Information is the simple accumulation of data, a capacity that requires certain gifts, but not something that produces wisdom; knowledge makes use of certain kinds of information, but its forms of analysis and synthesis are far more important to what it offers than the mere accumulation of data: one must know how to assess the data in order to have knowledge. Wisdom is not based on either information or knowledge. It is much closer to a form of divine inspiration, a specialized kind of intuition that isn't derived from the steady accumulation of facts or the assiduous analysis of those facts and the inferences that are drawn from them. Wisdom emanates from an intuitive sense of the world and its dynamics. It is found in those people who are most acutely aware of the ways in which their lives are attached to the relational dynamics around them. Without that profound sense of attachment to the world, wisdom is not possible. In this respect it is quite different from knowledge, which at least until recently was assumed to be based on neutrality, objectivity, and disinterestedness. Wisdom is neutral and disinterested in its own way, but not from lack of attachment. It is based on knowing that there is no separation between the world and one's being, that the one flows into and out of the other in a constant interplay.

In our own world, wisdom has almost disappeared. It cannot be easily employed for the accumulation of wealth, status, or power, the central goals of our social system. It follows that wisdom is beside the point. So we acknowledge it in various Eastern religions and note its presence in the Dalai Lama, but for the most part we are not interested. And because we see it as the possession of religious mystics, we lack the capacity to discern the wisdom of Socrates. He has some of the same existential features of the clichéd version of the Eastern mystic—he has no money, not much of a home, no particular place in the sociopolitical scheme of things, and seems about as central and as completely marginal as any holy figure might be. His indifference to status and wealth might also be seen as a mark of wisdom, particularly for individuals who seldom think about anything else.

At the same time, Socrates lacks the otherworldliness and piety of a religious mystic, and he is far from being mystical. However much he believes in the wisdom of his daimonion, or inner voice, he is not really a poet, prophet, or diviner. He no more chants the past, present, and future the way the poet does than he descries the nature of things by reading various signs, than he prophesies the future of Athens through his endless discussions in the agora. He is not a holy figure in any sense, pretends to no special form of awareness beyond his daimonion and his willingness to listen to what the gods tell him. And yet, he is said to be the wisest person in Athens.

What constitutes the nature of Socrates' wisdom beyond the fact that he is much more aware of what he doesn't know than we are? Should we assume, as Socrates does at times, that the Oracle meant nothing more than that no human being is wise? Or is he truly wise in some sense that we miss because we are too insistent on seeing the wonders of his irony or the splendid gift of reason so regularly on display? I would argue that Socrates is wise in specific ways that are linked to his keen awareness of what he doesn't know. The knowledge of his ignorance, for example, is crucial when it comes to listening to the voice of his daimonion: he does what it says, regardless of whether he realizes it is right or not, because he believes the voice speaks the truth. This response is based on his awareness that the daimonion has never steered him wrong in the past, but it is also a reflection of his ignorance: he doesn't know why the voice tells him what it does, but he goes along with it anyway.

Although Socrates never asserts that he relies on intuition for his sense of what to do next in his life—or in an argument, for that matter—he does precisely that on many occasions, just like everyone else. However much he is committed to reasoning things out, he is always attentive to the flow of discourse and knows how to respond to it. The very fact that he respects prophets, diviners, and poets in most of the dialogues shows that he has the greatest regard for the wisdom that is available to humans only through intuitive means. A brief glance at a typical dialogue quickly shows how much Socrates navigates by the same intuitional devices we employ. This is obvious, for example, when he considers a good spot for a dialogue: he takes in the ambience, assesses its virtues and limitations, and decides that, yes, by the plane tree would be a good place for a talk because it is quiet, remote, and comfortable. These are aesthetic decisions, based on intuition. They are the source of wisdom, however small and insignificant they may seem. Socrates is a master of such moments, even though he can get carried away by dialogue and lose sight of his local context as well.

Intuitive wisdom makes itself most apparent in Socrates' life in the various dialogues that involve a flow of conversation. Socrates characterizes this process as "divine wandering" on any number of occasions, reflecting his awareness that dialogues are works of magic, interchanges of words that have a life of their own, to which the interlocutors must respond if they are to heed the call of discourse. However much dialogues depend on reason, on setting one thing next to another and analyzing its pertinence, they are driven by the flow of words, by the omnipotence of the dialogue itself as it masters the participants. Socrates may seem in control of the dialogue because he is the one who is most attentive to the drift of things, knowing when the words have taken the interlocutors one place rather than another, responding in kind to whatever appears in the stream of discourse. Far from being in charge, though, Socrates achieves mastery through listening, from his acute awareness of where the words have gone as a result of the mutual exchange among the participants. There is no more intuitive source than this process through which a human assesses the appropriateness of something based on the relationships that have been established through the larger processes in which one participates. This is what Socrates has mastered, in dialogue and in life.

Socrates is the master of reason, but he is so only because he is even more a master of the intuitive nuances of contexts. He may be best known for analyzing questions from many angles, but we have been so taken up by his uses of reason that we have lost sight of the more basic manner in which he intuitively determines what goes next to what, what topic flows from what has already taken place, what argument moves forward and which one is circular, when to end the dialogue because nothing further will be learned in the current context. These all involve intuitive steps along an irrational path that is based on affective cues rather than the light of reason, and no rational argument could take place without careful attention to these nuances. Wisdom in the positive sense is an intuitive reliance on the irrational affects of contexts for cues on how to proceed, an endeavor that may also be connected to the insight that comes from knowing what one doesn't know. It is Socrates' greatest strength. If he were only a master reasoner, he would not have been able to maintain his place in our imaginations for so long.

If Socrates is both wise and wily, if he is both rational and yet highly dependent on the irrational flows of life, he is also an essential gadfly to the city of Athens and its greatest threat. Too often we assume he is one or the other when it is impossible to separate the two. Athens needs a gadfly to keep it from complacency, as does any thriving community; Socrates provides that necessary sting. It may be a mistake to regularly deflate the pompous figures in power, for they will lie in wait and seek their vengeance. But if someone isn't willing to point out when harmful errors are being made, the city will be doomed. Unfortunately, as Socrates' life makes clear, the need for acts of deflation never ends. The best possible light one could put on this matter is to say that Socrates' wisdom manifests itself in an acute ability to know the difference between self-interest and the interests of the city, something we might think is obvious. But every day humans confuse the two even when they aren't working from a ruthlessly selfish position. Their intelligence doesn't allow them to easily distinguish between the two, so they assume that what is good for them is good for the city as well. Only truly enlightened people are able to recognize the difference between the two on a regular basis, though others can discern the difference after the fact when the consequences become apparent.

This basic point cannot be emphasized too much: Socrates was able to distinguish between his own self-interest and the needs of the city, and he was able to act on that basis. Others are much less able to make this crucial distinction, regularly confusing the two at their own and the city's peril. Recent corporate scandals make this point all too well, however easy a target they might be. Surely many CEOs throughout the United States in the nineties convinced themselves that their greedy absorption of huge sums of money was a reflection of the good they were doing for society: their great powers produced wealth for shareholders, and the percentage of shareholders in the country grew to include the majority of the population by the end of the millennium, so the CEOs deserved to be rewarded excessively in order to encourage them and others to continue to produce such bountiful wealth for the country as a whole. However greedy they were, and however desperately wrong that greediness was, they doubtless went home at night feeling virtuous, convinced they had done wonders for their shareholders, for the company, and for the market economy itself. These kinds of mistakes are most prevalent when people strive to acquire wealth or power; they deceive themselves about the difference between their own good and the good of society. But the same is true for us every day: even the best of us only occasionally have qualms about whether this or that choice is good for everyone or only for us.

Our inclinations toward self-regard are only part of the problem. What we are dealing with is a question of perspective, the ability to see things from more than one angle, to be disinterested in our inquiries, to have a kind of parallax vision in which the various frames of reference can be measured against one another. Socrates possessed this rare gift, another function of his wisdom, so he became an essential gadfly to Athens because he was able to recognize what was good for the city and what would put it in peril. He held his ground in public because he became convinced of what was good and what wasn't, and more often than not he was right. Although the simplest way of recognizing his ability to distinguish self-interest from the good of the community is his poverty and his deliberate avoidance of power, his lack of self-interest is also regularly on display in the dialogues when he defends a point of view to the end because it seems the right thing to do. We must assume that this is why so many powerful Athenians considered him a threat. He did little more than sit around and talk, but he was incorruptible and knew the difference between what was good for him and what was good for others. Therefore, he endangered their own highly self-interested positions.

The great difficulty in being Athens's gadfly is apparent today in the fact that we often call such people whistleblowers. Their characteristics are similar to Socrates': they see inequities, gross mismanagement, or misrule and cannot abide it, insisting on pointing it out even when they know their future will likely be harmed by demanding that the problem be brought to light. Yet most whistleblowers are recognized for one significant incident in which they stayed the course and made the inequity known to a larger audience. However much they might be vigilant in similar, quieter ways for years at a time, in effect they push things to the limit only on one particular occasion. Socrates spent his entire life in such endeavors, regularly refusing to back down from positions he was convinced were for the good of Athens even when no one else sided with him.

Yet one can never go too far in this direction without recognizing the other side of things, for, complex as he was, Socrates was more than a simple gadfly who was committed to the good of the community. He was very much a threat as well. Like it or not, the good of the city isn't always served by severe taskmasters such as Socrates. No doubt societies need gadflies to keep them honest, for political regimes tend to run from the truth when it suits their purposes. If there is no one to call attention to the ill-conceived choices politicians make, they will make even larger mistakes or become more corrupt. Societies need people who will keep their citizens on the straight and narrow path of virtue as well, or at least as close to that path as large groups of people are likely to be. Without someone to set a standard for virtue, there would be even less of it than there is. Ralph Waldo Emerson reminded us many years ago that people naturally seek out money and power because those are the things that seem most worth pursuing.[1] If they don't have someone such as Socrates (or Emerson) to show them that there is a better way, greed and power-mongering will get out of control. As a public scourge, Socrates constantly reminds his fellow citizens that more is expected of them, that they too should think of the good of the community first rather than always basing their choices on self-interest.

But there are times when a gadfly such as Socrates can become a burden to society, a striking fact given that he is regarded as someone who is supremely attuned to his context. If that were always so, he would realize that no good would come from further humiliating this interlocutor or that politician. If one of the goals of a virtuous person is always to act in accord with the situation at hand, Socrates too often errs on the side of overkill. One can be grateful that he resisted poor political choices and pointed out the error of the leaders' ways, but beyond a certain point this behavior has negative effects. The public disgrace of fools serves a whole variety of useful social purposes and can benefit a city by leaving no doubt that such behavior will be exposed for what it is. But as the victims of such pillorying accumulate, they produce more and more corrosive effects on the polis. The *Apology* is testimony to the fact that even if Socrates had been right in each individual context to show the person the error of his ways, the accumulated burden of those situations produced a poisonous atmosphere that was good for no one. Recognizing this fact, Socrates should have eased up on his attacks. Instead, he did the opposite, seeking to flog even more intensely those who charged him with crimes. The desire to do so is understandable, and one might even think doing so is a necessary strategy. But it is not good for the community to call into question the power structure at a time when the results can only further poison the mood of the city.

It is a worthy endeavor to contend for the city's good throughout one's lifetime, and no one was more committed to this task than Socrates. But we should also see that, at least in retrospect, he made strategic mistakes along the way that reflect the limitations of his wisdom. If we think about the standard interpretation of the Delphic Oracle's declaration of Socrates' wisdom—that it meant only to highlight how ignorant all human beings are—we can also see how pertinent that interpretation is when we regard Socrates' contentiousness. Even the best human beings regularly err in the assessments of their context, are incapable of always knowing how best to act in a particular situation. All of us develop habitual ways of behaving and make the same decision over and over again without properly taking into account the cumulative ramifications of such choices. Thus, Socrates failed to consider what might happen if he persisted in his public humiliations over many years. If he did consider the potential consequences, he failed to reflect on the effects his trial might have on Athens and on the ideal of virtue that was central to his life. He could no more anticipate all the consequences of his choices than anyone else could, so in the end the accumulated malice that devolved from his dialogues with foolish but powerful people did him in and contributed to the weakening of Athens as a whole, undermining the ideal of virtue to which he had devoted his life. This is the best that human beings can do, so Socrates ends up being an exemplary model of the life of virtue, its necessities and limitations, and a perfect example of the fact that even those most virtuous among us produce patterns of mistakes over time that debilitate both them and society. Here too we understand the gist without wanting to admit it, for we know that those who constantly oppose others for the good of the community can also become highly unpleasant scourges who do no one any good. Socrates' situation wasn't that dire, but the accumulation of his mistakes undercut his otherwise noble imagination and undermined his own cause.

When one thinks of the variousness of Socrates and his effects on the world, one must also briefly consider the powerful results of Socrates' great invention, the dialectic of dialogue, and Plato's equivalent invention of the dialogue as a literary genre, both of which are wonders of Western civilization that produced great changes in our modes of thought. As Socrates imagines it, the dialogue is the equivalent of a divining rod. It is a process through which truths come to light, in which human character reveals itself, and through which the rhythm of the world manifests itself. Irony and contest aside, the purpose of dialogue is to put language in play while focusing it through a question: What is truth? What is justice? In the best of cases, the interlocutors remain open to what comes of the question, and they follow its drift wherever it goes. In the end, much if not most of what they learn is what can't be said about truth or justice, but this helps clarify what they are. They also learn about the processes of language, the mysterious means through which the world reveals itself to us. Without the flow of dialogue, our links to the world would be greatly attenuated, and we would know much less about the patterns that determine the nature of the universe. Socrates understands these great powers, which is why he takes them up as the means through which to determine the truths of existence. At their best his interlocutors also realize that the divining rod of language can have peculiar powers if one lets it have sway over the dialectic that proceeds from it.

As with the intellectual capacities of humans in general, the dialogue relies on various skills. First, it requires the acutely focused question and the determination to follow it where it will go. Second, it depends on analysis and reason, the ability to sort through what comes up in the discussion and determine what is pertinent and what is not. Third, it needs conscious attention to those details in order to establish what has taken place. Fourth, it insists on submission to the irrational processes at the center of both language and thought. The "divine wandering" inherent in all great dialogue depends on a willingness to let the question and the language have priority over the interlocutors rather than the other way around. It also requires a willing suspension of one's self-interested orientation to the world. One must give that up for the imperative of the question. One must be willing to forgo one's egocentric purposes if one is to be susceptible to the dynamic of language and the patterning of mind that allows things to come to light that would be unavailable through the stratagems of analysis and reason.

However much dialogue depends on a flow, on an ongoing interchange between two or more people who have ceded control of their thoughts to the drift of the dialogue, the dialectic of language is as overdetermined as we are. It is no more purely rational than it is completely irrational. It depends on a non-self-centered orientation, yet it also requires the pointed focus of the question. It gives up control of the flow of the dialogue to the play of language, yet at some level language is also shaped and given direction by the interlocutors' tacit sense of what goes with what.

All of this is another way of saying that the dialogue is an ingenious device, one with magical properties that defy our ability to make sense of them. It is no accident that, even after all these millennia, we still can't account for the synaptic leaps of insight that language is capable of producing on a regular basis. We are even less able to explain how the sincere engagement of individuals in a communal flow of language that is oriented around a specific question can produce insights that are unavailable in any other way, that defy reason even as they depend on it, that work as mysteriously as the reading of tea leaves or intuiting the direction of a thunderstorm. The dialogue can produce profound insights into our situation in the world if we allow it to occupy our psyches, yet it resists our analysis of its processes no matter what orientation we take.

The same can be said for the ingenuity of the dialogue as a literary form. Socrates "invented" the dialogue as an instrument of profound philosophical inquiry, and Plato adapted it into a literary form in order to suit his own philosophical and literary purposes. At the same time, both Socrates and Plato relied on earlier models of linguistic interchange among people, most notably in literary genres like tragic drama, a site where the power of language to dominate the minds of the characters and produce cruel truths about the nature of their lives was on display long before Socrates or Plato thought about dialogue. The tragedies of Aeschylus and Sophocles provide clear evidence of the power of language in play and reveal the ways in which its processes change the course of lives in a moment and forever alter the drift of civilization as well. But tragic drama lacks the self-awareness of the Platonic dialogue. It so thoroughly immerses its characters in the scenes in which they take part that the ways in which they are guided by language are usually off to the side, not observed at all.

Socrates and Plato take a tragic literary form that is designed to divine the irrevocable circumstances of human existence in order to induce us to accept the fated nature of our lives, and they turn it into an instrument of the greatest change of which the species has so far been capable. However much we believe that Western civilization is inaugurated by the Socratic and Platonic emphasis on reason, it is more accurate to say that the form of the dialogue took the fateful acceptance of the flows of life as seen in tragic drama and turned it into a means of moving our fates in directions more to our liking. We had to submit to the drift of the dialogue in the same way that the characters in a play like *Oedipus the King* had to accede to the force of history and the power of the oracle, but we could use these powers to imagine new ways of being human and to consider different ways of organizing our thoughts and our communities. Inasmuch as the dialogue depends on both reason and the irrational flow of language, it shows that we have long been mistaken in our assumption that reason transformed the world to produce the wonders and horrors of today's highly technologized society. Without the interplay of reason and unreason through the flow of dialogue, our world would never have come about.

Given the nature of the Socratic dialogue, I should also note that its classic form induces us to assume mistakenly that true discourse depends on multiple interlocutors. There is no doubt that the free interchange of multiple points of view is capable of producing stunning insights into the nature of things precisely because of the diversity of backgrounds. But just as we have been thinking about the diversity inherent in the man Socrates, so too we acknowledge our own multiplicity. Just as the point of this chapter is to remind us of the complex, overdetermined nature of Socrates, so too it should call attention to our equivalent complexities. Dialogue with "ourselves" is possible because we are not just one thing, because our processes always exceed our ability to understand them. More specifically, we need to note that various kinds of dialogue are both possible and necessary. Like Socrates, we have a voice in our head with which we are in conversation throughout life, though it would be better to assume that we have multiple voices. One of the virtues of Freud's invention of id, ego, and superego is that these terms suggest the kind of dialogue that is taking place in our minds at any given moment. We have yet to get a proper handle on these voices and the way they generate our lifelong dialogue with our situation in the world. But we know well enough that those conversations take place, and they were first produced with their most powerful literary equivalents in the dialogues that come down to us from Socrates and Plato. We have only now gotten to the point where we can once again take the dialogic model and apply it to the conversations we have with ourselves as well as with others, which suggests that perhaps we have finally returned to an understanding of the centrality of the dialogic relations that language plays out for us.

We come back, in the end, to the greatest virtue inherent in Socrates and the dialogue form for which he is most famous: they both present the variousness of our nature in play with the variousness of our contexts, demonstrating the powerful ways in which these ongoing interchanges produce the world in which we live. Not that Socrates himself is always insistent about this variousness. Particularly in such dialogues as the *Republic,* he can espouse a contrary view that embraces simplicity and unity over complexity and variousness. But if we observe Socrates in the dialogues where there is serious engagement with profound questions, we witness a man who is integrated into his world in a variety of ways, someone who manifests a range of perspectives during the course of a dialogue and who advocates an awareness of all of which humans are capable. Even if he speaks against these positions as well, he does no more than reflect that variousness and show that none of us is capable of avoiding contradiction. Those who are committed to facing the full burden of their overdetermined natures occasionally construe their behavior in simpler ways than they should. If at times Plato and Socrates argue for a reductive idea of humans with unified natures, one can well understand the appeal of that simplicity. How wonderful to think one perfectly understands one's situation. How comforting to give up the need to endlessly interpret one's own nature and others, to refrain from trying to figure out the ramifications of this or that utterance. In a simple world with unified human beings, we would all know where we stood once we had established the unity on the basis of which each individual's character was formed. We grow weary of having to deal with the consequences of our complexity, so there is always an urge to find easier ways of understanding the world.

We face the pressures of complexity on a regular basis, and we just as regularly desire an easier interpretive life. But the Socratic dialogue insists that complexity is inevitably part of the species, that serious questions can seldom be answered to our satisfaction, and that regular engagement in dialogue with our best interlocutors is the most important and one of the most interesting and enjoyable things we do. Dialogue produces a whole range of experiences as it unfolds, reveals a spectrum of emotional engagement with life, and encourages us to embrace that richness at every level. At the same time, it reveals the ways in which our lives are relational from the ground up. We are not free agents but rather contextually oriented creatures who are always in the process of discerning the parameters of our environment as best we can. Because we are part of the complex relations that unfold on this planet, we are always caught in time and place, which adds to the richness of our lives but which also irretrievably links us to everything else in the world. The dynamics of these endlessly enriching relations unfold best in conjunction with others as we pursue the nature of the existence we share with other living things. After all these millennia, we still have found no better way of addressing those complexities than the dialogic form.

In the Socratic dialogue, we find ourselves close to the divine, in the midst of the most powerful human states, those connected to love, prophecy, divination, and poetry. We also recognize our baser incarnations, from the crude self-interest and vanity that drive so much of our everyday behavior to the political calculations we undertake as we measure our relations to the power structures of which we are a part. We move among sincerity, irony, play, and desperate seriousness and recognize each of these states as essential to our idea of what it means to be human. We acknowledge the emotional range of our experiences too, from joy to sorrow, from sadness to distress over our lot, just as we comprehend the necessities that drive our behavior in so many ways. There is no greater portrait of our lives, and this is due both to the magic of Plato's pen and to the candor with which Socrates confronted the world throughout a long lifetime of engagements with the most compelling issues the species ever has to face. For these reasons, Socrates remains the most exemplary of human beings even as he is the most exceptional, the individual who reveals our full nature even as he exceeds us in his ability to live comfortably with who he is.

In order to see all of these elements in play in Socrates' life, though, we need to revise the standard notions we have developed of him. We must find ways of putting reason in its place as only one crucial aspect of Socrates' life, albeit one whose development would have been seriously retarded without Socrates' example of how to employ it. But if it is essential for us to recognize the importance of reason in Socrates' life and our own, it is also necessary to put it alongside all the other, irrational elements of our existence that are more fundamental to the quality of our lives and the overall shape of them as well. Only by investigating Socrates' deep, lifelong commitments to the irrationalities at the center of our being can we properly appreciate the mixture of qualities that contribute to Socrates' well-being and to our own.

ONE

THE HOLY

SOCRATES has come down to us as the master of reason, the one who is wisest because he admits his ignorance, and the eponymous practitioner of Socratic irony. At the same time, even a casual reader of Plato's dialogues realizes that there is more to the man than that. One of the most striking things about the dialogues is how thoroughly they allow us to come to know Socrates. Plato is the first novelist because his depiction of Socrates is so complex and thorough that the man far exceeds the stylized versions of human behavior one finds in the dramas of the time, however much they too are filled with specificity. After half a dozen dialogues or so, the reader comes to feel as though he knows Socrates, understands the ways in which he moves through his conversations, and also gets a sense of the probing disposition of the man.

Among Socrates' salient characteristics, one finds a persistence in thought and language that is unprecedented. Socrates keeps at the dialogue until he feels satisfied with what has been said, yet we fail to ask how he knows when the talk is finished. A good conversation—like Plato's dialogues—has a unique rhythm and pattern, and an attentive speaker knows when there is nothing more to be accomplished. The dialogue goes back and forth, a certain amount of repetition sets in, and eventually one of the interlocutors realizes that the discussants have come up with all that is likely to be said on that particular day. Socrates generally acknowledges that there may be more to discover on another occasion even as he recognizes that the specificity of the dialogic context only allows some things to manifest themselves in any single situation.

In addition, Socrates possesses various forms of reverence, for the dialogic form itself and also for the gods. He strives in the *Apology* to defend himself from the charge of introducing new gods into Athens and argues that he has never called the traditional gods into question. How he might reconcile these forms of piety with his unrelenting reason is yet another interesting feature of many of the dialogues. This combination of piety and reason is never better on display than in the *Ion,* where Socrates discusses the ways in which lives are governed by their respect for the gods and the truths they bring us. The dialogue may be specifically concerned with the ways in which rhapsodes rely on the inspiration they receive from the gods, but Socrates also delineates the manner in which pious individuals attend to the words of the gods and allow their lives to be directed by their suasion. It is easy enough to ironize Socrates' piety in this and other dialogues, but I would argue that the piety reveals itself in conjunction with the irony. Socrates loves to undermine the vanity of humans who think they know what they are talking about, but at the same time he can show his reverence for the pathway through which truth makes itself known to him.

One finds the rich mixture of characteristics early in the *Ion* when Socrates speaks to Ion's strengths: "I have often envied the profession of a rhapsode, Ion; for it is part of your art to wear fine clothes and to look as beautiful as you can, while at the same time you are obliged to be continually in the company of many good poets, and especially of Homer, who is the best and most divine of them, and to understand his mind, and not merely learn his words by rote; all this is a thing greatly to be envied. I am sure that no man can become a good rhapsode who does not understand the meaning of the poet. For the rhapsode ought to interpret the mind of the poet to his hearers, but how can he interpret him well unless he knows what he means?"[1] Socrates sets Ion up by repeatedly suggesting he envies him and his profession, as if he would rather be a rhapsode than a gadfly. He appeals to the desire to be envied in order to induce Ion to let down his guard. The flattery is quickly followed by the ironic assertion that Socrates envies rhapsodes because they get "to wear fine clothes and to look as beautiful as [they] can." This statement leads to the acknowledgment that the envy also comes from the fact that rhapsodes "are obliged to be continually in the company of many good poets, especially Homer," but the fine clothes seem to take precedence.

No doubt Socrates is amusing himself here, as Ion is well dressed and pleased by the impression he thinks he is making. One can infer that the average rhapsode is more caught up in the flummery and prestige of the role than in the task of mastering the poet's words. Those who chant poetry enjoy being rhapsodes because of the social display involved—everyone looks at them with rapt attention while they recite Homer's words—and not because this role allows them to discern the significance of the poets they study. Socrates implies that the typical rhapsode has a misguided sense of priorities, and much of what follows suggests that Ion doesn't properly understand what is involved in reciting other poets' words. Socrates' remarks also reveal how much he likes being "continually in the company of many good poets, and especially Homer." In suggesting that he values poetry, Socrates contrasts his hours in the presence of poets to the time spent with those who are less than good company. The poets' care with words, the richness with which they articulate the human situation, and the complexity of their texts affords the listener a vision of life that is far more rewarding than that which is usually found in conversation with one's neighbors. Ion's remarks throughout the dialogue reflect this difference, as he seems to know little and is far too imprecise in his use of language.

These remarks are a prelude to the main business of the dialogue, which is to discern the nature of the relationship between the rhapsode and the poets' words. Socrates establishes that it is not enough "merely [to] learn his words by rote": there must be some other capacity that makes a rhapsode worthy of the name, for if the rhapsode is to transport us into the world the poet articulates, he must first thoroughly know the parameters of that world. He must "understand [the poet's] mind," a far more difficult task than committing his words to memory. In many ways these remarks identify the great mystery underlying all communication: how does meaning get conveyed from one person to another? What brings to life the words we read on a page or hear someone recite? These are questions we regularly ignore, opting instead to discuss the ways in which social codes impress themselves on us through language. But the social relations that are worked out through discourse don't begin to get at the most powerful questions inherent in every moment of genuine discourse, as Socrates reminds us. It is never enough merely to recite words. One must first get into the mind of the poet, understand the rich mental context from which the words came, in order to interpret them in ways that move an audience.

If the *Ion* did nothing more than remind us that the rhapsode must understand the mind of the poet, it would be an important dialogue. In putting the matter this way, Socrates highlights the rarity of poetic discourse. In between merely reciting the words and knowing the poet's mind, for example, there are stages that might involve understanding how the words of the poem hang together, how the form of the poem brings the words to life. Instead of phrasing the issue that way, Socrates insists that Ion must know Homer's mind if he is such a good interpreter of his work. Socrates' orientation resembles the phenomenological view expressed by Georges Poulet after World War II as he attempted to show how we occupy a writer's consciousness when we take up his or her text.[2] Poulet's approach seems naive today, but both he and Socrates reveal something of the mysteries of interpretation that can never be made available from the perspective of the social critic. We may not exchange consciousnesses with the writer, but there is something akin to another consciousness that occupies us when we read, regardless of how we characterize the process through which that takes place.

Socrates, however, doesn't believe that the poet's consciousness occupies the rhapsode and then the audience. On the contrary, from the very beginning of the dialogue he suggests that a more profound process is at work. In claiming that Homer is "the best and most divine" of the poets, Socrates gets at the central question of his inquiry: how are the poet's words different from ordinary discourse? The answer is that poetry is divinely inspired; the rhapsode is taken up by the poem as he masters its words, and the inspiration is passed on to the audience. Although the *Ion* is a short dialogue, we are repeatedly exposed to Socrates' inquiry into what differentiates the rhapsode's approach to poetry from the ordinary arts of learning. The most famous aspects of the dialogue involve the scenes where Socrates reveals how little Ion knows about his gift. Does he know how to be a general? Ion manages to say both yes and no at various points because he is confused about the origin of his knowledge. If he understands the means of a general, he employs the art of knowledge in the same way a general does: he masters a specific set of skills in order to make sense of the world. The rhapsodic art would then mirror all the other task-based approaches to learning in the world: the craft would be mastered, the skills repeatedly employed, and the rhapsode would get better and better at what he did the longer he pursued the techniques of the trade. But Socrates shows that the rhapsode's work is neither an art nor a craft, for otherwise we would be left with the quandary of how the poet could speak of practices he himself doesn't know and hasn't mastered, such as the arts of the general or the cook.

Socrates insists that the truths of the poet have nothing to do with the degree to which he accurately describes the actions of specific people. To be sure, the plausibility of a narrative depends on the accuracy with which it describes the procedures people employ in their work, but we don't go to Homer to learn how to be a general. This specific form of "knowledge" is acquired elsewhere, in the army or in books on leadership. Poetry's truths occupy a different space, and both Ion and the audience need to know this if they are to appreciate the wonders that poets and rhapsodes bring to audiences through their work. What we call the content of the work is incidental to the truths the poet expresses. We might imagine this as the gist of the approach the New Critics took toward poetry half a century ago, in contrast to the social commentary we find ourselves in the midst of at present. Those whose main goal in life focuses on cultural criticism would meet with as much ridicule from Socrates as Ion does: they are supposed to express the fundamental truths of the poet, yet they spend all their time showing how generals act when they are being generals, a serious category mistake.

Both poet and rhapsode are divinely inspired. As long as this point makes sense to us, the work of the dialogue falls into place. If, like the average cultural critic, we insist that all discourse is of the same order, Socrates' labors are pointless: we will continue to reduce all forms of language to the same undifferentiated porridge of words that embraces everything from advertising in mass magazines to the most arcane forms of biblical scholarship and the most profound poetry. The art of words is nothing more than persuasion from this perspective, even when the writer thinks otherwise. After all, Ion has little idea of the energies that drive him, so he might just as well be a purveyor of social codes that oppress others while he thinks he is part of a higher calling. Socrates' words would be dismissed as irrelevant today because he insists there is a difference between the ways poets and rhapsodes use language and the purposes to which it is put by those who base their work on instrumental arts designed to achieve specific ends.

Socrates describes his viewpoint repeatedly in the *Ion,* but the variations reflect his most extensive description of the poet's powers:

> The gift which you possess of speaking excellently about Homer is not an art, but, as I was just saying, an inspiration; there is a divinity moving you, like that contained in the stone which Euripides calls a magnet, but which is commonly known as the stone of Heraclea. This stone not only attracts iron rings, but also imparts to them a similar power of attracting other rings; and sometimes you may see a number of pieces of iron and rings suspended from one another so as to form quite a long chain: and all of them derive their power of suspension from the original stone. In like manner the Muse first of all inspires men herself; and from these inspired persons a chain of other persons is suspended, who take the inspiration. For all good

poets, epic as well as lyric, compose their beautiful poems not by art, but because they are inspired and possessed. (14)

Socrates insists that poets and rhapsodes are divinely inspired and devotes his energies to convincing Ion of this fact. Thanks to Jowett's translation, we repeatedly get a good sense of just what is involved in this approach toward poetry, something that is more important than it otherwise would be because we have completely lost sight of what it might mean to be divinely inspired. If we grant any credence to a notion like inspiration, we certainly don't think of it as divine. God is dead, Nietzsche declared, and divine inspiration disappeared along with Him, however much Nietzsche seemed to believe in a form of it, and however much all great writers have in some sense been as divinely inspired as Homer or Ion.

The poet and rhapsode are divinely inspired, which means that "there is a divinity moving [them]." Socrates' metaphor for this process is the magnet: "This stone not only attracts iron rings, but also imparts to them a similar power of attracting other rings; and sometimes you may see a number of pieces of iron and rings suspended from one another so as to form quite a long chain: and all of them derive their power of suspension from the original stone." The magnetic attraction that inhabits the poet when the god moves within him is thus transferred to the rhapsode, who passes on the charge to the audience, and all end up being moved by the mysterious divinity that inhabits the words of the poet. It is worth noting that Socrates has a chance here to suggest that something is lost as the magnetic force gets passed from poet to rhapsode and from rhapsode to audience, but he doesn't avail himself of the opportunity. He sees the full force of the divinity as something that can be transmitted from one individual to the other: "In like manner the Muse first of all inspires men herself; and from these inspired persons a chain of other persons is suspended, who take the inspiration." There is no loss of message here; all are equally suspended in the magnetic chain, all equally taken up by the divine inspiration.

Just as quickly, Socrates moves the discussion to a slightly different register by his summation of the process: "For all good poets, epic as well as lyric, compose their beautiful poems not by art, but because they are inspired and possessed." To be inspired is to be possessed, but we have yet again lost sight of just what this might mean. The divinity moving within poet, rhapsode, and audience is not simply the power of words. It possesses the poet, rhapsode, and audience, takes over their being for the time during which the words exert their powers, and transforms the individuals in the process. Socrates explains this possession as follows: "And just as the Korybantian revelers when they dance are not in their right mind, so the lyric poets are not in their right mind when they are composing their beautiful strains: but when falling under the power of music and meter they are inspired and possessed; like Bacchic maidens who draw milk and honey from the rivers when they are under the influence of Dionysus but not when they are in their right mind. And the soul of the lyric poet does the same, as they themselves say; for they tell us that they bring songs from honeyed fountains, culling them out of the gardens and dells of the Muses; they, like the bees, winging their way from flower to flower" (14). Poets are "not in their right mind" when they are composing their lyrics, nor are the rhapsodes who chant them or the audiences who are taken up by them. The reference to the Bacchic maidens gives some sense of the powers of the poet, particularly since Socrates emphasizes that the process takes place when people fall "under the power of music and meter": the rhythmical incantations of the poet allow the mind to be taken over by something that is other. The result is a divine transformation as truth enters poet, rhapsode, and audience through the inspiration of the god.

One of the strengths of Jowett's translation is the way in which he defamiliarizes the process whereby poetry captivates the mind. Ordinarily we think of not being in our right mind as a form of madness, but we tend not to use the same phrase for those powerful moments when we seem to be in the presence of a god. I see much of Socrates' life work as being devoted to distinguishing among the various irrational states so that the most valuable ones can be prized while the negative forms can be avoided. The poet captivates by taking one out of one's right mind, by usurping the psychic place in one's being we might ordinarily think of as the self or soul. That is the great glory of the poet and a manifestation of his central role in society.

At his most straightforward, Socrates paints the picture of the rhapsodic mentality when he asks Ion, "Are you not carried out of yourself, and does not your soul in an ecstasy seem to be among the persons or places of which you are speaking[,] . . . whatever may be the scene of the poem?" As we know, the word *ecstasy* means to be taken out of oneself: the rhapsode and the audience are taken up by the characters and setting of the poem and "seem to be among the persons or places" to which the words of the poem refer. "Whatever may be the scene of the poem," rhapsode and audience are transported to it, taken away from their every-day lives and cares and occupied by foreign armies that usurp their imaginations while the meter and the rhyme of the poem work their magic. It may be that after all these millennia we can do no better than Socrates and speak about the powers that take over our minds in the midst of great writing, but anyone who has been caught by this power would attest to the fact that even if one can make no meaningful distinction between so-called ordinary and poetic language, there is a big difference between the effects produced by imaginative literature and those found in everyday conversation, reading the newspaper, or following a list of tasks to accomplish. The words may be the same, but at the very least the rhythms and cadences of the imaginatively conceived words have greater power over our minds—and in some way take us out of our "right" minds—than those we use in everyday circumstances.

Inasmuch as we are inclined to be skeptical of the effects of poetry, it is worth emphasizing that Socrates doesn't appear to be ironic when he discusses the magical properties of poems. He regularly pokes fun at Ion and his ignorance of what he does when he recites poems, and he makes it clear that Ion is in many respects a fool. But there is no reason why Ion must understand what overtakes him when he recites poetry because he is not working via art or various skills he has mastered. As Socrates points out: "For not by art does the poet sing, but by power divine; had he learned by rules of art, he would have known how to speak not of one theme only, but of all; and therefore God takes away reason from poets, and uses them as his ministers, as he also uses the pronouncers of oracles and holy prophets, in order that we who hear them may know them to be speaking not of themselves, who utter these priceless words while bereft of reason, but that God himself is the speaker, and that through them he is addressing us" (14). Socrates insists that there is no reason why the rhapsode should understand what he is doing. If he was working from artistic devices, reason would be in him. He would consciously craft an idea of how this or that phrase would produce specific reactions in the audience. The poet's powers would be little more than a manifestation of the sophist's persuasive means. If Ion were such a practitioner and remained ignorant of what he was doing, he would be more than silly or ignorant. Inasmuch as he works by inspiration rather than craft or reason, inasmuch as he is not in his right mind when he composes his strains, he has no easy way to access the means through which his recitations work.

Socrates has no doubt that poets bring godly things to humans, and he works hard to demonstrate this fact to Ion. He doesn't want only to convince Ion that he is possessed when he recites but also to explain the kind of conviction that comes with the poet's words. He asserts, for example, that "in this way God would seem to demonstrate to us and not to allow us to doubt that these beautiful poems are not human, nor the work of man, but divine and the work of God; and that the poets are only the interpreters of the gods by whom they are severally possessed." Socrates doesn't make the kind of category mistake we regularly employ in dealing with words. He wants us to know that poems "are not human, nor the work of man." Homer may be the poet, and Ion may be the rhapsode, but the words come from the gods, not from either Homer or Ion. Over the millennia we have described poetic discourse in a variety of ways, but the most powerful has always been to say that poets are inspired, whether we take that to mean, as Socrates does, that they are possessed by gods or, more generally, as the Romantics do, that their words come from some inhuman source, or from twentieth-century notions of the unconscious and its effects on language, or Jung's various descriptions of archetypes and their origin in the collective unconscious. Humans have repeatedly tried to make poetic language fit into the box of the self, reducing the force of discourse to some species of subjectivity that suggests words are nothing more than the poet's attempt to make sense of reality. Socrates insists that the poet's words are impersonal, that they come from god, that they don't derive from a human or social domain.

Socrates' remarks also speak to the conviction of the poet's words. The powerful forces of the poem do not "allow us to doubt that these beautiful poems are not human," an unusual way of saying that the power of the words carries such force that we are convinced we are experiencing more than a poet's view of reality. We are so captivated by the words that they convince us unequivocally of their divine origin. Yet again this is both a strength and a weakness, for if poetry carries its conviction in the power of the words and their ability to sway us without reason, we are left with no rational means of accounting for how they have the effects they do. We do not doubt it, yet we cannot properly explain why the poet's words transform us. As long as we assume that the purpose of poetry is to take us out of our right mind, we also have to acknowledge that that "right mind" will therefore never be able to make sense of that which poetry accomplishes. The best it can do is recognize that the poetic state is irrational, not to be explained by technique, definition, or rational argument. It convinces us by rhythm, meter, word choice, and rhyme. We are left with the impersonality of the poem, its apparent godlikeness.

Most people who read the *Ion* have already encountered the *Republic* in some form or another and therefore know that Plato banishes the poets. It is thus all the more difficult to take Socrates seriously when he argues for the divinity of poetic discourse. Surely he must not believe what he says, because his position goes against the grain of his argument in the *Republic*. Surely he is just setting up the poet as an irrationalist so he can expel him later for his complete lack of reason. This seems to me to be a serious misreading of Socrates' intent in the *Ion,* an abuse that destroys the careful delineation of Socrates' position. It may suit us to focus on the ways in which Socrates strips his interlocutors of dignity, but that was not the primary goal of his dialogic endeavors. At best that was a secondary effect. Socrates reveres the poets for their words even as he remains skeptical of the things they might say. He insists that "the poet is a light and winged and holy thing, and there is no invention in him until he has been inspired and is out of his senses, and reason is no longer in him: no man, while he retains that faculty, has the oracular gift of poetry." However ironic Socrates can be, it is hard to mistake the praise inherent in phrases that characterize the poet as a "light and winged and holy thing."

Notwithstanding the later charges against Socrates for impiety, it is difficult to believe he would say the poet is holy and then employ that holiness as a reason for expelling him from the community. And although there is a huge gap between this praise of the holiness of poets in the *Ion* and the expulsion of them in the *Republic,* Socrates sees the poets as the holy center of society in this dialogue. Whereas he was certainly aware of the limitations of poetic language even as he was chary of the effects of irrational states on the order of the community, he seems reverent throughout his life, distinguishing the holy from the secular and paying it proper respect. For this reason, his arguments on behalf of the poets in *Ion* are closer to what he thinks than what he says when he seeks to expel them in the *Republic.* At the same time, we also have to allow for potential changes of mind and the different goals of the two dialogues.

The above quotation speaks to the nature of poetic craft as well, which is important because otherwise the poet will be seen as someone who lacks control over his materials. Socrates' distinction is quite clear: there is "invention in him," but not "until he has been inspired and is out of his senses." He may be the mouthpiece of the gods, but he still employs technique. His stratagems are modulated through the divine energies that direct his words in the first place. Socrates manages to convey the fact that the poet's words are divine even as he leaves a secondary place for that which he would characterize as art, the devices through which one makes one's words more powerful and effective. The poet is a mouthpiece of the gods, but he is not devoid of the inclination to improve a line or change a word. Those impulses are directed by the force of the gods and work properly only when they are under their sway. When they are, the poet's choices are directed by the higher power, but his personal disposition is also in play.

|| One of the most important ramifications of Socrates' discussion of the poet's words is the conception of humanity inherent in them. Both Socrates and the Athenians had a more protean notion of the nature of our being. This is nowhere better represented than in the *Ion,* with its regular references to the fact that the poet is not in his right mind, that reason is not in him, that he is possessed, that divine inspiration implies all these things. Our own register has become so two-dimensional that we reduce the import of such words. We assume that Socrates is merely insisting that the poet's words are different from those that are found in ordinary discourse. This is true enough, but it doesn't begin to account for the richness of Socrates' views of our psychic pliability. In our own day we imagine a continuum of consciousness, based on levels of intensity, and we think that the extreme levels of intensity (both hyper- and hypo-) produce what we call altered states. The vast terrain in between tends to be reduced to more or less the same state with minor intensifiers added to distinguish one mode of being from another.

But when Socrates says that reason has been taken away from the poet and the rhapsode, he means quite literally that the state of reason has been displaced, taken over, occupied by another state, in this case divine inspiration. It is as though there are various states available to us at any given moment, and they come and go more or less of their own accord, often without notice. We may be in a reasonable state, or we may be in love, or we may be in the midst of sexual ecstasy or taken up by some other intensely sensuous state; each of these situations produces its own psychic conditions. There is no identifiable movement to and from these various states. One is simply taken over by them. The ruptures aren't noticeable because we have been inclined not to pay attention to them. Just as we assume our eyes are constantly moving smoothly over the field of vision rather than lurching about jerkily as they in fact do, so we believe that our stream of consciousness is continuous rather than regularly disrupted and displaced by the various states that fill out our sense of the world. One notes these differences particularly in ancient poetry. When Odysseus is crying or lamenting his fate, he is completely given over to that state. He moves into and out of states in accord with the circumstances he faces at any moment, and he makes no attempt to provide continuities between them. The differential movement into and out of psychic states doesn't trouble him at all.

One gets a similar view of human consciousness in the *Ion:* it is a turbulent site that can be occupied by various modes of being. Poetry itself makes this clear, for the audience is magnetically attracted by the poet's words, taken out of itself in an ecstasy and transported to a different domain. Socrates isn't simply describing the difference between imagination and reason, a distinction we also acknowledge. He believes that these states are radically different, and the ecstasy of the poetic state is not characterized by one's imagination placing one in Odysseus's situation. It is a state in which our consciousness is usurped by the gods, taken over by impersonal forces that direct our attention to things to which we might ordinarily not pay attention. That is why poetry is so powerful: it can take us out of ourselves, allow our minds to be organized by forces that have nothing to do with selfhood. And whereas the *Ion* is devoted to exposing the ways in which poetry rhapsodically transports us to psychic levels that aren't available in any other way, the implication of Socrates' arguments is that there are various states, each of which is discontinuous from the others, each of which links us to our environment uniquely, sometimes in highly personal, emotional ways, at other times in highly impersonal, godlike ways, and at still other times in abstracted and rational ways as we analytically consider the ramifications of various possibilities. There is no continuous, coherent whole of which these states are a part. They are different ways our consciousness is occupied at any given moment.

Having said as much, I also need to address the qualitative values inherent in such states, for some are more valuable than others. Clearly not all occasions are suitable for the ecstasy poetry produces. Much of the time we need reason to be in us, to use Jowett's diction. During such times it would be detrimental for us to be possessed by the energies of the divine. The same is true for states of powerful emotion, whether one thinks of love or grief: they are appropriate in some contexts, and, as with poetic ecstasy, they dispose us to the world in ways that are unrelated to our reasonable states. We need to know when to submit to them and when to let them unfold in accord with the way we feel. Works such as the *Odyssey* lead one to conjecture that millennia ago the movement between states was more fluid; the control exerted over them by the "self" or some other mechanism was not as centralized and imperious as it has come to be. The Athens of Socrates' day seems to be a halfway house between Homer's fluid psyche and our own relatively rigid and constrained forms of consciousness. Socrates has a much richer sense of the field of play of consciousness and is in a better position to understand the movements into and out of various states.

If one thinks briefly of the Homeric epics, one can see how thoroughly people of the time gave themselves over to their states, a situation reflected in Auerbach's powerful meditation many years ago on the two-dimensional nature of the Homeric corpus.[3] When Homer's warriors were in battle, they were wholly of the battle: that state completely occupied their minds. When they were safely ensconced in a sensuous paradise, as Odysseus was on Calypso's island, they gave themselves over to that. There is little sense of the passage of time or anything else on Calypso's island: Odysseus partakes of its delights until he decides he wants to return to his wife. There is no superego imposing coherence on the Odysseus who dallies with Calypso and the one who longs for home and Pene-lope. They are both the same Odysseus, but when he is with Calypso, the desire for the return home is muted. When we think of poetic contexts, the same is true for the powerful recitations of Demodocus: he fills the space of which he is a part, the audience is moved by him, and his voice transports the people away from their everyday context to another plane.

In some respects these situations are much like the ones we face today. What is different is the pliability of the psyche. We also see how important society is as a means through which people chan-nel these states. It occupies the role of superego much more than it seems to us today because we assume that most humans have a high degree of control over their being at any given moment. Given the pliability, one recognizes that the contexts that were invented for the expression of various states—poetic ecstasy, for example—were carefully, if intuitively, devised to deal with the variousness of the mind. Inasmuch as the inspired possession of one's psyche by the Muse places one in a vulnerable position, it makes sense for rhapsodes to do their work after a meal, among friends, in the safety of one's own hall, libations flowing freely, while the people have a chance to unwind. Easing up on one's focus isn't always useful; it certainly isn't a good idea to have one's mind filled with images of the battle at Troy when one is vulnerable to one's enemies and under attack. The Greeks evolved modes of organization that made such states available to individuals at times when they could temporarily put off the anxieties involved in daily living and allow themselves to *not* be in their right mind.

Lest we assume these rhapsodic moments in Greek culture were simply forms of what we today call entertainment, we need to remember how seriously Socrates takes the divine possession of the poet. Unlike us, he doesn't praise Ion for being able to take people away from their cares for a brief time, giving them a respite from their hard lives. On the contrary, he assumes that Ion will transport them to a domain of fundamental truths about the nature of things. The god of poetry fills people's minds because the truths of the Muse can only be revealed in this way. These transports also temporarily put off the cares of the self, and they offer what we call entertainment, gripping tales of battle or intrigue. We might be inclined to say that the poet and rhapsode are the constructors of the culture of which they are a part, and from a sociological angle that is part of what they do. But the displaced nature of the states they induce and the inspired possession they offer to the audience have less to do with constructing culture than with inducing the rhythms people need to find expression for their most fundamental connections to the world. That the poets also reinforce a religious system of gods that upholds the social codes, that they articulate stratagems of war that might be useful to the hoplite, that they describe things such as table manners that are essential to the organization of culture is certainly important. But to assume that these are the main "goals" of the poet is to lose sight of divine transportation, to ignore the ways in which humans orient themselves to the world in radically different ways.

If we no longer believe in divine transport, the Muses, or even inspiration, we must still make an effort to understand the power of these displaced states. Even if they aren't divine in any way that makes sense to us, they are clearly different from our normal states, and their specifics need to be identified. The first and most obvious difference is their relative impersonality. Most of the time our consciousness is taken up by self-oriented goals. We strive to maintain our existence as best we can, which involves regular consideration of the virtues and limitations *for us* of the various situations we occupy. The state of poetic transport isn't interested in individual selves or taken up by the concerns of specific people. That is what Socrates means when he says the poet, the rhapsode, and the audience are taken out of themselves: they are not thinking in self-centered ways. This is the most fundamental difference inherent in the poetic state. It shares this impersonality with other states—the god of war also usurps one's consciousness, and reasoning is impersonal too—but the character of the impersonality is different. Both the poetic state and the state of warring share impersonality and non-self-centeredness, and they share highly emotional orientations to that impersonality. But the furies of war focus those energies in different ways than the poetic state does, even though it is possible for one state to modulate into the other: the impersonality of the poetic state can lead the audience to tear the singer to pieces in an ecstasy, for example. But there is a focus to warring that is not intrinsic to the transport of the imagination, and the concentration of war energies always involves an individual or a self more than poetic transport does.

It may also be true that the emotional valences of poetic transport and warring are different—the ecstasy of violence differentiating itself from the transport of poetic harmony—but it is not always certain that the two states distinguish themselves in that way. However much we strive to separate the creative and synthetic impulses from the destructive and analytic ones, the differences are not always readily identifiable. Even so, the impersonal state characterized by the word *rage* manifests itself in different ways: the rage of extreme anger is different from Wallace Stevens's "blessed rage for order," that equally powerful urge to evolve a sense of pattern in the world.[4] And even if love and hate are not as far apart as many of us want to believe, we will soon be able to identify the various hormones that flow throughout the brain when we are in the midst of love and the ones that course through our nervous system when we are in the midst of anger and hatred.

What differentiates these two impersonal states from reason is that the reasonable state is relatively devoid of emotion, though we have contemporary writers like Antonio Damasio to thank for showing us that reason devoid of emotion produces paralysis rather than lucidity.[5] Love, war, and hate are intensely emotional, even if the emotions are different. Reason prides itself on being both impersonal and unemotional: what is at stake is not an individual fate or even how an individual might feel about a given context but an analytical attempt to get at the specific nature of a particular situation. The tools of reason don't, in theory, speak differently from one person to another: they are a means through which our emotional biases can be put out of play while we consider the nature of things from a less self-interested perspective. As with the highly emotional impersonal states, reason's impersonality is crucial to our development as human beings. Without some ability to reason in dispassionate ways, orderly discourse cannot take place. Without some common standards of analysis that transcend any particular individual, no meaningful accord can be reached. We need the click-clack of reason's blades to hew a path through contexts that are saturated by bias, mistake, and self-interest.

We know that Socrates is the master of reason, the individual more than any other in Athens who could make the reasonable discriminations that were necessary to separate foolishness from truth. We also know that he considers reason a supreme virtue, to which he devotes his life. In the end, though, Socrates' protean version of the human psyche depends on a compelling awareness of our various discontinuous states and the places they take up in society. He suggests that we need to know when the impersonality of reason should take precedence over self-interested states or emotional impersonal states, just as he insists that we must understand the importance of divine transport and find a place for its dynamics, discerning its essential role in human virtue. Without the full range of personal and impersonal, emotional and non-emotional states, we lose an essential part of our heritage.

|| Another crucial aspect of the divine inspiration to which the *Ion* is devoted is the nature of poetic utterance in general. It is not enough that it transports us; it does much more than that. Socrates makes the crucial links to other forms of divine inspiration in one of the passages where he seeks to explain why poets and rhapsodes are limited in their inspiration. Ion can recite Homer with great power but not Hesiod or the other poets: "For not by art does the poet sing, but by power divine; had he learned by rules of art, he would have known how to speak not of one theme only, but of all; and therefore God takes away reason from poets, and uses them as his ministers, as he also uses the pronouncers of oracles and holy prophets, in order that we who hear them may know them to be speaking not of themselves, who utter these priceless words while bereft of reason, but that God himself is the speaker, and that through them he is addressing us" (14). The core argument of *Ion*

is that the rhapsode sings by divine power rather than art, a point that is emphasized because Ion "specializes" in Homer. He cannot transport himself or his audience with other poets. So, Socrates concludes, he could not have mastered the practices of the rhapsode by learning techniques, for they would apply to all poetry and not just to one writer. I will have more to say about this in a minute. For the moment I am concerned with the statement that "god takes away reason from poets, and uses them as his ministers, as he also uses the pronouncers of oracles and holy prophets." Socrates is careful as always with his distinctions, but he clearly associates the poet and rhapsode with oracles and holy prophets, yet he distinguishes them from one another as well. In all of them, god takes away reason, usurps the psyche for his own ends. In all of them, god uses specific human beings "as his ministers," which is why they are all holy: they permit themselves to be possessed by the spirit of god and allow his work to be done among humans through divine possession.

Socrates couldn't be praising Ion any more than he is here in associating his work with those who are oracular or prophetic. And whereas it has been quite some time since someone like Percy Shelley has characterized poets as "the unacknowledged legislators of the world" or argued that they are numbered among the great race of prophets, Socrates comes close to anticipating Shelley's assertions here. Poets are not oracles, nor do they get their music by listening to one. They are not prophets and don't speak through the revelations of various divine signs they have learned how to read. But they are interpreters of the gods' words, even if those words occupy a still-curious space somewhere between the oracular and the prophetic on the one side and ordinary forms of discourse on the other. If they don't prophesy, the words of the poets present us with a full version of humanity that clearly suggests what we are and what we will become. They are not oracles, yet their rich, complex accounts of the historical and mythical scenes of society are capable of revealing the past and projecting that past into a future. Their prophetic truths come from the divinely inspired evocation of what it means to be human, to be

Athenian, to be part of a physical world whose processes are magically revealed through certain kinds of discourse that involve divine possession.

Still, even Socrates avoids saying what a poet gives his people. The poet brings the truth, but that truth remains elusive. The poet may be a light and winged and holy thing, but he earns that characterization by inducing us to inhabit a divine space during the recitation of poetry. We note the feelings, we understand that in some way we have been possessed by a force that has displaced our normal modes of consciousness, and the power of this force convinces us it is divine, or some equivalent. But to this day those who take these different psychic states seriously have no good way of articulating what particular things these states offer to humans. We are always left with the dross of the experience: we talk about hormonal changes in the brain, we note the non-self-centeredness of them, we speak of the "therapeutic" effects engendered by being taken away from one's cares for a brief time, or we say that the poet provides bourgeois comforts that allow people to escape from their anxiety. We could likewise say they bring fundamental truths to people that can't be found in newspapers, or we could insist that their work is devoted to nothing more than the pleasures of rhythm and meter—the meaning of the words becomes irrelevant, the patterns they induce in us through their movement being that which most affects our well-being.

The poet ranks at the top of human importance along with the oracular voice and the prophet as far as Socrates is concerned, and any fitting measure of the nature of poets and poetry must take that high estimation into account. If today's social critics refuse to do so, poetry has also fallen into disrepute among other segments of the population. In contrast to Socrates' insistence that the poet is a highly rarefied type whose willingness to be the mouthpiece of the gods is crucially important, demotic culture in the United States assumes that anyone who possesses a modest facility with words and who also has feelings is capable of being a poet. Such an approach coincides with Socrates' view that poets don't really need to learn technique, but it also denies that there is anything beyond personal expression involved in poetry. We sing ourselves, to paraphrase Whitman, rather than becoming the voices of god as modulated through particular individuals, and a great many people can express themselves well enough to qualify as poets.[6] Poetry becomes so democratized that it is little different from the forms of speech we learned in elementary school. The result is a form so debased that the line between sacred and secular utterance becomes irrelevant.

We might think the poet's plight in our day stems from the fact that poetry is no longer much of an oral form. Even if there are more poetry readings now than at any time in the past, for the most part the poem has been reduced to words on the page. This shift means that any transport the poem brings will be produced by the reader rather than by the rhapsode or some other third party. We might put this another way and say that in the current environment the reader him- or herself becomes the rhapsode, the one who allows the divine voice of the poet to sing. But even in Socrates' time the rhapsode's capacities are almost as rare as the poet's: not everyone has the ability to move audiences into states of divine possession. The infrequency of this gift is one of the elements of the rhapsode's world that makes his work so valuable. If readers are called upon to achieve the same forms of mastery as the rhapsode, few will manage to do so, which in turn means that most readers will fail to become the last link in the magnetic chain that goes from the gods to the poet to the rhapsode to the audience. And if the reader is not a fitting link, it follows that he or she will not recognize the difference between a poem that comes from the breath of god and one that is merely an individual's personal grumble. If there are no such distinctions now, this is in part because there are no longer sufficient people—poets or rhapsodic readers—who are capable of manifesting the true power of poetry to audiences. Poetry is debased because nothing but the base of poetry is left—words measured out in more or less metrical lines.

The undifferentiated mess that poetry has become also speaks to the conundrum at the center of the *Ion:* Ion is a master of Homer, but his gift doesn't extend to other poets. Ion can recite

Hesiod but remains incapable of transporting the audience through this poet. And although both Ion and Socrates make clear that Homer stands alone, Hesiod's poetry is imbued with the inspiration of the gods as well. For some reason, though, Ion isn't capable of bringing Hesiod to life. Socrates addresses this situation repeatedly in order to convince Ion that he is divinely inspired. If he worked by art or technique, he could as easily master Hesiod as Homer or anyone else. However important this line of inquiry might be, it hardly satisfies us when it comes to the question of why Ion is such a good rhapsode of Homer's verses but is ineffective with other writers. Divine inspiration almost makes sense of the situation, but then why wouldn't such inspiration be broad enough to allow a good rhapsode equal powers over a whole range of poets and poetry? This question never comes up in the dialogue, yet it remains the most intriguing of all.

Ion knows his gift is highly localized, and he remains satisfied with Socrates' argument that it is specialized because he is divinely inspired. This is a flattering way of describing the high powers of the poet and rhapsode, so why shouldn't Ion be pleased with what Socrates says? But as we look at the issues involved in Ion's specialized capacities, we must ask yet again why he can perform magic with Homer while failing to make Hesiod sing. In the academic world, this question is related to the various areas of concentration available in a given discipline. People choose specializations for a whole variety of reasons—market concerns, the relative ease or difficulty of a person or period, the types and forms of literature that are most appealing at any moment, consideration of the individuals with whom one will have to work if one undertakes this or that field—but often individuals are "chosen" by their areas of specialization. A Shakespearean is someone who thinks Shakespeare is everything. A Romantic assumes that the great poets at the beginning of the nineteenth century spoke more compellingly to the human situation than anyone before or since. If we imagine such a context, we can ask why a Shakespearean would be a Shakespearean and a Romantic a Romantic.

In the best of cases, one would assume that there are complex attachments between individuals and their area of specialization. If someone wanted to devote her life to Shakespeare, one would think there were multifarious links that made the critic feel best when she was in his midst. Shakespeare is a writer of such magnitude that it is impossible to isolate any particular reason for the attachment: one could love his linguistic dexterity, his dramatic flair, the compelling way he represents the human condition in play after play, the specificity and complexity of characterization in so many of his plays, or even the aura of the Renaissance that is presented in his works. Any one of these could be reason enough for powerful links to develop between the playwright and the critic, establishing a lifelong communion that is as deep as the best of friendships.

Equally important, that "friendship" is likely to be as affective in nature as it is a function of specific things the writer does. Deep emotional and intuitive bonds develop that make the writer the equivalent of a twin. When one spends a long time with a writer of any quality, one comes to feel as though one could imagine what that individual would think about specific situations in the contemporary world. A complex literary work allows one to inhabit a different universe, and in some ways the difference is much more akin to inhabiting Homer's mind than the shores of Troy. One can get a good sense of both Homer and Troy in the great epics, but the so-called Homeric viewpoint is far more compelling than any particular description of battles, cities, or mythological figures. The affective tentacles of the poem work their way into one's mind and allow one to feel as though one genuinely knows what it means to inhabit the Homeric world, the Shakespearean one, or the Whitmanian one.

The difficulty in speaking of these forms of attachment goes far beyond our current skepticism about them and our conviction that the author is dead. Our instruments for describing literary interactions remain crude, as Shakespeare again demonstrates. It wouldn't do to say one was attached to Shakespeare's work because one had a similar psychological makeup. However much one gets a sense of the "Shakespearean world" or the "Shakespearean viewpoint," we still have no idea what "Shakespeare the man" was like, and it would be a mistake to assume we inhabit his psyche through the plays. Whatever the Shakespearean view is, it is not William Shakespeare's psychology or his specific ways of linking himself to the world. At best we get glimmers of such things. What we understand is a cluster of complex associations that seem to fill out a world and an idea of what it means to be human. But when it comes to the very best writers, we can't say with certainty just how the writer feels about human behavior. What was Shakespeare's religious viewpoint? Did he have a tragic or a comic orientation to life? The multifariousness of the texts undermines such ways of thinking about the writer. Surely Shakespeare embraced both the comic and tragic aspects of life, just as he evoked a sense of the Royalist position as much as he was capable of undermining it or was able to present both Christian and pagan orientations in the same play, confusing us by doing so. We could say he isn't interested in such distinctions, which seems likely, or that his greatness stems from the fact that at any given moment he could easily enough adopt any of a number of positions with utter conviction.

At the same time, although it may be true that someone loves Shakespeare because of his rich psychological portraits of human behavior, that is insufficient for a love affair with an author. Likewise for the current manias that insist on seeing the plays as a workshop for gender, ideas of the orient, visions of religious conflict, or other social problems. Shakespeare involves himself in these contexts, but he exceeds their narrow focus, just as any serious critical attachment to him would go beyond the particular viewpoint that was brought to the texts. No disciplinary, biographical, or psychological approach can adequately capture the relationship between Shakespeare and his most ardent suitors.

We need to remember that the *Ion* insists that the attachments inherent in the poetic relationship are divinely inspired, a function of not being in one's right mind and not, therefore, concerned with the personal or the disciplinary; those are social functions, whereas the poet's work has to do with the transport inherent in the magnetic powers the gods pass down to the poet and the rhapsode to the audience. Even if we don't speak of divine inspiration, and even if we don't believe in being possessed by a text, these Socratic ways of characterizing the poet's power focus on the affective mode of our body. Ion "specializes" in Homer because there are compelling affective links that attach him to the Homeric texts. He didn't "choose" Homer but was chosen by him: the iron filings lined up in a particular way, and he began to recite Homer with the kind of power he couldn't bring to other poets. Ion no more knows why he fits so snugly with Homer than we are capable of describing why a Shakespearean becomes a Shakespearean. This "gift from god" comes to anyone who has been captivated by poetry and devoted his life to it through particular attachments to texts. It manifests our most compelling intuitive powers, those tacit links to the world, to other people, and to poetic discourse that make life worth living.

The larger mystery addresses the basic affective and intuitive attachments we have to the world, out of which the specific links develop over time. The affective world—the emotional and intuitive aspects of our being—has been discredited for so long that we fail to notice Socrates' commitments to these great gifts. We regularly ignore that the most powerful Socratic dialogues focus on some part of the human mystery that devolves from our affective links to the world. This is most obvious in works such as the *Ion* or the *Symposium* that are devoted to material like poetic inspiration or love, but even in dialogues where justice or truth is the center of attention, the same affective field of play enters in at every level. At some point, for example, one might be inclined to ask why Socrates can't make up his mind about whether humans can be taught, whether learning is a kind of recollection or a form of divine communication between gods and humans. Surely such a wise man should have some answers to these fundamental questions. The same applies for truth, justice, and arete: why does Socrates leave us with so little that helps us understand them?

The only pertinent answer is that any specific response to the basics of human existence is so caught up in the particular affective linkages through which it manifests itself that we cannot produce a simple declarative response about the nature of this or that. Our world is encircled by great affective powers about which we are more or less ignorant, in spite of the fact that we remain confident we can answer questions about the nature of truth, justice, or love. Even if we think the most skeptical response is the most accurate one—truth, justice, and love are social constructs we manipulate within linguistic games for our own self-serving ends— we too easily convince ourselves that we really know what these things are. There are doubtless many academics today who are completely skeptical about truth, justice, and love, who make a living by declaring themselves so, who at the same time are deeply in love with someone, who speak in a variety of contexts with full conviction that they know the truth, and who have a strong viewpoint on what justice would be in any specific situation. The logic choppers of the world would exult in the contradiction between theory and practice in such lives, but they would miss the more important point: the affective elements of our existence are invariably undercut by the logical statements we make about our lives because that aspect of our being is completely irrational.

We are affective creatures from the ground up. Even the scientific world has begun to investigate the emotional contexts of our lives,[7] though it continues to do so in the crudest of fashions and hasn't begun to probe the links to the world that are so important to a dialogue like the *Ion:* why does poetry have power over us, how does it works its charms on us, and what are its effects on our lives? We are intuitive creatures, but most often we are hardly aware of this fact and are even more ignorant of the power of intuition in our daily interactions with the world. How are we able to make imaginative leaps from across a large room that allow us to know what someone else is saying when we can't hear the words? How do we sense danger or comfort in a specific context? How do we manage on occasion to know what another person says and means in complex utterances? These situations require what has long been called intuition, yet for the most part the word is associated with negative irrational states, or nonexistent states that are erroneously interpreted as intuitions when they are only bad interpretations. When God died, so did the world of affect and intuition. Nietzsche had read Plato well enough to know that Socrates considered the affective/intuitive domain of humans the province of divine inspiration and various forms of possession, and his own commitments to inspiration show that Nietzsche recognized the centrality of the affective to our lives as well. His insistence that we revalue the world on the basis of our bodily hebetude suggests the same thing. But when God died, inspiration died, and we have yet to resuscitate it, though our increasing awareness of the affective elements of our being suggest a reappraisal is in order.

Poetry and intuition: a necessary relationship, the one that most fundamentally articulates our attachments to the world and reminds us of the divine powers that move through our lives. If we are convinced of these facts, the most curious element of the *Ion* comes not in what Socrates says about the divine powers of inspiration but rather in what he doesn't say. He is so intent on proving the divine nature of poetic discourse that he blinks when it comes to the potentially negative offshoots of this realization. I have already mentioned the most curious omission: he speaks of the magnetic power of poetic discourse while ignoring the fact that magnetic power declines as the attraction moves from level to level. Inasmuch as Socrates chose the metaphor as a fitting way of speaking of poetry's power, one might think he would mention that the power lessens as the words move down the chain. The failure to note this weakening of effect is striking, all the more so since we know it will later be a primary source of attack against the poets. Even worse, Socrates at no point discusses misinterpretation at any level. Given what he knows about the ways in which words get misconstrued, we can only be struck by his failure to acknowledge that the gods' words can be mistaken by humans, with destructive results. Short of assuming that Socrates was trying to make the best case for poetic possession without trying to contaminate the process by things that can go wrong, we are left wondering why more isn't said about this potential problem.

An even greater omission is the failure to talk about the possibility of divinely inspired states that get out of control. Socrates makes reference to the Korybantian revelers, for example, who "when they dance are not in their right mind." He compares the poet to "Bacchic maidens who draw milk and honey from the rivers when they are under the influence of Dionysus but not when they are in their right mind." This parallel exposes the poetic state of possession, but it ignores the fact that these irrational states can easily become violent. The Bacchic maidens tear the singer apart in their madness, and there are other stories of divine revels gone awry; they flow from the inspired ecstasy that produces harmony and joy to the violence that threatens people's lives. Anyone who knows about powerful irrational states understands that this is always a potential outcome and can only wonder why Socrates doesn't mention it. It is as though he deliberately hides the negative underside of one of the most powerful human states. The dialogue itself might be more effective as a paean to the poet's powers if it acknowledged these limitations. The poet may well be a light, winged, and holy thing, but not all those who listen to him are, and there is no telling what they will do when the charm of the magnet overtakes them.

Nevertheless, these omissions should not undermine our confidence in Socrates' defense of the power and importance of poetry any more than they should keep us from seeing the psychic dislocations to which he so adeptly calls our attention. Socrates convinces us of the sacred nature of the poet's craft even as he insists that it is based on a form of possession, even as he declares that the gods make their truths known to us in this fashion as much as they make use of oracles and prophets. It may be that our feelings for this dialogue are always tinged by our knowledge that Plato finally argues that the poets should be banished from the republic. But we also recognize that Socrates was acutely aware of the powerfully positive irrational forces that flow through the lives of individuals and communities, he knew how central these forces were to the good life, and he understood how important the poet was to the well-being of everyone taken up by his magnetic powers. Without him, the community loses its magnetic powers. Without him, life loses the charm that makes it worth living. Without him, humans remain devoid of the powerful emotional and intuitive truths upon which their confidence in daily life depends. In these respects, poets are as prominent and important as anyone in the community; without them, politicians and generals have nothing to hold together. They may maintain order and peace as best they can, but the poet provides the community with the words that sustain it even in its darkest hour. Socrates celebrated the divine poetic energies that redeem the day and convince us that life is worth living.

TWO

ON THE SIGN OF SOCRATES

IF WE consider the variousness of our ways of looking at the world, no one better embodies our concerns than Socrates, that ever-enigmatic figure who means many things to many people. The more one reads in and around Socrates, the more one is struck by how resistant he is to our interpretations. If our goal is to reduce the world to cause-and-effect chains that make sense of human experience, Socrates suggests the impossibility of such a task. Of course, our relations to him are made more problematic because we don't have him firsthand. We see him through Plato, Xenophon, and the countless interpreters who have considered him and his importance for millennia. There can be no fresh view of Socrates, but that doesn't mean he is completely elusive. It is relatively easy to get a good sense of him even if it is also difficult to understand the overall implications of his life for the civilization that follows.

Any consideration of Socrates should begin with the fact that the oracle at Delphi said he was the wisest of all Athenians. Socrates explains in the *Apology:* "Chaerephon, as you know, was very impetuous in all his doings, and he went to Delphi and boldly asked the oracle to tell him whether . . . there was any one wiser than I was, and the Pythian prophetess answered, that there was no man wiser."[1] Inasmuch as Socrates found it hard to believe he was wise, he sought out those who were presumed to be the wisest in order to test the value of the oracle. Here we are already confronted with a multiple array of elements in Socrates' basic situation. He only tells us that he didn't believe he was the wisest person in Athens, but we have to wonder why he works so hard to refute the oracle. If he were to refute it, he would be superior to Apollo's sacred word. How could a wise and reverent man deliberately seek out occasions to discredit an oracle? Socrates never even acknowledges that he could end up casting doubt on the value of the words of the priestess. He defends himself before his fellow Athenians against the accusation of impiety for putting new gods in place of the old, yet no reference is made to the fact that he called the old gods into question by his inveterate inquiries of those presumed to be wise.

Socrates appears to be asking a deliberately simple question about the oracle's words: "When I heard the answer, I said to myself, What can the god mean? And what is the interpretation of the riddle?" (450). It is inexplicable to him that he should be thought of as the wisest, so he decides the best method for pursuing the implications of the oracle is to make inquiries of others, on the theory that "if I could only find a man wiser than myself, then I might go to the god with a refutation in my hand" (451). The burden the oracle places on Socrates also ends up giving him an orientation to his life's work. As he puts it: "And so I go my way, obedient to the god, and make inquisition into the wisdom of any one, whether citizen or stranger, who appears to be wise; and if he is not wise, then in vindication of the oracle I show him that he is not wise; and this occupation quite absorbs me, and I have no time to give either to any public matter of interest or to any concern of my own, but I am in utter poverty by reason of my devotion to the god" (452).

Socrates shows his piety and devotion to the gods in order to overcome the charge of impiety that has been leveled at him, but we should find it curious that the oracle induces him to give over his entire life to its refutation. At the same time, we can see a pattern develop in the nature of Socrates' inquiries, as he learns time and again that the person to whom he is asking questions "knows nothing, and thinks that he knows. I neither know nor think that I know. In this latter particular, then, I seem to have slightly the advantage of him" (452). The ritual profession of ignorance always devolves from the two-fold inquiry: Socrates shows that the best Athenians may possess skills or ability of a particular kind, but they too easily transfer that skill to everything and assume they are capable of passing judgment on anything that comes their way. They are ignorant because they can't see the limits of their knowledge, whereas Socrates is always acutely aware of how little he knows and thus always assumes he has a "slight" advantage in wisdom over his interlocutors.

Socrates concludes that "the truth is . . . that God only is wise; and in this oracle he means to say that the wisdom of men is little or nothing; he is not speaking of Socrates, he is only using my name as an illustration" (452). Inasmuch as the oracle's pronouncement was negative rather than positive—it doesn't say that Socrates is the wisest person, only that there is no one wiser than he—Socrates chooses to infer that the point is that humans lack wisdom. In his account of his life, it is as though he devoted his time to the work of the god in order to refute the god, gradually realizing that he is a means through which the gods could test and keep humble those individuals who thought too highly of their intelligence. By showing them they were more ignorant than they thought, Socrates prevents them from getting out of control.

As though to ask for their pity, Socrates repeatedly reminds his audience of the great cost involved in his life's task: "I went to one man after another, being not unconscious of the enmity which I provoked, and I lamented and feared this: but necessity was laid upon me—the word of God, I thought, ought to be considered first" (452). Needless to say, those who were shown to know less than they thought they did weren't happy and grew to hate Socrates. Their rancor has much to do with the fact that Socrates was finally placed on trial, even if it is not listed in the bill of particulars against him. Socrates wants to defend himself against people's enmity by reminding everyone that a "necessity was laid upon" him to do this work, and he felt that the words of the oracle had precedence over his own well-being. He thus continued in spite of the fact that "this investigation has led to my having many enemies of the worst and most dangerous kind, and has given occasion also to many calumnies" (452).

What is so striking about Socrates' explanation is how improbable it is. Does he really expect his interrogators to believe what he says? He doesn't once suggest that he also takes pleasure in making fools of those who think they are wise, though he admits that the people who listen to him "like to hear the cross-examination of the pretenders to wisdom; there is amusement in this" (462). Doesn't Socrates enjoy deflating other people's ideas of themselves? He seems not to, insisting that he is simply doing the god's work. From an ordinary perspective, Socrates' argument lacks credibility in a variety of ways: it strips his motives of anything smacking of self-interest, even the pleasure of finding oneself better than one's interlocutors. It is based on an interpretation of the oracle that seems in excess of the facts: we can imagine Socrates trying to refute the oracle, but not using the priestess's words as a means through which to organize his entire life.

To his credit, Socrates insists that his pursuit of the implications of the god's words wasn't without its own tests. If he has concluded that his inquiries are "a duty which the god has imposed upon [him]," he strove in a variety of ways to ascertain the necessity of that duty. He tells us: "I am assured by oracles, visions, and in every sort of way in which the will of divine power was ever signified to any one" (462). We can infer that Socrates' life was a dual challenge: he was driven to make inquiries of the wisest wherever he found them, whatever the cost, and he was compelled to question and re-question the oracle that placed him on his pathway. We might assume that the repeated questioning of the oracle through dreams, other oracles, and visions reflects a fair degree of uncertainty about his mission. If Socrates was well aware of the enemies he was making, he would want to be regularly convinced of his duty in order to face the risk of alienating so many people. For this reason alone it was wise to continue his inquiries of the gods along with those of men.

To use a Heideggerian formulation, we might think of Socrates' work as a mode of inquiry that brought together the gods and the humans. If he doubts the veracity of humans who profess to be wise, he also questions the power of an oracle that declares he is wiser than he thinks. If he probes the limits of human knowledge, he also digs deeply into the utterances of the gods in order to fit their words into the human domain. Socrates is thus a fundamental site in the Athenian world where gods and humans come together, where what is known is interpreted and carried forth into new areas through an assessment of the enigmatic utterances of the gods and the reductions of those utterances by the humans who profess to know what they mean. If Socrates did nothing more than keep the oracles and other signs from being grossly misinterpreted, he would have had a crucial role in Athens.

Socrates' words to the jury nevertheless call into question the view of him as a reasonable man. First, we have already seen that much of what he says by way of self-justification doesn't make sense. That he was driven by an imperative from god—derived from an interpretation of an oracle—to question people so assiduously that many grew to hate him isn't reasonable. It is even questionable whether Socrates' line of argument has any plausibility to it. Second, his justification contradicts itself: he is paying great fealty to the gods throughout his life by trying to cast doubt on their oracles. Even more, Socrates makes no serious attempt to address this contradiction. He doesn't see that he is refuting the accusation of one kind of impiety by providing evidence of another kind. His arguments are hardly logical or rational.

In addition, Socrates makes clear that his entire life has been organized by irrational means. He has become who he is by listening to the words of oracles, dreams, and visions, and by attending to his daimonion. None of these means of understanding is rational. They are intuitive forms of appraisal that have little to do with analyzing the truth of this or that context. They depend on a richer, more complex assessment of things than reason can provide. Many Socratic dialogues make powerful use of analytic modes of inquiry, but the assessments of their results come down to the same things we see on display in the *Apology*: affective, aesthetic, intuitive measures of how well what is being put forth fits into the context in which it is placed. Socrates' strength as an interlocutor derives much more from his willingness to go with the flow of things and test the plausibility of what comes out of it than from the analytic processes he uses to probe the relationship between the one and the many.

When we listen to Socrates' defense against the charges leveled at him, we are forced to consider the implications of his self-justification: why does he think what he says is a credible response to the attacks on his personal character? Why would he assume that "the god made me do it" is a sufficient explanation? What is so pleasing to me about the *Apology* is how human it makes Socrates look. He has his arguments, but they are also self-justifications that don't work as well as he might think. He whines a bit, argues that only a fool would deliberately alienate so many people unless there were larger imperatives driving him, insists that he was doing the work of the gods when no one else was, declares himself highly important to the state as a result of his work, and concedes that he didn't expect to win and was surprised how close the vote against him was. One can't help but see a welter of motives, arguments, and affective stances in play in Socrates' apologia, precisely the kind of mixture we would use in such circumstances.

When contemplating the conflict between Socrates and the other Athenians, we need to pay attention to Socrates' awareness of what drives the accusations against him. He imagines one of the Athenians asking, "'What is the origin of these accusations of you: for there must have been something strange which you have been doing? All this great fame and talk about you would never have arisen if you had been like other men'" (450). Socrates is not like others. As a result, his fellow citizens don't understand him. One might assume Socrates' difference comes out in the fact that he has not pursued self-seeking goals. His poverty is a badge of honor, a mark of recognition that he doesn't think of himself first but is committed to the pursuit of knowledge instead: "I did not go where I could do no good to you or to myself; but where I could do the greatest good privately to every one of you, thither I went, and sought to persuade every man among you, that he must look to himself, and seek virtue and wisdom before he looks to his private interests, and look to the state before he looks to the interests of the state; and that this should be the order which he observes in all his actions" (465). Socrates has never once said that others should ignore their own personal interests as he has. Nor has he argued that the Athenians should pay no attention to the interests of the state. On the contrary, he wants to promote virtue in order to create the ideal polis, a state most worth living in because everyone is virtuous.

We can get some idea of the Athenians' problems with Socrates if we consider the nature of the word *arete* that does so much to define Socrates' uniqueness. Always a tricky word to translate into English, *virtue* is the standard way of rendering it, though *excellence* is a powerful alternative. Both manage to capture the complexity of the term even as their difference suggests our troubles in understanding it. Arete involves the daily practice of excellence. It is not based on contemplating the nature of what is good in the quiet of one's home. *Virtue* involves right action, filling out one's space in the social and natural worlds as well as one can. *Excellence* articulates the active part of Socrates' ideal of the good, for by definition the word means standing out at what one does, performing one's actions to the utmost of one's capacities. This idea of the good presupposes an aesthetic standard of judgment, finding the fitting proportions of a situation and fitting oneself properly into them. All modes of excellence are based on this fundamental principle in Socrates' mind, in contrast to earlier uses of the term, which assumed that arete was measured by one's physical prowess and cunning. Odysseus possessed arete because of his strength and his wiliness, his ability to turn situations to his advantage. Socrates and Plato move the word away from this more pragmatic form of excellence and transform it into a moral standard that is based on the carefully measured life in which nothing is done to excess.

Arete is a function of fit: the more harmonious the relationship between oneself and one's environment, the more virtuous one is. When one applies this general rule to the various tasks and forms of work in the world, it follows that the individual who makes the best baskets is likely to do better than the one whose work doesn't measure up. Because Socrates' idea of the good is predicated on the aesthetic standard of that which is fitting, it translates readily into both the social and natural worlds. Instead of assuming that what is fitting is preordained in some Platonic world of ideas, Socrates sees arete as the means of assessing each individual context for that which is most appropriate to it—the better one is at doing this, the better one is. Given this, there is every reason to think that the practice of arete can lead to wealth and social prominence: one's work will stand out as excellent, one's skills will be highly valued, and the rest will follow. Socrates is far from arguing that the Athenians need to adopt abstemious or ascetic ways of life in order to be good, though what is fitting is by definition not excessive—the principle of moderation is built into this idea of the good. But Socrates has no trouble arguing that the true pursuit of the good is as easily a path to wealth and esteem as the more typical ways of organizing a life.

Arete is further based on a non-self-centered mode of existence. If it can lead to wealth and status, it does so not through the pursuit of self-interested goals but rather by posing non-self-centered questions about the nature of things. One doesn't address the world by asking, "What's in it for me?" One sees one's life in a larger context, assesses the situation as a whole, and seeks to fit one's own activity in the flow or dynamic of the context of which one is a part. Arete doesn't produce ancient warriors of great physical prowess or medieval knights on personal quests for the good. It engenders individuals who are devoted to a contextually based form of excellence that finds the good in every fitting situation rather than in something derived abstractly from one's experience or achieved at the end of a long line of social and natural trials. Arete ought to be a function of one's actions every moment of the day.

Arete is fundamentally non-self-centered in its orientation because it doesn't split the world into subjects and objects in order to achieve its effects. It doesn't say, "I have a great facility for throwing the javelin, and I shall master that skill in order to achieve great fame." It says, "I have a great facility for throwing the javelin and shall pursue the dynamics between my body and the javelin as fully as I can because that is the best way I can express my relations to the world." Fame may or may not follow, but it is not the goal of this form of excellence. For Socrates, arete is never the self-interested practice we so often think of when we imagine the various contests around which Greek life revolved. We assume that the goal for every great athlete was fame, social prominence, and wealth, and we are probably more right about this than Socrates. But from his viewpoint, excellence is found in the expression of the relationship between skill and activity rather than in the pursuit of fame.

The Greeks didn't have a word exactly like *self,* so we need to be careful in our application of it to their context. Still, we can't help but recognize that what makes Socrates strange to the Athenians is his non-self-centered pursuit of the things of the world. This is incomprehensible to them because they organize their thinking around self-interest. They fail to understand that Socrates' inquiries are a form of giving that expects nothing in return. Socrates doesn't live in the world of double-entry bookkeeping that most people inhabit. He doesn't spend his days toting up what he has gotten in return for his actions any more than he is busy marking off the places where he got less of a return than he expected to. The bookkeeping life tallies things on the basis of the finite self that knows it will not live forever and wants to get what it thinks it has coming to it every day. To do otherwise from a self-centered perspective is to waste one's energies. The Socratic life of arete is opposed to this viewpoint, insisting that as long as one constantly evaluates what is fitting in one's life, the problem of self and the question of payoffs become pointless and uninteresting. They are shoddy means for organizing one's relations to the world. The unexamined life is not worth living for Socrates because it fails to see the unimportance of the self, just as it can't discern the proper relations between the individual and the world.

From another angle, we might think the Athenians fail to understand Socrates because of their own laziness. It may be that wealth and status are available either with or without Socrates' commitment to the good, but, given the choice, the majority of people tend to pursue wealth and status in the old-fashioned self-centered way. Socrates' approach might be thought harder for a variety of reasons. It is not the typical mode of organization, so one has to devote extra energy to think in a non-self-centered way and has to have energy left over to fend off society's complaints about one's rebellion against its rules. That combination makes it more difficult to work through arete than to go along with the ordinary modes of achieving social goals. Arete may be the better way to conduct one's life, and it may be easier in some respects, but it looks more difficult to one who doesn't practice it.

We all know good work when we see it, but perhaps it is harder to understand how good work is accomplished than it might seem. More to the point would be a simpler fact: too many people don't receive the same kind of "reward" for good work that Socrates does. They don't take satisfaction in efforts employed to good purpose. Why this should be so is a mystery too, for there is great pleasure in accomplishment that comes from hard work. Yet somehow that form of pleasure isn't as evident to most people as it is to Socrates. This explanation for the difference between Socrates and the other Athenians makes more sense than laziness, for many people will work hard at things that have nothing to do with the practice of arete. Individuals expend enormous amounts of energy pursuing sexual objects of desire, for example, because their pleasures are intense. They can also devote tremendous energy to their children. Unwillingness to work hard doesn't seem to be the main problem in the Socratic difference, then, even if it is part of the scenario.

What gives Socrates pleasure—organizing his life around the daily pursuit of arete—doesn't seem to provide the same satisfaction for others. Is this because their minds are improperly organized to appreciate the pleasures of arete? Or are their minds organized so that there is no ready reinforcement for that which Socrates most desires? This would seem to be a chicken-and-egg question: one could argue that the pleasures of arete are unavailable because the organizational discipline hasn't been established

to produce them, or one could assert that the organizational structures don't exist because most minds don't adequately reinforce
the pleasures of arete. No matter what they do, individuals who
aren't "made" to seek out such satisfaction are not going to be
inclined to do so. Even if Socrates became rich as a result of his
pursuit of excellence and provided a model for public success, his
way of doing so would not reinforce the same neural circuitry in
the majority of people.

One could phrase the matter a different way and say that some
humans are more inclined to take their pleasures in a public way
whereas others' satisfactions are more intrinsically motivated. For
some, pleasure is defined by the status quo; for others, the true
pleasures of life have little to do with what anyone else might be
thinking at any given moment. Here, too, we come up against a
wall, first because human situations are never this clear-cut: we all
derive a certain amount of satisfaction from public pleasures and
from private ones—the dividing line between the two is never
neat. More to the point, Socrates organizes his life around public
pleasures too: he is always out among the people asking questions,
pursuing his inquiries. He is not an asocial individual. It is simply
that his public pleasures are different from other people's.

Another approach can be framed on the basis of one of Socrates'
most enduring questions: can arete be taught? The Platonic dialogues suggest both that it can and that it cannot. This has always
been the most troubling of Socratic questions because the health
of the community depends on how we respond to it and organize our social systems. If arete can be taught, good people will be
able to pass on their notion of excellence to their children. Yet
time and again, as we see in *Meno,* parents are unable to do this:
prominent, honorable people end up producing troubled, dishon-
orable children. Yet surely a person committed to arete would
strive to pass on virtue to his or her children. It follows that excellence cannot be taught. There must be some truth to this viewpoint, or else noble houses would become more noble as the generations move forward, and they don't.

Whatever it takes to pass along excellence to others remains as

elusive as it ever did. We know this because we have regular public crises that point to the problem. We always seem to be agoniz-
ing over murders of children in schools, corporate thievery, racial
abominations, or some other form of degradation. When such terrible things happen, we struggle to discover what could have pre-
vented them. If we think about children killing other children in
schools, some will blame the ready access kids have to guns, which
unquestionably plays a part. Others will attribute the problem to
a subculture that attracts some teenagers—whether it be computer
games and their attendant mythologies or devil worship—and
there will often be truth to that as well. Still others will blame the
parents and insist they must have been neglectful, which is often
true too. Or we might think that society's general indifference to
teenagers and their problems produces these unfortunate situations. This has plausibility as well, as in the "bad seed" theory,
which suggests that certain brains at specific periods in their development derive pleasure from uncivil acts of violence. Where is the
truth to be found? In some mix of all of these possibilities? Or do
we make a choice based on our disciplinary biases?

To me it is clear that none of our explanations is sufficient.
However much our culture glamorizes guns and makes them too
readily available, only a few individuals ever shoot other kids in
schools. It would be good to get rid of the tremendous surplus of
guns, and it would also be an excellent idea to de-emphasize the
human attraction to violence. But there would still be kids doing
evil things to other kids. Could the children who do these things
have been taught otherwise? Could they have found a commitment to excellence? Perhaps. Did such a lesson fail to take because
of this or that specific factor? Probably not. Has American culture
always been more or less indifferent to excellence? It would seem
so. Might this have something to do with young people's lack of
interest in arete? No doubt. After all, by Socrates' standards most
adults aren't committed to excellence either. They are interested
in the pursuit of money and power. One might think that such
self-centered goals are the problem far more than what any particular person says or does at any given point. But the same thing

could be said for Athenian culture: it was organized around status and greed. That was precisely what Socrates was trying to change.

Can virtue be taught? I am Socratic enough to think that in an ideal world there would be a point of entry into everyone's orientation to life that would lead to a commitment to arete. We need to go back to the fact that Socrates is on trial chiefly because people envy him. They instinctively know he possesses something they do not. He has been unable to show them how to achieve the arete around which his life is organized, yet he is among them every day showing that he is driven by the most honorable pursuits. The Athenians know at some level that Socrates has the most worthy orientation to life, and they would be eager to possess it under the right circumstances.

I spend a considerable amount of time on the notion of arete in the courses I teach, and almost everyone in my classes has a good idea of what is being discussed and has an attraction to it. There are few students who are totally indifferent to excellence. They find the idea attractive in the way I suggested earlier: there is something about it that produces pleasure, that satisfies them, that draws them out of themselves and makes them think that maybe there are other ways of doing things. Yet somehow the appeal of arete doesn't take hold with sufficient force to become central to their lives.

I have pursued these questions for so long that invariably I even make the point in class: I will say to the students that they are obviously moved by the idea of arete and can feel its powerful attraction, yet most of them will end up letting the idea pass them by. Why, I ask? The answers are never sufficient, and they are usually the ones I already put forth. Social pressures push students to do other things with their time, and they feel they must choose between arete and what society says. Other students will say they are attracted to arete but find it too elusive a concept around which to structure their lives. Just what *is* this thing called arete when all is said and done, and what is one to do with it, they might ask? Still others will say—notwithstanding Socrates' argument to the contrary—that there is no payoff in the choice of arete. Organizing one's life on that basis doesn't necessarily produce wealth and status, and therefore it is too big a risk to invest in the principle when the outcome is not clear. Still others—myself included—might come back to a dispositional argument: some people are inclined to seek out arete, but most are not. Some people are intrinsically attracted to the pursuit of excellence, while others see its appeal but aren't interested in rethinking their lives.

In the end there may well be an intrinsic appeal to arete, but, for whatever reason, it is hard to integrate into one's life. It is difficult to understand, problematic to find organizational schemes that make use of it, and even harder to produce a discipline on one's own that is a function of excellence. Without any ready reinforcement for arete in the larger world, it tends to disappear, leaving behind the memory that there are indeed other, better ways of organizing one's life that one has abandoned for one reason or another. But if students respond to the attractiveness of the idea, most of them already know their lives will not be centered on arete. They may or may not make excuses for this fact, may or may not feel defensive about it or hostile to one who challenges their lassitude. But they recognize the power of arete and have already decided it is not for them.

These thoughts suggest that most of us are capable of appreciating the great power of the idea of excellence. I conclude from this that there is a theoretical point of entry into the life of arete for all of us. It may be that many are called and few are chosen, but that seems as much a function of the circumstances that govern everyday life as it is a necessity built into the character of humanity. The problem is that there are six billion people on the planet, and the amount of labor that would be needed to unfold the possibilities of arete in any individual is too daunting. It is inconceivable that enough humans would have the time, energy, and determination to allow whole societies to evolve in accord with an idea of arete. It is hypothetically possible but pragmatically beyond the capacities of the human beings who currently exist. And the current population doesn't seem proportionately any different from the one that existed in Socrates' day, suggesting that there has been no "progress" in this respect.

As noted, Socrates' difficulty in many ways stems from the fact that the average well-bred Athenian is more than capable of appreciating the appeal of Socrates' vision. That is precisely why Socrates is a threat to the state. Too many Athenians are afraid that his ideas might take hold among the young and breed a revolution in sensibility. If Socrates were a harmless old fool who went around spouting truisms no one took seriously, even a troubled Athens could tolerate his presence. The Socratic enigma is that most people are capable of appreciating the value of what he says but are incapable of integrating it into their lives. The result is that Socrates becomes a threat to them.

What is most curious is that the Socratic message has produced the same reactions in every society in which it has manifested itself. It is derided, ignored, or lambasted, but in the end it is also seen as a threat. When one asks why, one concludes that it isn't just because it is different, though that is part of the problem. If humans instinctively react negatively to the differences in their environment, it would follow that their initial response to what Socrates says would be hostile. But the problem seems to be that they also react positively, appreciate the worth of the goods Socrates is purveying, and would like to follow him into town for further discussion on the matter. Socrates' message is so dangerous because it is appealing even as it is beyond the capacity of most individuals. Having been exposed to the virtuous life and been unable to measure up to it, one can only spend the rest of one's life dealing with the rancor that follows from an awareness of one's incapacity. It makes perfect sense that the Athenians would be eager to get rid of this reminder of their weakness.

The ambiguous attitudes people have toward the Socratic way of life reinforce the problem Socrates poses for the Athenians. They want to keep things simple. They think there must be a root to cure every ailment. They dislike things that are too complicated, that are mixed, that are both attractive and yet difficult at the same time, that are plausible ways of construing experience yet elusive as well. Therefore, they would just as soon get rid of Socrates to eliminate the troubling multiplicities that spring forth in their minds whenever they confront their various reactions to his presence among them. Better to remove the questioner than to attempt to answer the questions. Socrates is tellingly blunt in laying such a viewpoint before the jury in the *Apology:* "Me you have killed because you wanted to escape the accuser, and not to give an account of your lives" (468). They know that what Socrates says has value; they simply don't want to measure their own lives in accord with that standard and thereby have no choice but to eliminate the standard-bearer.

Socrates also recognizes how things will turn out. He must be surprised that he managed to live seventy years, given the difficulties he produces for society. He is equally clear that his demise will not be caused by the error of his ways but rather by his probity, the forcefulness that pushed his inquiries to the point where people came to dislike him. He was able to cut through the persuasive rhetoric that dominates public life and show what was true and what was not. The result, says Socrates, is that "I certainly have many enemies, and this is what will be my destruction if I am destroyed; of that I am certain;—not Meletus, nor yet Anytus, but the envy and detraction of the world, which has been the death of many good men, and will probably be the death of many more; there is no danger of my being the last of them" (458). Socrates is wise enough to know both the short view and the long one: he will be convicted out of envy, but he is by no means the first person to suffer such a fate, and "there is no danger of [his] being the last of them." On the contrary, there is an inevitable social dynamic when it comes to Socratic types. They produce turbulence, usefully stir things up, and then must be eliminated lest things remain in a perpetual state of uncertainty.

|| Socrates' relationship to Athenian society is curious in that he is devoted to the betterment of the polis yet is generally not regarded as having Athens's best interests at heart. Part of this has to

do with his incendiary ideas, but he also doesn't think of social duty the way other Athenians do. This comes up several times at his trial and is especially worth considering because Socrates is so insistent that one should think of the good and the good of society before one thinks of oneself. At the same time he is accused of putting his own self-interests before the state's in continuing to question the way things are done. Given this charge, Socrates feels compelled to discuss his anomalous sense of public duty repeatedly at some length.

The problem is most pointedly addressed when Socrates speaks of the time when he was a senator and was called upon with others to try "the generals who had not taken up the bodies of the slain after the battle of Arginusae" (461). He reminds his accusers that "you proposed to try them all together, which was illegal, as you all thought afterwards; but at the time I was the only one of the Prytanes who was opposed to the illegality, and I gave my vote against you; and when the orators threatened to impeach and arrest me, and have me taken away, and you called and shouted, I made up my mind that I would run this risk, having law and justice with me, rather than take part in your injustice because I feared imprisonment and death" (461). The first thing we learn here is that Socrates tried to take up a useful role in the civic structure of Athens, thinking it his duty to be a senator. He did not decide to stay out of politics without any experience of that world but rather learned firsthand why it was not for him.

Socrates reminds the Athenians that whereas the other senators wanted to try the generals en masse for failing to take up the bodies of the dead, he objected that this was against the law. He opposed the sense of the community, and "the orators threatened to impeach and arrest me, and have me taken away." Nevertheless, Socrates persisted in his opposition, knowing that he might face serious consequences for standing up for law and justice rather than political expedience. Even though he stood his ground, Socrates emphasizes that he "feared imprisonment and death"; he simply acted on his principles rather than his fears. In the end, his argument against trying the generals together was the proper one, and the rest of Athens finally came around to his position: "as you all thought afterwards." But before the others changed their minds, Socrates felt imperiled by the stand he had taken.

It is not unusual for someone in a political role to face a conflict between his principles and the pressures of social expediency, so Socrates is hardly the first to have experienced this difficulty. But he uses this particular case to articulate a general tendency: among the senators, there are typically two points of view—political expediency and a commitment to uphold the law regardless of the consequences—and Socrates was the only senator who wanted to uphold the law above all else. One might think this is not the best thing to say to people who will determine whether one will be put to death. But Socrates makes another, more problematic, point as well: his standards of judgment are so different from the rest of the Athenians that he would end up regularly opposing the general view and thus would never be a fitting member of the senatorial group.

Most harshly, Socrates draws the point for himself and for anyone else who would stand on his or her principles: "If I had engaged in politics, I should have perished long ago, and done no good either to you or to myself. And don't be offended at my telling you the truth: for the truth is, that no man who goes to war with you or any other multitude, honestly struggling against the commission of unrighteousness and wrong in the state, will save his life" (461). Constant opposition to those in power can only result in one form of death or another. However much one might defend honorable action in the abstract, in everyday life such a choice doesn't work to one's benefit. Socrates insists that this rule doesn't apply only to him. *Anyone* who "goes to war with you or any other multitude, honestly struggling against the commission of unrighteousness and wrong in the state" places his life at risk. Everyday politics and principle don't go together and never will.

Socrates then asks: "Do you really imagine that I could have survived all these years, if I had led a public life, supposing that like a good man I had always supported the right and had made justice, as I ought, the first thing?" (462). Again, we note the affront to his audience in these remarks, but they also reflect Socrates' problem with the mechanisms of the state. It is not that he doesn't want to serve Athens. It is that he can only do so in some ways and not others. Ordinarily one might think a man of such intelligence would be just what the state needs: more thoughtful people could only enhance its decisions. One might also assume that Socrates would be ideal for such public roles because he has repeatedly made the good of the community his primary concern. Anyone who has spent so much time prodding people to think more clearly about their choices in order to improve the life of the city should surely do even more good if he were put on an adjudicatory board that could make best use of his subtle interpretive abilities. One can even imagine some of Socrates' friends repeatedly making precisely this argument. One can imagine further that, having resisted these appeals, Socrates finds the more political Athenians are hostile to him because he hasn't taken up his share of the daily affairs of the community. Socrates knows that this behavior is considered both strange and self-serving and feels compelled to explain his choice in detail. Otherwise, he will just look like a selfish person who wants to do nothing more than cultivate his own garden.

What about Socrates' excuses for his lack of public roles? Are we to take them seriously? If we use the logic of common sense, Socrates sounds more like a rationalizer than someone who is sincere. Who more than Socrates could find the words to mediate between the differences he faces with the other senators? If disagreement arises, he more than anyone else should be able to work the problem out through dialectical means. And if he is not satisfied with bridging the gap between positions, he should be enough of an orator to convince others of the probity of his view. From such an angle, Socrates merely needs to accept the context in which politics takes place: self-interest, compromise, and the law tussle with one another in every situation, and senators do the best they can to work among these unhappy house guests.

Socrates suggests, though, that there is something about his life and mode of thought that is antithetical to this way of conducting business. There is an incommensurability that makes it impossible for him to bridge the gap between his view and that of the typical politician. The specific points of difference are obvious but perhaps less important than they might seem. Clearly Socrates is offended by the idea of filtering the law through one's own self-interests. This above all creates an insuperable barrier between him and the others because everything he does is committed to overcoming self-centered viewpoints. For him it is not a question of accommodating oneself to the pragmatic facts of decision making; it is rather whether one's life is organized around arete, a mode of thought that resists construing everything in the world on the basis of its value for the individual. There can be no compromise between a self-centered view and the approach from arete. Socrates is astute enough to realize this and to accept the consequences: it is not fitting for him to take up a public role.

In most respects all the other problems derive from the difference between arete and the self-centered approach to politics. But it is also true that Socrates sees the law as something sacred, to be upheld at all costs, whereas the typical politician is inclined to see it as something to bend to his own will or to fit the current circumstances. Socrates finds this offensive too, for if taken seriously, it means that laws are merely declarations of expediency, to be twisted and fit into a context on the basis of people's petty needs rather than the highest principles that govern the land. In turn, the fact that Socrates would be threatened in order to induce him to go along with the majority shows how little integrity others have. They can't bring themselves to accept Socrates' difference, even, perhaps, to accede to it now and then, because Socrates expresses his views with vehemence and refuses to back down. He leaves the senators no choice but to go along with him or find some way of stunning him into silence. They can't really do either, so they want him out of politics. They know the business of the state would grind to a halt if Socrates had a role.

A typical individual might ask Socrates why he cannot accept the terms of public service. After all, there is no reason why he couldn't state his position, do everything he could to convince others, and then abstain if the proceedings didn't accord with the law. The argument would run that even if Socrates didn't win many— or even most—battles, he would at least make a public case for an idea of the good. If Socrates won't do this, who will? And where will Athens be if no one is willing to object to the corrupt nature of the proceedings? Socrates should take the honorable role of noble opposition and accept his marginalized status as a given. But aside from the fact that Athenian politics doesn't seem able to accommodate such a person, Socrates has already made clear that this role would have led to his exile or death. Those in power would not have put up with his regular opposition to their plans.

Although he doesn't stress personal questions, Socrates has other problems in dealing with the Athenian leaders. Even if he didn't run the risk of serious punishment for his opposition, he would face the psychic burden of being isolated by his position. Such continued negativity wears one down, forces one to call into question one's own values. One might well imagine Socrates in his earlier days earnestly questioning whether he wasn't making excuses for avoiding public service when the main problem was that he found it unpleasant. He must have wondered whether he was merely rationalizing his position in order to defend himself against the complaint of selfishness. Who more than Socrates could come up with such a defense? Who more than Socrates could turn a simple case of public opposition into a potential threat to his life? Any intelligent person in his place would have had to work through such thoughts in order to determine how legitimate his concerns were.

One might imagine, for example, that Socrates would have been regularly attacked for his self-righteousness. The first challenge would be the most obvious one: if he and he alone opposes a stratagem, why would he think his viewpoint would take priority? The law of numbers would suggest that the majority is right. But the next challenge would be to the unreality of the principles on the basis of which Socrates functioned: it is all well and good to be right, but one also has to govern the land, which takes precedence over principles, particularly when the majority at any given time believes that principles are just a disguise for one's own interests. Socrates would be assaulted for his inflexibility, even if he argued that a legal system that one can bend in accord with one's needs is just a front for the will to power. Still, it does no one any good to be seen as piously committed to values that don't work in the everyday world. Regardless of the potential doubts and second thoughts Socrates would face on a regular basis, his public posture would end up being shaped by the senators rather than vice versa. He would take up a role that would appear to be designed merely to call attention to his own putative superiority over other Athenians.

At the risk of pushing Socrates' position too hard, I want to emphasize once more the necessity of his decision to avoid politics. In his world and ours, it is too easily assumed that certain characteristics constitute sufficiency for certain roles, public and private. There is no doubt that Socrates is wise. There is even less doubt that he is a master rhetorician, if by that we mean one who has allowed the nuances of language to master him. In addition, he is a subtle interpreter of words and actions, and he has an acute sense of what humans are and are not capable of doing. Finally, he has a great desire to do well by his community. Ordinarily, these characteristics cry out for a political role. We might assume that Socrates once thought he would take up a prominent political position in Athens. What a hard truth it must have been when he came to see that the way in which he regarded the good of the community ended up disqualifying him for any meaningful political service. Inasmuch as we think of his characteristics as ideal for a well-meaning politician, we must conclude that we have missed something: Socrates has all the right attributes, yet somehow they come together in him in ways that work against a political career. What makes the difference?

The long and the short answers to this question are the same: Socrates has a compelling intuitive sense of what is fitting in any given context that takes priority over everything else and must be preserved at all costs. Yet the more Socrates persists in refining his arete, the less fitting he is for public office, the more aberrant his views on the polis become. Like many individuals who have thought that the pursuit of knowledge was a pure good, Socrates realizes that excellence has its limits, that it alienates one from the status quo. However much we remain committed to the idea that a common pursuit of the truth brings us together, in fact knowledge produces exclusions everywhere it is found. This is most obvious in our own times in disciplines such as physics and biochemistry, where in order to commune with others through the shared viewpoint one must spend many years mastering a highly intricate vocabulary and mode of thought. In so doing, one ends up being able to converse meaningfully with the twenty or fifty or one hundred others who have developed the same complex understanding through the same "language game." This fact is less obvious in the case of someone like Socrates, for he seems only to be asking simple questions in language that almost anyone can understand.

Why, then, should Socrates have such trouble finding meaningful discussion? And why can't he discover ways of bringing his own deft sense of language and life to others so they may share it with him? We tend to think that Plato must have gone out of his way to come up with fools for Socratic interlocutors in many of the dialogues just to make Socrates stand out, but perhaps there are so many fools in the dialogues because Socrates is that rarest of individuals, a wise man. Protagoras and a few others aside, Socrates has no one to talk to, and not just because his language has become rarefied. Rather, he organizes his life and thought in such a way that words mean different things to him and concepts take on different colors when he discusses them. We might imagine him endlessly saying, "No, that is not what I meant at all." No doubt Socrates emphasizes his common traits for a variety of reasons, not the least of which would be to make himself less conspicuous. But his commitment to arete places him in a universe that is fundamentally different from the rest of the Athenian world, and there can be no meaningful converse between the two. Self-preservation would dictate a retreat from politics, then, as would the goal of keeping alive an awareness of the great virtue inherent in a commitment to excellence.

‖ Socrates was right to avoid politics. But his refusal of political roles doesn't mean that he chose not to devote himself to the polis. On the contrary, Socrates replaced political investments with other forms of public service, most notably his endless questioning. Even as Socrates suggests he would have been put to death if he had chosen a political life, he insists on the importance of his own forms of service. The most compelling statement of Socrates' social commitment comes when he warns the Athenians of what they will lose if they take his life: "For if you kill me you will not easily find another like me, who, if I may use such a ludicrous figure of speech, am a sort of gadfly, given to the state by the God; and the state is like a great and noble steed who is tardy in his motions owing to his very size, and requires to be stirred into life. I am that gadfly which God has given the state, and all day long and in all places am always fastening upon you, arousing and persuading and reproaching you" (460). As a gadfly that continually nips at the flesh of the state, Socrates manages to spur the animal to greater lengths than it would otherwise be capable of reaching. The state has an inherent tendency toward inertia, bolstered by the status quo that is always more or less content with the way things are because of its privileges. For this reason alone Athens needs someone to prod it when it would otherwise nod off.

Socrates believes that his public role is "arousing and persuading and reproaching" the leaders of Athens in order to get them to do the things they know are right but are hesitant to undertake. And although no one likes a gadfly, Socrates doesn't mind taking up this role. As always, he even recognizes the multiplicity inherent in this ad hoc position. The state needs to be roused from its dogmatic slumbers. Likewise, there are occasions when it needs to be reproached for a self-serving action that doesn't help the community, even if the leaders are content to move forward with their plans. By working through these various roles, Socrates modulates the effects of the state and improves its movement, pushing its actions closer to the ideal of greatness.

How, we might think, does the role of gadfly differ from that of senator? Why does Socrates think it is bad for him to be politically involved in a direct way whereas being a gadfly is suitable? Surely both roles are political, for Socrates urges people to consider things that will affect their policy decisions, just as his reproaches also have effects on the city. Similarly, anyone who devotes his time to being a gadfly is likely to offend people. If Socrates was so concerned about being put to death for his views as a politician, why isn't he worried about the problems that are likely to come from being a gadfly? The main difference between gadfly and politician would seem to be the unofficial, scrappy, ad hoc nature of the gadfly's role. Socrates will urge many of the same things upon the leaders of the community, but he won't be directly making policy. Why might Socrates think this would be a good role for him? Primarily, it would seem, because this position allows him to work in his most favored format: one-on-one or in small groups. However eloquent and rhetorically persuasive Socrates can be, he doesn't like the role of public speaker. Among other things, it calls too much attention to him. For someone who is as brazen as he is in conversation, Socrates has a surprising unwillingness to display himself in larger public forums. This might seem strange to us, but it makes perfect sense that someone could thrive in dialogic contexts while not performing well in large public venues. The one situation involves intimate conversation in a small setting; the other puts one in an environment where people mass together and most of the individuals are relative strangers. The one evolves from an exchange where the nature of the discourse is shaped by both interlocutors; the other is a hierarchical form of speech that moves from those who know to those who don't.

However ironic Socrates' endless protestations of his ignorance may be, we must believe him. Anyone who witnesses Socrates in action on a regular basis can't help but see how totally dependent his sense of things is on the context in which he finds himself. If his interlocutor supplies words and context too, there are other elements in the mix that are also beyond Socrates' control. When he asks about the nature of virtue, he does so because he really doesn't know what it is. If he asks whether arete can or cannot be taught, he does so because he has ruminated on the subject long enough to know that he doesn't know. He can't make up his mind about whether or not it can be taught. If we assume Socrates is sincere in expressing his lack of specific knowledge, it would make perfect sense that he would work best in situations where definitive answers weren't necessary, where one person wasn't in charge of the conversation, where it unfolded on the basis of its own momentum.

One thinks as well of the essentially non-self-centered element of Socrates' orientation. Excellence is the product of a carefully thought-out calibration of the relationship between human capacity and the situations where those capacities take up their place. One doesn't ask, "How might I best distinguish myself in this situation?" but rather "What is the best use of my skills and capacities in this particular context?" One isn't concerned with profiting socially from what one does but is interested in the best way of deploying one's limited resources in the world for the benefit of all. This is a mode that decenters the individual, places him in relation to a larger framework. It diminishes the importance of the person and focuses on whatever is in play between the individual and the context.

A politician's role, in contrast, involves a variety of different assumptions. To begin with, from Socrates' perspective a politician should be set apart as an expert. Rather than working from the questioning context of Socratic ignorance, a politician should be trained to address the issues that face him in the same way a doctor would consider the problems of a body. As a specialist in political machinery, such an individual places himself above the context and the other people who are part of it. His discourse with individuals is informed by his greater knowledge of the situation and his firmer grasp on the possibilities. His persuasive discourse is far more pragmatic than Socrates' mode and is one-way rather than dialogic. The politician works by convincing others whom he doesn't know of the probity of his views. Socrates works by endlessly considering the implications of what has already been said in the context of the question with which the conversation began.

In our own day we recognize that some individuals thrive best in large public venues while others excel in smaller forums with a more intimate dynamic. Both contexts can produce change, but they do so in different ways. Each context has different requirements for its participants. Socrates has regarded these differences carefully, on the basis of his own experience as a senator and as a result of his regular engagement with the problems of the polis when he talks to people in the marketplace. He has determined that for a variety of reasons his skills lend themselves to the more intimate forum and are not appropriate for the public venues of statecraft. Although Socrates doesn't flesh out his reasoning for us in the *Apology,* we know enough about him to assume that this precise fit between his skills and the intimate context inclines him in that direction and dissuades him from moving in the larger circles of political life.

In a dialogic context driven by a question rather than a questioner, Socrates can work out the implications of a problem with other people so that the question itself forces individuals to think without being preoccupied by their own self-interests. The questions don't have predetermined answers any more than one asks them in order to consider how best to prosper. Language is also deployed in a different manner. It depends on the willingness of the interlocutors to take their time in working out the nuances of words, patiently teasing out whether they are using this or that term in the same way, pushing and probing at the implications of one idea or another to see if they are really agreeing on the essential points or only covering up disagreements by not recognizing varying connotations in words. There is an open-endedness to this use of language that is not fitting for politics, even in the best of cases when we imagine politicians looking out for interests besides their own. The mentality that goes with open-endedness doesn't suit the different imperatives of political discourse.

We remember too that Socrates was bothered by the fact that he ended up opposing the majority's ideas rather than providing a positive approach to whatever situation was at hand. This form of negativity—action by reaction, choice by opposition—is deleterious to one's health in a variety of ways and generally unpleasant regardless of its overall effects. No one wants to always be saying no. At the same time, Socrates' role in the basic dialogic context is curious in another way, for he seldom puts forth specific propositions of his own, at least if we concern ourselves with those dialogues that question general concepts, the early dialogues in which we can assume we are nearer to the Socratic mode than in the later ones where Plato's interests take priority over what Socrates might have said. We might think that Socrates moves from the political role of opposition and negativity to the dialogic role in which he really has no position at all beyond the fact that he is the one who listens most intelligently to the implications of the question at hand. He is personally disengaged from the implications of the question beyond what it says about an idea of humanity. This might be seen as an empty rather than a negative view, a perspective that works itself out by determining what isn't the case. We recall that many dialogues end up with no meaningful conclusion. Yet in these venues where Socrates has nothing to say for himself, he ends up being far more positively and pragmatically oriented than he ever could be in the political realm. The indirection of his method produces results, whereas his direct opposition in public forums produces hostility and negativity.

There is another way in which Socrates' decision to remain situated in dialogic forums is the better choice for him and the community as a whole, and that has to do with the general effectiveness of smaller groups. Although today they seem to be used more by advertisers and political handlers than anyone else, this in itself suggests that there are things that can be learned in small groups that can't be discovered in other ways. Presumably the focus group's greater intimacy allows the "real" issues to come to the fore. People are more likely to discover what they really think in such a group than in another forum where they might be more inclined to side with the status quo. At the very least, the focused prodding of such group dynamics induces people to think things through in depth, producing greater clarity. To the extent this is true, Socrates performs a necessary public role that no one else can do as well.

There is one final element of Socrates' role that we must reinforce: in taking up the position of gadfly, Socrates willingly becomes an irritant to the body politic. He agrees to be placed in a less than glorious position because it suits him best. No young person is ever likely to declare that when she grows up she wants to be a gadfly. Anyone who has seen a horse bedeviled by a horsefly knows what a torment that fly can be. The best the horse can do is try to shake it off by muscle contractions or the wave of its tail. Short of that, it is reduced to moving to another part of the pasture in the hope that the fly won't tag along. Humans too can be pursued by gadflies, but we have better means of dealing with them and usually can escape from them. For all practical purposes horses cannot, and to the horse the gadfly can only mean a degradation of living conditions. To choose such a role for the good of the community is to take upon oneself great difficulties, not the least of which are the indictments Socrates faces in his old age.

|| In the end, Socrates can only conclude: "I did not go where I could do no good to you or to myself; but where I could do the greatest good privately to every one of you, thither I went, and sought to persuade every man among you, that he must look to himself, and seek virtue and wisdom before he looks to his private interests, and look to the state before he looks to the interests of the state; and that this should be the order which he observes in all his actions" (465). The average Athenian may not understand the reasoning processes through which Socrates determined what to do with his life, but Socrates concludes that the only thing worth doing is to regularly urge his fellow Athenians to pursue arete. Everything follows from this personal commitment, and therefore nothing is worth more insistent discussion than the manner in which people might pursue excellence in their lives.

Perhaps what produces the incommensurability between the average citizen and Socrates is not the different views of wealth and status but rather Socrates' fundamental organizing principle: his daimonion. The charge of impiety—the argument that he is attempting to replace the Greek gods with new ones—is a specific attack on the fact that Socrates' life is determined by the voice that tells him what not to do. Socrates has a daimonion and his fellow Athenians do not. From some angles this too can be seen as little more than an irritating tic: the Athenians are bothered by the fact that Socrates' voice is always mentioned as though it were sufficient reason for action when they appear to have no idea what Socrates is talking about. After a while, they must have grown weary of hearing about the daimonion and tried to find ways of getting rid of the man who endlessly spoke of it.

In order to assess the problems inherent in Socrates' daimonion, we need to have a better sense of its importance. Socrates' most comprehensive expression of his voice occurs about midway through his defense:

> You have often heard me speak of an oracle or sign which comes to me, and is the divinity which Meletus ridicules in the indictment. This sign I have had ever since I was a child. The sign is a voice which comes to me and always forbids me to do something which I am going to do, but never commands me to do anything, and this is what stands in the way of my being a politician. And rightly, as I think. For I am certain, O men of Athens, that if I had engaged in politics, I should have perished long ago, and done no good either to you or to myself. And don't be offended at my telling you the truth: for the truth is, that no man who goes to war with you or any other multitude, honestly struggling against the commission of un-righteousness and wrong in the state, will save his life. (461)

Socrates' voice is clearly the organizing principle of his life, the mechanism through which he determines what is and is not appropriate behavior in a given situation. He mentions that the daimonion has been with him since he was a child and states that the voice prompted him not to become a politician, adding to our understanding of that choice. It "forbids" him to undertake an action without explaining why. In this respect it is very much like other signs and the Oracle at Delphi, which more often than not make cryptic declarations that need to be interpreted by the individual who attends to them. The Oracle, we remember, didn't say that Socrates was the wisest person in Athens. It declared that no one was wiser than he. That doesn't necessarily make Socrates wise, nor does it offer a positive proposal about the value of his wisdom.

So too with Socrates' daimonion: it prohibits but never tells him anything specific. It doesn't insist he should run for office; it will comment on his ability to be a politician by urging him against it when he considers it. In this way the daimonion becomes a fundamental ethical check for Socrates, the ideal moral guide. He is able to think about a situation, decide on a particular course, and then listen for the voice. If it speaks out, he knows his choice is wrong. If it doesn't, he assumes he is on the right track. Socrates is so confident of this voice that he relies on it for the basic guidance he needs in everyday life. If Socrates is always committed to moderation, to a middle path through which only the most carefully calibrated choices are made, the daimonion assists him by speaking up whenever he strays from the path. If he thinks incorrectly about a situation or starts moving in the wrong direction, it urges him back to the right road. Such a voice is a tremendous asset, and we can well imagine that it is Socrates' distinguishing feature. Even if he hadn't regularly declared his reliance on it, his behavior suggests how much he depended on a resolute moral compass.

We need to remember that Socrates' daimonion is something for which we lack a word. It isn't conscience per se, though much of what we mean by the word *conscience* is built into it. Both are guiding forces, both often work in "negative" ways by proscribing activity rather than promoting it, and both are conceived of as the fundamental ethical guide in a person's life, intrinsically linked to the life the gods have allocated to the person. But Socrates' voice was not nearly as Christian as the word *conscience* suggests. First,

Socrates hears the voice over a wide range of significant and commonplace contexts. It isn't just there when grave decisions must be made. He tells us that it bedevils him about the smallest matters. We can almost hear the voice telling him he shouldn't stop brushing his teeth yet because they need a bit more work. It thereby broadens itself from a purely moral force into something more akin to an aesthetic impetus: it is the telemetry device that informs Socrates of the formal appropriateness of his actions. It determines how well they fit into the situation at hand and allows him to consider the patterns and rhythms of which he is a part rather than seeing his action as an independent force.

What distinguishes Socrates' great probity is that he has an ethical vision predicated on an aesthetic awareness of the world. He determines what is fitting, what belongs within the self-disciplined path of his life, through an acute awareness of the dynamics of existence, the patterns into which his life falls in relation to the other phenomena on the planet. He is good in the ethical sense because he is so sensitive to the aesthetic good, to the way his actions mesh with the world about him. Christian conscience has nothing to do with aesthetic patterns and everything to do with a paternalistic voice that either comes from God or is imposed on people when they are young by some authority figure. All daimonions are different, but conscience says the same thing.

Socrates' daimonion is his and his alone. At the same time, it is not exactly Socrates either. The standard definition of a daimonion is that it is a sharer or apportioner of fates. As such it cannot be reduced to a person's identity. It is the leading edge of the individual, the interface between the person and the world that induces one to take a specific pathway in life, but the individual and his identity are always more than this leading edge. The daimonion apportions and organizes one's life without being of it. It is the formal mechanism of the universe that is grafted onto one. It is the impersonal voice of the universe declaring what is apposite even as it can speak meaningfully only to the one whose daimonion it is. It both shares one's fate and apportions it at the same time, being neither quite here nor there.

The manner of the daimonion is most pertinently exemplified in the *Apology* toward the end when Socrates explains why he hasn't tried to escape from the death sentence in spite of the fact that he knows he is innocent:

> I should like to tell you of a wonderful circumstance. Hitherto the familiar oracle within me has constantly been in the habit of opposing me even about trifles, if I was going to make a slip or error about anything; and now as you see there has come upon me that which may be thought, and is generally believed to be, the last and worst evil. But the oracle made no sign of opposition, either as I was leaving my house and going out in the morning, or when I was going up into this court, or while I was speaking, at anything which I was going to say; and yet I have often been stopped in the middle of a speech, but now in nothing I either said or did touching this matter has the oracle opposed me. What do I take to be the explanation of this? I will tell you. I regard this as a proof that what has happened to me is a good, and that those of us who think that death is an evil are in error. (468)

Socrates is used to the regular intervention of the daimonion. He explains that it "has constantly been in the habit of opposing me even about trifles," so we see the degree to which it saturates all elements of his being. Yet he is shocked when the daimonion chooses not to speak up at the most crucial moment of his life: he has been sentenced to death, yet at no time did the voice rebel against his decision to go along with the sentence. It as though Socrates accepts the decree just to see if the daimonion will oppose his willingness to be put to death. Then, when he doesn't hear the voice, he is both astonished at its failure to dictate anything to him and surprised—almost happy—that the daimonion has helped him by not putting in an appearance. Because it didn't speak to him, he knows it is right for him to go along with the penalty and die.

I want to emphasize how thoroughly the daimonion is part of Socrates' being, as we see here in the elliptical way it governs him even when it doesn't appear. Socrates mentions at least three occasions: he left his house to go to court, he entered the court, and he started to speak. He presumably did these things with the intention of acceding to the court's will, but part of him also assumed that the daimonion would object to his decision to die. It is as though he leaves the house waiting for the daimonion to stop him; then he enters the court waiting for the daimonion to stop him; finally he starts to speak, confident that the daimonion will urge his words away from his decision to accept the penalty of death. Yet the voice never comes in spite of his expectation that it will. This is why when Socrates tells the jury that the daimonion didn't appear, he characterizes it as "a wonderful circumstance": he had expected otherwise, and his own ideas were once again surprised by the doings—or in this case, the lack of doing—of the voice. Far from assuming that he has been abandoned by his life-long companion, he infers that the daimonion is offering him the greatest assurance it possibly could: it agrees with his choice. What better way to make the final momentous decision of one's life? If the daimonion had overridden Socrates, it would suggest that its wisdom was in excess of Socrates' even after a lifetime of learning both the most and least important lessons in daily life. It is only fitting that Socrates should be wise enough to make the right decision and to find comfort in the fact that the daimonion agrees with him.

An essential part of Socrates' decision derives from the strange powers of the daimonion and the manner in which it goes against what Socrates might have thought. He concludes: "I regard this as a proof that what has happened to me is a good, and that those of us who think that death is an evil are in error." Other Greeks would have assumed that life is the most important thing, that death should be resisted at all costs. Regardless of whether we think of the religious duty to preserve life or the life instinct, there is something that prompts us to live, to try to maintain what we already have. On the negative side of the equation, we all fear death, not knowing what it brings, at worst assuming it will result in nonlife or the torments of some kind of afterlife. Socrates is sufficiently human to have these thoughts too. Why, after all, would he bother to use the lack of the daimonion as an occasion to tell people that death is not the evil they think it is? He is no doubt surprised to learn that his daimonion doesn't consider impending death an awful thing. It is also worth noting that even here Socrates uses his experience and the wisdom of his voice to educate the Athenian people: his own situation could allow people to see that there is no reason to fear death.

But Socrates' choice is once again in opposition to the status quo. It reflects his difference from other Athenians. The whole train of events leading up to Socrates' execution reflects the same pattern of "unconventionality." We can assume that the average Athenian would have placed himself before the mercy of the court in a position of abjection; instead, Socrates proudly declares his difference by insisting that his actions were fitting, articulating with vehemence the righteousness of his viewpoint. After he was found guilty, we can assume that the average Athenian would propose a reasonable counterpenalty to death; Socrates doesn't offer a meaningful alternative, leaving the Athenians no choice but to apply their own. He goes out of his way to eliminate all the other possibilities: he insists that he can't bring himself to go into exile, nor can he conceive of promising not to ask questions in the agora again. He is not about to change his ways at this point in his life no matter what the consequences, and he knows what the likely consequences are. After being condemned to death, the average Athenian would have done any number of things to avoid his end, from pleading with the court to trying to escape; Socrates refuses to do anything other than accept the fate that has been meted out to him through the interaction of the Athenians, the specific context in which they find themselves, and the ministrations of the daimonion: it is right that he should die.

It makes perfect sense that the desire to keep life would be the organizing principle for most people—where would the species be without such an imperative? But it can force one to give up everything one holds dear. We are inclined to take that road if it is forced upon us, though we all hope it won't be. But Socrates' life is organized differently. In conjunction with his deeply felt aesthetic orientation, his strong self-discipline, his deep moral probity, and the powerful voice of his daimonion, he declares there is a different standard that places some values above the desire to remain alive. If the Athenians were to take Socrates' display during the trial seriously, they would have to revise their idea of what life is about, something they are unwilling to do. So they condemn him to death rather than face any more of his daimonic difference.

Socrates does have some control over the other powerful element in play here, though: he could refrain from telling people about the voice he hears. We remember that he knowingly keeps humiliating the so-called wise people of Athens through his inquiries, willingly makes enemies because he feels the god compels him to persist in his questioning even when the number of his enemies rises to dangerous proportions. We might think this too is honorable: Socrates persists in the pursuit of right even when it takes a toll on his social standing, even when it places his life at risk. Still, aren't there other ways of determining the relative wisdom of individuals in the community? Couldn't Socrates find a way of pursuing his inquiries that was less humiliating? Isn't there something hubristic in this desire for inquiry that prods Socrates to go for the kill even when it is against his own interests? How is Athens served by having everyone's pretensions cut down to size?

The same line of inquiry comes up vis-à-vis the daimonion. Socrates' insistence on this special voice is at best a dual-edged sword: it distinguishes him from the rest of the community, but it also creates hostility. It is as though Socrates regularly irritates people by implicitly suggesting that his daimonion makes him superior to them. He has a voice that tells him what to do and they don't. Past a certain point, wouldn't it be best for Socrates to stop talking about the daimonion? Does his probity depend so much on this near equivalent of a deus ex machina to require his regular insistence that his word is better than other people's because he attends to the voice of the daimonion? There is a weakness here, a worry, perhaps, that his words won't mean as much, won't be sufficiently persuasive on their own: they need to be bolstered by the authority of the daimonion. Or is it pride that keeps word of the daimonion on Socrates' tongue?

|| Socrates insistently declared the centrality of the daimonion to his life, and that was part of the reason he was on trial. As he tells us, it is this ready reference to the daimonion that "Meletus ridicules in the indictment" by saying that Socrates introduced new divinities into the community. This is a trumped-up charge, the kind of thing people invent when they want to get rid of someone. Still, any serious inquiry into the nature of the Socratic temperament must finally ask in what sense the daimonion could be a replacement for the Athenian gods. Even if Socrates demonstrates proper fealty toward the traditional gods, is there any way in which his daimonion could be considered a new god? In a localized sense, the answer would have to be yes: Socrates' daimonion allows him to make choices in a way that is disconnected from the traditional gods. Even if he consults oracles and makes use of other forms of divination, the most powerful force in his life is the voice that proscribes things on a regular basis in matters large and small.

Socrates' daimonion is an internalization of the roles the gods have played in Greek society and is thus a mechanism that moves the people away from their traditional roots. It is not that Socrates is filled with pride, seeking to usurp Zeus's place through his voice, for the daimonion is not a personal characteristic. The charge, after all, is not that Socrates declares himself a god or arrogates roles formerly assigned to the gods to himself; it is that he introduces new gods. This reflects the fact that both he and the Athenians realize the daimonion is not Socrates the man. It is the voice that directs rather than the man who acts, and that distinction is never breached. Still, even if the voice is not Socrates' but another entity, it remains in contention with the gods for priority.

If we imagine a world in which everyone has his or her own daimonion, much of the work of the gods is taken over by individuals who heed the voice. This produces a breakdown of collective order, the shared agreement to let the laws of the gods dictate the parameters of social unity. If everyone listens to his or her own "god" and acts in response to the imperatives of the "inner" voice, there can be no consensus on the nature of things unless everyone's voice is in accord. From a traditional social perspective,

this is more than a casual threat. It could undermine the basic structures that constitute the community. One could argue that such
voices would contribute to rather than take away from the general harmony of the community, but Socrates never speaks to this
problem.

The threat of Socrates' daimonion is readily apparent if we consider the offshoots of the word. The Greeks conceived of the daimonion as either a good or an evil force. It might apportion one's
destiny as it does Socrates', carefully counseling him against specific choices and guiding him to the best of all possible lives; or
it might be a device of fate that leaps out at one and permanently
changes the direction of one's life—when Oedipus stabs out his
eyes with Jocasta's brooches, we find the chorus asking what daimonion made Oedipus do this evil deed.[2] If Socrates' voice resembles our idea of conscience, it also hovers near negative human states, as we see when the word *daimonion* modulates itself
into *demon* and *demonic possession*. Whatever that voice is, it is not
Socrates himself; it is visited upon him rather than a possession of
his. It comes from an unknown source rather than being a moral
guide that Socrates develops through consistent right action in the
world. It doesn't caution Socrates to reconsider; it tells him that
the choice he is about to make is wrong.

When people hear Socrates speak of his daimonion, we can assume that the more thoughtful of them consider what he says. If
they don't hear such a voice themselves, how can they imagine
what he means when he insists that his voice just told him not to
object to the sentence of death? One of the more intelligent ren-
derings of this possibility comes in Plutarch's essay "On the Sign
of Socrates" when the interlocutors consider what Socrates' voice
might be. Theanor proposes the following connection between
Socrates and the rest of us:

> But whereas some men actually have this sort of apprehension in
> dreams, hearing better asleep, when the body is quiet and undis-
> turbed, while when they are awake their soul can hear the higher
> powers but faintly, and moreover, as they are overwhelmed by the
> tumult of their passions and the distractions of their wants, they can-

not listen or attend to the message; Socrates, on the other hand, had an understanding which, being pure and free from passion, and commingling with the body but little, for necessary ends, was so sensitive and delicate as to respond at once to what reached him. What reached him, one would conjecture, was not spoken language, but the unuttered words of a daemon, making voiceless contact with his intelligence by their sense alone.[3]

What differentiates Socrates from ordinary people in this view is not that he has a daimonion and they do not but that they are insufficiently attuned to the nature of things to be able to hear their voice. They might apprehend it in dreams when the rest of their consciousness is damped down—"when the body is quiet and undisturbed"—but when they are awake they "can hear the higher powers but faintly" because they are "overwhelmed by the tumult of their passions and the distractions of their wants." What makes Socrates different is not that he hears a voice but that he has the self-discipline to constrain his passions and needs so he can hear its commands.

Those who are less disciplined than Socrates allow their minds to be overrun by other voices, the noise of desire, or the jabber of a disorganized consciousness that hears nothing but its own chatter because it has found no way to quiet itself. At the same time, if the Athenians possess daimonic intimations in their dreams or in other contexts, they know what Socrates is talking about when he refers to his daimonion. They hear that voice too, only they have chosen not to bother with it. Socrates threatens them by attending to the voice they cannot quite grasp. He produces envy because they have glimmers of the potential power of the daimonion and know the value of the certitude it brings to one who properly heeds it. In this respect Socrates threatens to undermine the polis by reflecting the great need all individuals have to organize their behavior, to discipline their energies so they are not wasted. People must train themselves to know what they really need rather than what they think they need. If they do that, they can quiet themselves enough to be able to hear the voice of the daimonion.

The Delphic imperative to know oneself is bound up with the voice of the daimonion, even if Socrates himself never makes this point. And although the need to know oneself is presumably central to the Athenian way of life, it is so only in the nominal way contemporary society seems committed to wisdom and learning. All recognize at some level that they should investigate the parameters of their existence, but few do so. Socrates devotes so much of his life to questioning the nature of arete because it is the source of wisdom about humanity, the root of discipline, the site through which the ordered life can manifest itself and the voice of the daimonion can be heard. One comes back to the fact that Socrates repeatedly insists that a life devoted to excellence is not devoid of wealth and status: "I tell you that virtue is not given by money, but that from virtue come money and every other good of man, public as well as private" (459). We might assume that the discipline of arete organizes one's energies sufficiently so that one knows what one wants and understands one's capacities. One is not bedeviled by false dreams or overwhelmed by fantasies of one's omnipotence: one knows one can do this and not that, has these skills and not those; one discerns that the best way to make use of one's particular skills is in this area rather than that. The result is a life that has coherence and is devoid of the internal noise that misleads one with its illusions of grandeur and the external noise of the community.

Do the Athenians have an intuitive sense of the ways in which the examined life, the disciplined existence, and the voice of the daimonion come together? Without doubt. Do they have some awareness that it is possible for them to imagine lives like this for themselves? No doubt. Do they regard such a life as the best of all possible lives? Perhaps. Are they willing to devote all their energies to the pursuit of arete? Unquestionably not. Are their excuses for not doing so legitimate or simply rationalizations for their own laziness? We can never know for sure. We only recognize that in the course of human history the majority of individuals seem unable to follow a pathway remotely akin to Socrates'.

Socrates is a revolutionary. He believes that arete can be achieved by carefully honing one's intuitive awareness of the world. As one attunes oneself to one's context, one hears the voice of the daimonion directing one in large and small ways: it will tell one not to eat that, not to use that word, not to make that choice. The more it does this, the more one's actions fit into the intuitive context with which one begins and from which springs the voice of the daimonion. It is, again, the interface between body and world, the site where the two work out their relationship, the self-conscious moment when the intuitions of choice are made known to one through the inner voice. It is important to remember how Socrates' quest for arete and the centrality of his daimonion are linked to his unwillingness to dictate how others should live. This makes sense because the unexamined life must be examined by the one whose life it is. Socrates can only prod people to ask themselves about the nature of their existence and hope they do the rest. He is not didactic, he is not prescriptive, he doesn't tell others how to live beyond one point: they need to organize their energies around the pursuit of arete rather than seeing excellence as something that accrues from the acquisition of money and power.

Socrates' moral habits are very much like the daimonion's, as is strikingly reflected in the form of the dialogue itself. The voice doesn't tell Socrates what to think or to do. It only tells him what is not the case: that is not the right thought, word, or choice. Similarly, Socrates doesn't tell his interlocutors what justice is: he allows an idea of it to emerge from the mistaken assumptions about what it might be; as the talkers eliminate this or that possibility, they are left with a better idea of justice, but they don't have a straightforward formulation of it because no such thing exists. The dialogue moves back and forth, driven by questions that prod the interlocutors as a daimonion would, forcing them to ask again and again: If that is so, what about this? And if that is so, what then? The question drives the questioner rather than the other way around. Socrates is always saying "whither the argument may go, there shall we will follow," knowing that he and his interlocutors are being directed by the inquiry rather than self-interest.

Through arete, Socrates proposes a curious shift in thought

toward an individualized and yet completely non-self-centered ethos that doesn't depend on the community for its sense of right and wrong. We understand a part of this viewpoint because we readily contrast the ethos of individualism with community-centered values. For better or worse, the community-centered morality has always prevailed, even in individualistic societies such as the United States. The values of the people are determined by the status quo, by the communal agreement of various groups about what is and is not appropriate behavior. Likewise, these communal arrangements are invariably prescriptive: they tell people what they can and cannot do. We may pretend otherwise in a consumer culture, but it is obvious that such communities are slavish and derivative. Today, we still fight a pointless battle between individual values and communal ones: at the extreme left and right wings of our politics, we have communal value systems that others seek to impose on everyone—the values of the Lord as seen through the most literal rendition of Christianity, or the values of the commune as seen through the imperatives of race, class, and gender. In between the extremes, lip service is paid to the values of the individual, but the word *individual* in this context is really only a displacement of the word *secular,* which means that the values are determined by peer pressure rather than through some putatively objective means such as the Bible or human rights.

We are so taken with this language and its ruses that Socrates' position doesn't make sense to us: we are back once more to its incommensurability with our ways of construing things. Socrates' ethos is individualized but non-self-centered. We must all examine our own lives, but from a perspective that derives from our relations to the world rather than from self-interest. We each need to discipline ourselves in accord with a commitment to arete so we can hear the voice of our daimonion, yet the voice is not ours alone, somehow not ours at all: it is the universe speaking to us from our place within it. To the extent that we listen to the voice, we will be working from interests other than our own. Our daimonion leads us to a place of shared accord with others, but we get there by working out of our own context rather than beginning with a communal view and applying it to our situation. The daimonion tells us all we need to know, but it doesn't explain how to get rich and famous or how to enhance our self-interests; it establishes how to make the best possible choices in the contexts in which we find ourselves. To the extent that we heed the voice, we end up with lives that fit their circumstances. To the extent that other people organize their lives in the same way, humans find points of interchange through which the individualized voice of the daimonion produces a community of values. This is the Socratic ideal, and it is found in the daimonion, in the commitment to arete, and in the method of the dialogue itself, which is an attempt to let the voices within us achieve accord through the questioning of fundamental values.

Socrates prods the Athenians with these values, spurred by his daimonion, which insists that he keep at it. He cannot move elsewhere or remain quiet. Those would be self-centered choices that would negate the value of Socrates' entire life:

> Some one will say: Yes, Socrates, but can not you hold your tongue, and then you may go into a foreign city, and no one will interfere with you? Now I have great difficulty in making you understand my answer to this. For if I tell you that this would be a disobedience to a divine command, and therefore that I can not hold my tongue, you will not believe that I am serious; and if I say again that the greatest good of man is daily to converse about virtue, and all that concerning which you hear me examining myself and others, and that the life which is unexamined is not worth living—that you are still less likely to believe. And yet what I say is true, although a thing of which it is hard for me to persuade you. (466)

The self-centered choice would be to preserve one's life at all costs, but Socrates decides to converse about arete as long as he can. The self-centered thing would have been to pursue wealth and status from the beginning, but Socrates chose to attend to the divine command that directed him to inquire endlessly about the nature of virtue so that others might see the benefit of doing so. Yet Socrates realizes he can never persuade the jury that his actions are a result of the non-self-centered commands of the god. That explanation is inconceivable to them because they never learned how to live outside the calculation of self-interest.

No matter what Socrates says, he loses. So he is reduced to the most telling, most incriminating statement of all: "For if, O men of Athens, by force of persuasion and entreaty, I could overpower your oaths, then I should be teaching you to believe that there are no gods, and convict myself, in my own defense, of not believing in them. But that is not the case; for I do believe that there are gods, and in a far higher sense than that in which any of my accusers believe in them" (464–65). The Athenians pretend to worship the gods but have lives organized in accord with their self-interest. Socrates willingly accedes to the power of the gods in a variety of ways but also believes in the gods "in a far higher sense than that in which any of [his] accusers believe in them" because he has allowed his daimonion and other forms of divination to determine the parameters of his life. That makes Socrates the most pious of men, the individual who shames others by practicing what he preaches, by organizing his life on the basis of a humble subordination to the larger voices that hold sway over the forces of the universe. Socrates is also wise enough to know that any purely self-centered commitment to rhetoric, any attempt to use the "force of persuasion and entreaty" to "overpower" the Athenians' oaths against him would only play into their hands by demonstrating that he was committed to self-interested persuasion rather than truth. He can only trust the truth of his voice and let his fate fall out as he fully expected it would in the first place: it is time for him to die.

‖ One final approach to the intersection of arete, the dialogic form, and the daimonion would focus on why so little has been made of the irrational aspects of Socrates' life and so much has been devoted to his commitment to reason. The daimonion is a highly irrational force that intrudes on Socrates without any thought from him, the farthest thing from reason one might imagine. The dialogue form itself may have self-corrective mechanisms within it that could be thought of as the guiding hand of reason, but for the most part its powers reside in the force of words. Arete in and of itself has nothing to do with reason either. It is a commitment to know what is the most appropriate thing to do in any particular context, but that is more a function of an aesthetic awareness of the dynamics of the universe than a reasoning process. If so, why do we always think of reason first when we contemplate the virtues and limitations of Socrates? Why don't we see his reasoning powers for what they are, a subordinate, secondary factor in the overall dynamics of his life and thought?

The most obvious answer is Plato. As he moves along the pathway of his own career, Plato is more and more intent on making Socrates into someone whose sole guide is reason. Socrates himself praised the virtues of reason, and rightly so, but in the end he is far more committed to an idea of arete than to reasoning per se. And excellence is a function of a moderate, self-disciplined, careful assessment of one's relations to the world, only a part of which is covered by the act of analysis. Socrates never suggests otherwise, and when we look at the early dialogues of Plato, we find a wise man who relies more on his daimonion and on other forms of divination than on reasoning. The daimonion is hard to find in the later dialogues, but the record shows that Socrates' voice was a powerful factor in his life from beginning to end. Otherwise it would not be so prominent in Xenophon's account of Socrates' life, nor would it have been picked up by Plutarch. The daimonion is the most striking feature of Socrates' mode of being. The reason is obvious, as Theanor explains in Plutarch's essay on the daimonion: "For while the paths of life are numberless, yet those are few on which men are guided by daemons" (437). Anyone who is lucky enough to have a voice that guides him is going to know what a precious resource it is. Given the rarity of such individuals, a daimonion would be the most noticeable feature of anyone who possessed it, regardless of how it was characterized. Plato's later reticence on the subject therefore speaks to revisions in

Socrates' character he produces for his own ends: he transforms Socrates from someone whose chief characteristic is his daimonion to one who stands out because of his ability to reason.

We see this most obviously in the final, fatal employment of the voice in Socrates' decision to abide by the death penalty. Socrates almost dares the voice to object to his decision to accept the death penalty, perhaps even hoping it will protest. He uses the daimonion as the final call to order in his life, the ultimate arbiter of his fate. He waits for the word, even if it is a nonword in this case. When he gets it, he knows the time to die has come. But this is hardly confirmation of a reasoning process Socrates has undertaken. On the contrary, his reasoning about the death penalty comes later, backing up the daimonion rather than initiating its prompt. We imagine that Socrates is concerned that his decision to accept the death penalty is wrong. Shouldn't he live to fight another day, regardless of the context? What if he is mistaken in this most crucial of decisions? The daimonion brings him comfort by supporting his choice.

The significance of the daimonion is all the more obvious when we keep in mind Xenophon's rendition of the trial in which—though ready reference is made to Socrates' reliance on his voice—we find more explanation for Socrates' choice: "I would have guaranteed for myself a death made burdensome by illness or old age—old age is a pit into which flows everything which is intolerable and devoid of pleasure."[4] Regardless of whether Socrates actually made such an argument in defense of his decision to die, this sounds more like rationalizing than reasoning. It flows from the words we invent to justify a decision after the fact rather than to help make one. And just as Xenophon's Socrates is less captivating than Plato's because Xenophon doesn't grasp the essence of the man, so we would expect him to buttress Socrates' decision to go along with his daimonion by saying nothing with arguments that aren't very convincing.

Although Xenophon hears the word about Socrates' daimonion more insistently than Plato does, a comparison of his account with

Plato's provides an interesting triangulation through which we are better able to imagine what Socrates' mode of being must have been like. If Plato's early acknowledgment of the Socratic daimonion fades into the light of reason over time, Xenophon's Socrates is more of a didactic moralist than anything else. It is as though Xenophon's account of Socrates' life manages to capture specific judgments Socrates might have made at various times without getting at the essence of the man. If we could make a distinction between a way of life devoted to the ethical practice of arete—a commitment to excellence that requires the careful judgment and aesthetic calibration of every event of which one is a part—and a moralist who is intent on offering specific principles through which daily life can be patterned, Xenophon sees Socrates as a moralist rather than one committed to arete. Yet when we put the accounts of Plato and Xenophon together, they suggest that arete and the voice are the center of the man rather than reasoning on the one hand or moralizing on the other. Reasoning and moralizing are what are left behind when one fails to grasp the central essence, the daimonic voice that governs the pathway through arete.

I would argue that the great strength of Socrates' orientation to the world and his wise commitment to arete is that they are based on an affective, intuitive assessment of his experience rather than on a rational or moral mode of thought. Socrates' wisdom inheres in his willingness to make sense of that which doesn't make literal sense. He is so attuned to his environment that he is able to pick up the "irrational" nuances of things and fit them into an appropriate pattern. Socrates' great strength is the intuitive ability to sniff things out, to get what is in the air. The crucial capacity to reason about it afterward, to interpret the smells in the air, is also important, but it relies on the priority of the affective assessment of the world rather than the other way around. Socrates' wisdom depends on this two-stroke engine: an adept, intuitive assessment of the affects through which the world is assimilated, and an equally adept, reasonable interpretation of what those affects might mean: intuition moves toward reason, not reason toward intuition. Yet Plato repeatedly prevents us from coming to this conclusion by erasing the daimonic manner in which Socrates' intuitions come to him.

Xenophon does a fine job of reflecting Socrates' intuitive awareness of existence through one of Socrates' speeches at his trial. The remarks flesh out Socrates' role in Athens and other people's reaction to it:

> So, do you know anyone who is less of a slave to bodily desires than I am? Do you know anyone more free, since I accept no gratuities or payment from anyone? Could you plausibly regard anyone as more upright than the man who is so in tune with his immediate circumstances that he has no need of anything extraneous? Mustn't it be reasonable to describe me as wise, seeing that, ever since I began to understand speech, I have never stopped investigating and learning any good thing I could? Don't you think that the success of my efforts is proved by the fact that many Athenians and non-Athenians, who have made virtue their goal, choose to associate with me rather than anyone else? To what shall we attribute the fact that although everyone knows that repayment is entirely beyond my means, nevertheless people often want to give me something? What about the fact that there is not a single person to whom I owe a debt of service, but there are many people who admit that they are in my debt for services rendered? What about the fact that during the blockade, although others were filled with self-pity, I was no worse off than when the city's prosperity was at its peak? What about the fact that while others acquire their shop-bought luxuries at a high price, I arrange for greater, mental luxuries at no cost at all? Suppose that all I've said about myself is irrefutably true: doesn't it follow that I deserve congratulations from gods and men alike? (45)

What ties these queries together is Socrates' intuitive assessment of the world. The pregnant line is that he is a "man who is so in tune with his immediate circumstances that he has no need of anything extraneous." Socrates is above all one who is in tune with his environment. His arete is manifested in being perfectly placed within the situation in which he finds himself. Being in tune with one's circumstances is simply having an adept intuitive awareness of the world, adjusted repeatedly over time through the voice of the daimonion.

From another angle, Plutarch also helps us see the centrality of the daimonion in Socrates. He attempts to describe Socrates' wisdom in this manner: "Exactly as Homer has represented Athena as 'standing at' Odysseus's 'side in all his labours,' so Heaven seems to have attached to Socrates from his earliest years as his guide in life a vision of this kind . . . , which alone 'Showed him the way, illumining his path' in matters dark and inscrutable to human wisdom, through the frequent concordance of the sign with his own decisions, to which it lent a divine sanction" (405). Just as Odysseus was able to make his way through his journeys because Athena was there to show him what to do, so Socrates' daimonion guides him, illuminates his path "through the frequent concordance of the sign with his own decisions, to which it lent a divine sanction." The source of Socrates' wisdom is a divine dispensation that helps him understand the patterns of his life. But in order to achieve "concordance of the sign with his own decisions," Socrates must labor to assess the affective "information" that pours into and through him every moment of the day.

There is an ongoing dialectic between Socrates' acute assessments of his world and the voice of the daimonion. We always need to remember that the daimonion is not the equivalent of an internalized, domesticated god. It is always other than Socrates even if it is also always only Socrates' daimonion who is speaking. This is the aspect we are never quite equipped to understand. We think the daimonion is just a part of Socrates speaking to him, but it is more the manifestation of the universe "inside" of him. It is other than Socrates, yet it doesn't deliver its judgments generically, as oracles do. Its statements are always highly specific, relevant only to the one to whom the voice is speaking. That Socrates' daimonion induces him to agree to the death penalty because it doesn't object to it is as specific as one can get. The voice doesn't declare that anyone in Socrates' position should accept his death—that would be equivalent to the voice of God pronouncing a general judgment on how all humans should behave. It speaks only to

Socrates and only of his context. This is why it is a mistake for Xenophon to reduce Socrates to a purveyor of homilies; he only showed how his decisions were perfectly fitting in his own life.

In the end, one might be inclined to give up the idea of the daimonion because it resists our intelligence almost entirely. But Plato, Xenophon, and Plutarch provide strong evidence of its fundamental importance, and Plutarch has the great virtue of suggesting that all of us have a daimonion, if only we can find ways of quieting our needs and desires sufficiently so we can acutely attend to the affective world of which we are a part and to the voice that helps us navigate within that world. The link to Homer and his wisdom and the attentions of Athena allow us to see the quasi-divine nature of the daimonic dispensation. Plutarch understands the other side as well, reminding us that we should be circumspect in the face of mysteries we don't comprehend: "Take heed lest it be simplicity in us, in our ignorance of the significance for the future of the various signs interpreted by the art of divination, to resent the notion that a man of intelligence can draw from them some statement about things hidden from our view—and that too when it is the man himself who says that it is no sneeze or utterance that guides his acts, but something divine" (415). Because our intuitive assessment of the world is less adept than Socrates', we want to reduce him to our understanding. We take umbrage at the man's pride: *he* thinks he is driven by a divine force. The incommensurability of Socrates deserves our respect and attention because it proclaims that we too can imagine a life organized around an intuitive appraisal of the world that is guided by the voice that hovers around us, if only we are sufficiently quiet and disciplined to hear it.

THREE

DIVINE MADNESS

As we have seen, the more one reads the Platonic dialogues in which Socrates plays a central role, the more apparent it becomes that reason has a relatively small part in the processes through which the interlocutors of the dialogue arrive at their conclusions. Socrates repeatedly emphasizes how important it is for humans to sort things into their proper categories and to distinguish their qualitative elements, and reason is the means whereby these distinctions are made. One might even assume that the process of definition itself is rational, putting everything precisely into its own place. Even if one grants reason the powers through which the relations among things are established, though, one cannot read very far into most Socratic dialogues without recognizing the fundamental ways in which dialogue itself is an irrational process that employs reason chiefly as a curb to its potential excesses. In this light, reason is more a handmaiden than that which organizes human energies; it is a means to direct the flow of the more deeply rooted irrational processes, the mechanism through which individuals learn how to manage the various forces that govern their lives.

Similarly, Socrates is repeatedly clear about the centrality of the daimonion to his life. In the *Phaedrus,* for example, after he has finished arguing for the superiority of the nonlover over the lover, he is ready to head home when he tells Phaedrus that "as I was about to cross the stream the usual sign was given to me; that is the sign which never bids but always forbids me to do what I am

going to do."[1] Here again we see that "the usual sign" of the daimonion is the irrational principle at the heart of Socrates' being.
It provides him with no guidelines he can consciously build on,
though we might assume that repeated daimonic remonstrances
over the years induce Socrates to choose one course of action
rather than another. But Socrates never says that a particular pattern of choices is a function of rules he deduced from the voice
that forbids. He never organizes the implications of the voice and
in this way reinforces its fundamental irrationality. It comes to him
only when he cannot make the right choice on his own; then it
calls out and forbids him to do what he is about to do. Once his
actions are corrected, the voice disappears until the next time he
is in error.

If Socrates' fate is determined at his trial by the failure of his
daimonion to speak, his everyday life is also dictated by the voice,
as we see in his further remarks about his decision not to cross the
river in his speech to Phaedrus: "I thought that I heard a voice
saying in my ear that I had been guilty of impiety, and that I must
not go away until I had made an atonement. Now I am a diviner,
though not a very good one, but I have enough religion for my
own needs, as you might say of a bad writer—his writing is good
enough for him. And, O my friend, how singularly prophetic is
the soul! For at the time I had a sort of misgiving, and, like Ibycus, 'I was troubled,' and I suspected that I might be receiving
honor from men at the expense of sinning against the gods. Now
I am aware of the error" (58). Having declaimed on the virtues of
the nonlover in response to the provocation of Lysias's speech and
Phaedrus's regard for it, Socrates finds himself arguing for show
rather than to get at the truth: his decision to speak on behalf of
the nonlover had nothing to do with whether he believes the
nonlover is better than the lover. Socrates thus finds himself in a
situation where "receiving honor from men" takes precedence
over the truth. Even worse, his rhetorical deceits lead him into
"sinning against the gods" because he maligns Eros while uphold-
ing the priority of the nonlover.

Before his speech, Socrates "was troubled," "had a sort of misgiving," and therefore knew from the outset that his remarks were wrong. Afterward, his daimonion informs him of the same fact, "saying in my ear that I had been guilty of impiety, and that I must not go away until I had made an atonement." Ordinarily one might think that giving a short speech in a playful contest would be no matter for concern. It was clearly nothing more than a rhetorical exercise designed to point up the shortcomings of Lysias's speech. But for Socrates even this idle misuse of language is cause for shame: one should always mean what one says and say what one means. One should never use rhetoric for self-serving purposes but should instead employ it to seek out the truth. Small though this indiscretion is, it unsettles Socrates and prompts him to redress his wrong by a speech in favor of love that reflects the truth of the case.

In this situation, we see the daimonion offering confirmation of Socrates' initial suspicions. The flow of his dialogue with Phaedrus, we might assume, induced him to continue as he did even when he had promptings that told him otherwise, just as people find themselves making remarks at social events they know are mistaken before they utter them: wrong though they be, people often continue in spite of their awareness that they shouldn't. In such situations, one usually feels little more than a bit of guilt and lets the moment pass. For Socrates, the daimonion confirms the gravity of his misdemeanor by telling him he has made a double mistake, first by letting words fly free of the truth and second by maligning the gods in the process, impiety that requires prompt attention. The careful balance of a good individual's life must be constantly calibrated: the bad must be compensated by the good, an act of impiety followed by an acknowledgment of guilt and a pious act.

The small call of the daimonion in the *Phaedrus* reveals the ethical machinery at the heart of Socrates and shows how much his piety is connected to his sense of wisdom and his profession of ignorance as well. We might say that Socrates intuitively knew before he gave his first speech that he shouldn't do it, but it seemed a harmless enough peroration. After the fact, his conscience takes over and insists he has been impious and needs to atone for his sin. I would argue, however, that the language of sin and conscience is not pertinent because it derives from a Christian dynamic that doesn't apply. For Socrates the question of how best to live is more aesthetic than theological: the goal is always to choose appropriately, to make one's action fitting for the situation in which one finds oneself. The question of fit is more involved with beauty, with a match between individual and context that perfectly expresses them both. Socrates' speech is impious, and we may even think he is sincere in his concern that Eros might deprive him of love if he doesn't atone for his mistake. But the larger issue is the violation of rhetoric itself. The pattern and balance in Socrates' life depend on a non-self-centered orientation to the questions his experiences generate, and only when he addresses those questions in a disinterested fashion can he hope to maintain the harmony of his life and depend on the truth of his dialogue with others.

Like the rest of us, Socrates is ignorant because more often than not his choices depend on intuition. He has inklings—tacit, hardly noticed proddings—that induce him to move in this or that direction. The inklings are cues that suggest an orientation to whatever is taking place at the moment. Sometimes they are noted, just as Socrates suggests he had hints before he gave his speech that it was a mistake to do so; at other times they pass without any awareness of them. Perhaps after the fact we remember a certain feeling we had before we made our choice that we couldn't understand at the time, but quite often such cues are not recognized either before or after. Socrates' wisdom comes from these cues. I would call them the wisdom of the body, the intuitive links to his world that are based on the history of his body and thought that tell him what he should be doing at any moment. The wisdom and the ignorance are irretrievably linked because such knowledge can never be systematized. That, among other things, is what we mean when we say it is intuitive: it resists our intelligence.

Socrates' wisdom inheres in his willingness to listen to the small cues of his body, his acute attention to the intuitions that are always present to help situate a body in a context. His wisdom comes from the long-developed confidence he has in these mechanisms, his assumption that the initial orientation to a context his body provides will direct him intelligently, and his knowledge that the voice of the daimonion will come forth if he fails to attend properly to the inklings of his body. I am not suggesting that Socrates would describe his wisdom in this way. Among other things, he doesn't think of his daimonion as the call of his body. Nor do we see him going on at length about the cues of his body and the way they place him in a situation. He is more inclined to see such cues as mental or spiritual phenomena. Today, however, we would be more likely to think of the daimonion and intuition as bodily events. The intuitive cues don't manifest themselves with the same degree of self-awareness as the daimonion does, and the daimonion is a self-conscious response to a choice that has already been made, whereas the cues of the body orient us to a choice before it is made and while it is being undertaken. The intuitive cues and the voice of the daimonion are essential parts of the regulating mechanisms of the body that preserve its sense of wholeness and well-being. If they are driven by an aesthetic sense of what is fitting, they nevertheless show the intelligence of the body in different ways.

Given our view that Socrates is such a prominent exponent of reason, it may seem egregious to argue that his wisdom is a function of his willingness to listen to the cues of his body. But it is hard not to notice how carefully Socrates attends to these little signs, how intricately he considers the nature of his body and its responses to the contexts of which it is a part. We could begin with the setting as an example: the plane tree is a good place for a dialogue because, as Phaedrus puts it, "there are shade and gentle breezes, and grass on which we may either sit or lie down" (47). A dialogue is only possible when one can place the existential concerns of life off to the side, including the weather, insignificant though it may seem to be. The *Phaedrus* continues as long as it does because when Socrates wants to run away from his first speech as quickly as he can, Phaedrus says, "Not yet, Socrates; not until the heat of the day has passed" (57).

The subtle cues of dialogue must also reflect the disinterestedness of the inquiry. As long as the self is at the center of concern, a genuine dialogue is not possible, though it is often not easy to tell when we are being deceived by self-centered preoccupations. One of the strengths of *Phaedrus* is that it shows Socrates' ignorance, for he is clearly led astray by self-interest in the first speech. He may try to get out from under the effects of his speech by blaming them on Phaedrus, but Socrates too readily took up his part because he was determined to exceed the eloquence of Lysias, showing him up and thereby gaining greater regard in Phaedrus's eyes. We might also assume that Socrates is irritated by the fact that Phaedrus can't properly tell the difference between a good and a bad speech and therefore doesn't see that Lysias's remarks are flawed in technique and false as well. Socrates might have thought he was standing up for truth in discourse—a disinterested motive— but if that were so, he wouldn't have defended the nonlover. In doing so, he violated one of the greatest gifts the gods have given humans, the love of another person that produces the best happiness of which people are capable.

If we think about the first part of the dialogue, we find that Socrates is prompted to give his initial speech as a result of a typically thick context, one that involves everything I just mentioned. There are relatively self-centered concerns that stem from one's belief that one knows better than one's interlocutor, from one's irritation over the incapacities of the person to whom one is speaking. But non–self-centered concerns also enter the mix, those that come from a body's distrust for the gist of its situation: something about Phaedrus's remarks (and what Lysias says as well) isn't right, and Socrates sniffs it out. There is a relative crudeness to their responses to the world: Lysias glibly speaks on behalf of the nonlover and thereby desecrates the lover merely for the sake of displaying his own rhetorical skills. Phaedrus mistakes Lysias's speech as a masterful display of rhetoric rather than a structurally and philosophically flawed piece of work. Just as Socrates' body informs him of mistakes in his own choices, so too it responds when others produce error. When it does, it calls forth the need to rectify things, to introduce nuance into the situation so the mistakes are redressed and the balance is restored: Socrates must set Phaedrus right.

Socrates' initial encounter with Phaedrus is thus a mix of self-centered and disinterested motivations. In such contexts, dialogue can lead to the priority of the disinterested motivations or the self-centered ones. We might think of a genuine conversation as one where the disinterested inquiry wins out over the other interests: self-regard takes a back seat to the question in play. Socrates' goal is always to participate in disinterested inquiry, but even wise individuals can't always control the flow of discourse or attend to all the cues in play, so Socrates finds himself undertaking a speech for the lesser rather than the greater motives: self-centered interests win out. Fortunately, he has time to correct his mistake, so he offers a second speech that overcomes the self-centered impulses inherent in the first one. In the end balance is restored and the true value of the lover manifests itself, but only because Socrates is unwilling to settle for anything less than the best discourse, even when he starts off on the wrong foot.

|| If Socrates' wisdom is a function of the intuitions of the body as they manifest themselves in the cues of sense and feeling on one side and the voice of the daimonion (or the lack thereof) on the other, the organizing impulses in Socrates' life are about as far from reason as one can get. He is driven by irrational inclinations from beginning to end, and these impulses are not negative elements he must learn to overcome but the subtle gestures of a body to which he must learn to be endlessly attentive. It is not surprising, then, that the rest of the discourse is peppered with other signs of irrationality, up to and including the great perorations on the fundamental importance of irrationality to the good life. Early on, for example, Socrates says to Phaedrus, "Can I be wrong in supposing that Lysias gave you a feast of discourse?" (45). The em-

phasis on the word *feast* demonstrates how avidly Socrates seeks out meaningful interchanges. He sees them as the equivalent of a great meal, hardly the kind of language one would employ if one thought of discourse as a site for rational discussion. It is thus impossible to separate the pleasure of discourse from whatever truths it might purvey.

The irrationality at the center of dialogue is also on display in many of the offhanded remarks that punctuate the discussion. In tune with expressions found in other Platonic dialogues, Socrates explains the power of Lysias's speech by saying that "the effect on me was ravishing. And this I owe to you, Phaedrus, for I observed you while reading to be in an ecstasy, and thinking that you are more experienced in these matters than I am, I followed your example, and, like you, became inspired with a divine frenzy" (51). As with *feast, ravishing* is an intense expression of a person overwhelmed by feeling, stated even more vehemently in the remarks that follow: Phaedrus does such a good job of presenting Lysias's speech because he is "in an ecstasy," and Socrates "followed [his] example" and "became inspired with a divine frenzy himself." Socrates is no doubt poking fun at Phaedrus here, but such terminology repeatedly demonstrates that the effects of powerful discourse are hardly rational. They take one out of oneself and transport one to the world of the divine, overwhelming one with affect. Rhetoric has the power to persuade not because it is based on reason or logic but rather because it is capable of creating a divine frenzy in the listener that overcomes all rational barriers: the words move one to conviction because of their beauty, their rhythmical, intoxicating effects.

But such ecstasy is not the only manifestation of irrationality in the dialogue. There are many smaller examples that reflect how completely human existence is controlled by impulses that lie just beyond the realm of our understanding. When Phaedrus is done reciting Lysias's speech, for example, he declares, "I do not think that any one could have made a fuller or better" presentation, but Socrates quickly distances himself from such effusiveness by saying, "I can not go so far as that with you. Ancient sages, men and women, who have spoken and written of these things, would rise up in judgment against me, if I lightly assented to you" (52). Socrates has yet to formulate the reasons why he has problems with Lysias's speech, but he instinctively feels that such high praise is unmerited. He has internalized a standard of discourse that is based on what "ancient sages, men and women, who have spoken and written of these things" might say about the speech. If he believes it would satisfy them, he approves; if not, he senses that the sages "would rise up in judgment against" him, so he carefully assesses the quality of the speech in order to avoid the opprobrium inherent in such a judgment. The standards of the sages don't have much to do with reason, as they are more concerned with composition and style, though the truth value of the speech also comes into play. Socrates will shortly provide a more rational critique of Lysias's speech and demonstrate the ways in which it falls short, but initially his response is framed on the basis of the affective assumptions he derives from his reading of the ancients and his internalization of their judgments.

Immediately after Socrates' cautious response to Lysias's words, Phaedrus asks him where he has heard any better speeches, and once again Socrates suggests the intuitive means through which he measures the effects of rhetoric: "I am sure that I must have heard; I don't remember at the moment from whom; perhaps from Sappho the fair, Anacreon the wise, or, possibly, from a prose writer. What makes me say this? Why because I perceive that my bosom is full, and that I could make another speech as good as that of Lysias, and different. Now I am certain that this is not an invention of my own, for I am conscious that I know nothing, and therefore I can only infer that I have been filled through the ears, like a pitcher from the waters of another, though I have actually forgotten in my stupidity who was my informant" (52). Like most of us, Socrates cannot immediately recall a particular speech or speaker to whom he might attribute more powerful discourse, but then possibilities emerge: perhaps something that Sappho might have uttered, or Anacreon. As if stumbling about for an explanation for his reservations, Socrates gets to the heart of the matter when he asks, "What makes me say this?" and responds that the central criterion is "because I perceive that my bosom is full, and that I could make another speech as good as that of Lysias." In declaring that a full bosom prods him to doubt the quality of Lysias's speech, Socrates admits that the powerful feeling he has that he could do it better indicates that there must be problems with what Lysias has said. Here again Socrates uses a standard familiar to most of us, for we regularly encounter speech that leaves us feeling there is more to be said. We sense that we could do a better job of presenting the issues, so much so that our body prods us to provide our own discourse on the matter.

Socrates thus shows that one of the most compelling standards of judgment available to humans is the spontaneous feeling that they have more and better things to say on a subject than the speaker to whom they have been listening. This criterion works precisely because it is formed out of our direct responses to what has been said: as the speech progresses, we immediately feel that this should have been said rather than that, that the speaker forgot to mention this or stumbled on an important point, expressing himself poorly at the most significant moment. These are genuine responses to the nature of the speech and our sense of how well it fits the context it purports to fill out. In many ways there is no better gauge for the quality of speech, and even the most rational people begin with these kinds of intuitive appraisal.

Socrates' way of speaking about this impulsive response does an excellent job of fleshing out the context of his full bosom even as it demonstrates his conviction of his own ignorance. Admitting that he knows nothing about Lysias's subject matter that would lead him to think he could do a better job, Socrates concedes that the feeling "is not an invention of my own," that, on the contrary, he feels as though he has "been filled through the ears, like a pitcher from the waters of another." Once again, though, he concedes that "I have actually forgotten in my stupidity who was my informant." These remarks speak to a completely intuitive judgment of the quality of the speech. Socrates may be embarrassed that he cannot readily account for his instinctive reservations about the speech, but he knows with affective certainty that he is right to reserve praise for the speech until he has a chance to marshal his thoughts so they accord with his original emotional response to the speech.

Given the affective relation to words on the basis of which Socrates makes his initial judgments of rhetoric, it is no surprise that he suggests others make use of the same processes. In the middle of his first speech, for example, he declares, "And now, dear Phaedrus, I shall pause for an instant to ask whether you do not think me, as I appear to myself, inspired?" (54). Ordinarily we might consider this statement contradictory, for if Socrates were inspired, he wouldn't be self-conscious enough to ask if he appeared so. Inspiration is by definition a state in which one is carried out of oneself, so how could Socrates so coolly insist his words reveal his state of transport? The statement suggests that the inspiration of Socrates' words is less powerful than it might be if he actually believed what he was saying.

Phaedrus nevertheless concedes that Socrates' words are having powerful effects when he says, "Yes, Socrates, you seem to have a very unusual flow of words" (54). Here we note that inspired versus uninspired discourse can be determined at least in part by the "flow of words." The rhythm of ordinary discourse is different from that which is found in powerful rhetorical utterances, and although Phaedrus doesn't take the time to delineate the difference between the two rhythms, he is capable of distinguishing words that flow forth with inspiration from those that come from self-conscious or rational talk. Part of the difference is that the words flow smoothly, without effort; part comes from the quickened pace of the words and their patterned, insistent rhythms that reinforce the power of the thoughts; and part from word order and word choice: some words are more appropriate to inspired states than others. If Phaedrus is confident in his intuitive judgment that the flow of Socrates' words reflects his inspired state, we can assume that the aesthetic standards he uses to assess the quality of the remarks satisfies his sense of judgment without regard for a rational gauge.

One of the best things about the *Phaedrus* is the manner in which it shows how intuitive assessments of discourse guide the interlocutors on their way. If Socrates holds forth for a while and then pauses to see how his speech is going, remarking that he clearly seems inspired, we see him taking the temperature of his own discourse. As the dialogue continues, we have similar moments where he judges the value of his words, as when he says, "Listen to me, then, in silence; for surely the place is holy; so that you must not wonder, if, as I proceed, I appear to be in a divine fury, for already I am getting into dithyrambics" (55). Here again the reader can only be struck by the self-conscious way in which Socrates appears to be gauging the level of inspiration that drives his words. One is not accustomed to speakers stopping along the way and wondering whether they are "in a divine fury." Socrates seems to be attempting to heighten the inspired effects of his speech by calling attention to them, as if Phaedrus would wonder how Socrates could make such powerful utterances.

Two other interesting things emerge from Socrates' aside to Phaedrus. First, Socrates measures the quality of his discourse in terms of the degree to which he is employing dithyrambics, which are themselves a reflection of an inspired state. Their carefully measured cadences reflect the divine fury that pushes all inspired discourse, yet one cannot simply force the dithyrambics to come. The quality of an affective state is gauged implicitly by the appearance of specially modulated forms of language rather than anything rational. Second, Socrates carefully links his ability to get into dithyrambics to the specific site of his discourse. Realizing that he is moving into a divine fury, he infers that "surely the place is holy," for otherwise he wouldn't be capable of rising to such heights. At the same time, the declaration that the site must be holy is yet another intuitive assessment of the quality of his words: inspired discourse flows forth only in sacred spaces, so the fact that his words are capable of transport reflects the sacred nature of the site from which he speaks.

Still, Socrates realizes that complex and special circumstances are required for divine fury to manifest itself, and the place from

which one speaks is as important to the discourse as are the interlocutors and the speaker himself. It is not clear whether the place
becomes holy and sacred because Socrates finds himself producing inspired discourse or whether a site is declared holy when
such discourse is produced, but in some respects these are different sides of the same coin. Sacred discourse always suggests both,
as, for example, when the site of Jesus's Sermon on the Mount
becomes sacred because of the power of the sermon itself. Anyone who had been present at the inspired event would thereafter
recognize that place as a site of sacred energies because it was able
to call forth Jesus's great sermon. At the same time, only a space
removed from the commerce of everyday life has the potential for
this kind of holiness, and some places are more appropriately
"designed" for that purpose, either because they are at the top of
hill or are in a clearing that is both open and yet protected by
woods on its periphery or simply because the site is beautiful.

As a final manifestation of the ways in which discourse is guided
by irrational forces throughout the *Phaedrus,* one could look at the
moment when Phaedrus asks Socrates why he has stopped speaking. Socrates replies: "Does not your simplicity observe that I have
got out of dithyrambics into epics; and if my censure was in verse,
what will my praise be? Don't you see that I am already overtaken
by the Nymphs to whom you have mischievously exposed me?
And therefore I will only add that the nonlover has all the advan-
tages in which the lover is charged with being deficient. And now
I will say no more; there has been enough said of both of them.
Leaving the tale to its fate, I will cross the river and make the best
of my way home, lest a worse thing be inflicted upon me by you"
(57). Socrates stops his speech because he is irritated by the direction it is taking, and his distress is manifested in several ways. First,
unlike Phaedrus, he notes the change in his discourse from dithy-
ramb to epic, marking a qualitative difference that would undercut the unity of the discourse. This shift reflects Socrates' irritation over the fact that he has been "overtaken by the Nymphs to
whom you [Phaedrus] have mischievously exposed me." These
words suggest that Socrates was overcome by an irrational force,

but it was induced by Phaedrus's crude and misguided sense of the nature of discourse. Most important, Socrates' speech was driven by the imperative to justify the virtues of the nonlover over the lover. But in any great discourse, the choice of lover or nonlover shouldn't be determined by a wager. The "mischief" in the discourse comes from the fact that Phaedrus dictated that it had to support the nonlover regardless of Socrates' own views and regardless of where the discourse itself might go. It is as though a toxin in the air captured Socrates' mind, and he was driven by inspiration to speak what he didn't really believe. When he realizes this, he stops talking before he makes matters worse. Socrates thus comes to understand that one can speak in a divine fury even when one has no real conviction about one's speech. And although he admits to impiety because he has degraded the god of love, there is at least as much impiety in the fact that Socrates' speech is driven by a wager rather than by a commitment to the truth.

Socrates is understandably disgusted with himself. His speech, though powerful, was insincere, a violation of a holy spot. So he resolves to "say no more," convinced that there has already been more than "enough said of both of them." Socrates is so upset with himself that he brusquely dismisses the speech and the larger discourse of which it is a part: "Leaving the tale to its fate, I will cross the river and make the best of my way home, lest a worse thing be inflicted upon me by you." He wants to remove himself from the spot he desecrated as quickly as possible out of fear that he might be induced to produce further abominations.

When Socrates decides to leave his speech behind, he has acknowledged the fundamental problem on which the dialogue of *Phaedrus* hinges: what separates genuine dialogue, or dialectic, from mere rhetoric? Both dialectic and speeches of the kind Socrates has just uttered function through rhetoric, and both are capable of taking the participants outside of themselves. Divine fury can be present in both of them, as we have seen in Socrates' transport even when he didn't believe that the nonlover was superior to the lover. But if divine fury can manifest itself in good and evil speech, words driven by truth and words driven by pride and self-centered concerns, what distinguishes true speech from false? This dilemma has always been at the center of human discourse, and it is that with which Socrates and Phaedrus wrestle. The genius of Plato first presents this terrible problem in a homely way when Socrates himself, the wisest of men, allows his divine flow of words to be driven by the worst of motivations, a wager in which nothing serious is at stake.

‖ Before we consider the fundamental problem of true and false discourse, we need to look more carefully at Socrates' various statements about the irrational aspects of existence. The most crucial distinction Socrates makes in the entire dialogue is found in his recapitulation of what he has said in his speech: "And there were two kinds of madness; one produced by human infirmity, the other by a divine release from the ordinary ways of men" (79). This simple statement flies in the face of much of what we think about Socrates, Plato, and Western civilization. Throughout the dialogue Socrates insists that the choices in life are not limited to rational and irrational ones. Instead, there are rational decisions to be made, but there are also two kinds of irrationality in play in human existence, the kind that is "produced by human infirmity" and the type that is "a divine release from the ordinary ways of men." The dialogue is designed to engender respect for the divine forms of irrationality, such as love, that make life worth living. Without them, all that is charming in life would disappear, and we would be left with the choice to live either like Swift's Houyhnhnms or his Yahoos.

Our society still tacitly assumes that all forms of irrationality are bad, but in fact only those produced by human infirmity deserve such disapprobation. Various forms of anger, rage, and hostility are irrational in the worst, most destructive way. We are right to think that such irrationality is bad, right to contrast these baser forms of human experience with the rationality that shows us how to choose dispassionately among various options. The irrationality that stems from weakness produces negative effects, and we have as a result constructed various ethical systems to contain these human energies. Nevertheless, we have been unsuccessful in our efforts and doubtless always will be, notwithstanding the absurd hopefulness about the future that comes from those who think a little more knowledge about the genome or brain chemistry will give us the means to eradicate such things as negative human irrationality. If that were possible, we would become an entirely different species. After all, we cannot think of our past without recognizing the degree to which it has been driven by the irrationality that stems from human infirmity. Like it or not, this is a crucial aspect of our nature.

Few of us are eager to celebrate the negative forms of irrationality, though, which brings us back to the problems that derive from our reductive vision of Socrates: in conflating the two forms of irrationality, we misinterpret his basic concerns. Socrates may be very reasonable, and much of his wisdom may derive from things about which he has reasoned. But it also comes from the divine form of irrationality that is always at the center of a good Platonic dialogue. Socrates' best discussions invariably involve the good irrationality of divine wandering. The *Phaedrus* is a perfect example because it shows us this irrationality in so many ways. We have already seen how the direction of the dialogue derives from the subtle intuitive cues Socrates picks up as he goes along. We note the ways in which the conversation moves from the original provocation of Lysias's speech and Phaedrus's regard for it to Socrates' own speech, his rejection of that effort as stemming from the wrong impulses, the new flight that produces the famous articulation of the human soul in terms of the charioteer and the two winged horses, and finally the discussions about rhetoric and writing that bring the dialogue to a close. This is wandering indeed, always driven by the interpretation of gestures that defy reason, that resist our intelligence, that move through irrational processes to arrive at the essential conclusions about the nature of love, irrationality, and rhetoric.

If Socrates did nothing more than insist there were good and useful forms of irrationality, he would continue to open our eyes to a fundamental aspect of human experience that is too often disregarded because we assume that all forms of irrationality are bad, or that it is too difficult to distinguish between the good and bad manifestations of irrationality. But Socrates provides us with much more, beginning with his assumption that the good form of irrationality is "a divine release from the ordinary ways of men." In contrast to the bad form, which derives from self-centered impulses, good irrationality comes from the gods. Whatever such an idea might mean for a skeptical time like our own, it asserts that good irrationality differs fundamentally from bad irrationality. It is not that sometimes our irrational impulses turn out for the best while at other times they have destructive effects, nor is it that they spring from the same source. One has a divine origin, the other is a product of human infirmity, the incapacity to see beyond the affective responses that derive from our limitations.

If, for example, we take Socrates literally in the dialogue, he believes that love, a form of irrationality, comes from the god Eros, or at least from Aphrodite in some way. Among other things, this assumes that humans cannot produce love on their own. It also suggests the intrusion of certain energies into human situations that don't regularly drive our actions. We might have difficulty believing in Eros at this point in our history, but it is possible that Socrates had no more conviction about Eros as a real, divine entity than we do. Eros could as easily be a figure of speech for Socrates as he is for us. What matters is not the specific existence of a putatively divine entity called Eros but the cluster of assumptions that develops around his formation within human discourse. The most pertinent of these is as true today as it ever was: people cannot make themselves love anyone. If love were a lifestyle choice or a rational decision, it would by definition not be love. Whatever else it is, love is not under human control. The best we can do is heed its call and revere it as Socrates does in the *Phaedrus*. We can learn to have a high regard for an individual, to respect the virtues of someone, to appreciate the kindnesses of others and the like, but all of these situations are different from being in love, which always lies beyond our control.

Even those who have been most skeptical about the existence

of the gods often realize the useful purposes they have served, and the most pertinent is that they explain aspects of our existence that otherwise evade our understanding. Love is a good example because we couldn't begin to determine its origin. We may currently better understand some of the elements that come into play when one falls in love—everything from compatible dispositions to complex pheremonic interactions that make some people's smells more attractive to us than others'—but even if we arrive at the point where we can establish what fits and what doesn't, we will still be doing little more than offering a more sophisticated version of a dating service. What makes two people fall in love will always resist our intelligence, even if we come closer to establishing some of the elements that make relationships work. We may be happy about or distressed by the fact that love is beyond our intelligence; either way, we have no choice but to accept it, even if we don't construe it as divine intervention in our lives.

Two other aspects of Socrates' statement demonstrate how important the irrationally good aspects of our lives are, first because Socrates characterizes them as a "release," second because such a release gives us a respite from the "ordinary ways of men." The assumptions built into these words suggest relief from the rhythms and patterns that govern our everyday lives. Existence tends to be organized around routine, self-centered concerns, some of which are rational, many of which are not. These patterns are essential, but they also produce tedium, boredom, and worse: the eruption of negative irrational impulses that threaten to overwhelm the constraints of our usual ways of being who we are. More pertinently, we all know what it is like to be sick of who we are. However much we are committed to our own uniqueness, and however much our life plans unfold in accord with the dictates of our individuality, we still actively desire not to be who we are, or, rather, we ardently seek out states in which who we are is not a part of our awareness. If our lives depend on regular, self-centered consideration of who we are and what we should do, they also require non-self-centered states when we don't have to use the calculus of self-interest to sort things out. Such release can be achieved in a variety of ways, some of which, such as the consumption of alcohol, are more or less under our control. Other forms of release, such as love, are not. The best we can do is make ourselves available for them and hope they appear.

One cannot make oneself fall in love. But one can actively seek release from the ordinary ways one has established to be who one is. In doing so, one opens oneself up to the prospect of good forms of irrational behavior, though they might not manifest themselves. Still, one must be open to the possibility in order to achieve the release. Socrates' elaborate defense of Eros in the *Phaedrus* may seem a part of an ironic hoax to convince Phaedrus of a belief he really doesn't have, but more likely it reflects the ways Socrates regularly seeks to make himself available for the intrusion of the irrational good into his life. He knows that love is the greatest gift humans have, so he respects its force. The appeals to the god of love, the speech that is meant to recompense his betrayal of love in his earlier peroration, and his prayers to Eros are all ways of disciplining himself so he can be receptive to the irrational impulses that might make love come his way. These ritual procedures and the rhetoric through which they manifest themselves need be no more real for Socrates than the charioteer of the soul is: they can "merely" be figures of speech, for figures are never "merely" anything. They are always ways of organizing our thoughts about who we are, a means through which we orient ourselves to our experience that makes some aspects of life available to us and forecloses others.

In its crudest formulation, we might suggest the following: our lives are composed of disciplines and structures that are essential to the daily business of being who we are, but those forms inevitably call forth the need for other human states, irrational frames of mind that allow us to dispense with self-centered considerations. Given this basic need for non-self-centered states to relieve us of the constraints of our ordinary ways, we have two possibilities: we can take up the negative forms of irrationality and make use of them to create obliviousness, or we can make ourselves available for the intrusion of the good forms of irrationality. The negative way produces a life organized around various violent, de-structive, nihilistic impulses. The positive way provides us with the point of entry into the divine irrationality that most charms us into a conviction that life is good. The main virtue of negative forms of irrationality is that we have some control over them: we can more or less choose a violent form of expression, whereas the good forms of irrationality are not under our control.

We could once again use Socrates' attention to the small cues of his environment to emphasize what is at stake in the discipline that makes the good irrational forces in life available to us. Socrates has disciplined his intelligence, so he is capable of acutely attend-ing to the relations his environment evokes for him. In the *Phae-drus*, this means everything from his ability to hear the voice of his daimonion to his awareness of the ways in which those who have produced great discourse in the past might evaluate the words of Lysias or his own. These forms of acuity appear in Socrates' deft sense that good discourse is contingent on a variety of factors, including a congenial site like the cool of a plane tree that has been marked sacred by others because they have had good forms of irra-tionality come forth from the place. Although the dialogue is quite specific about the ongoing manifestation of these cues in Socrates' environment, only an unusual individual would be aware of them. Most of us spend our time blundering through life without regard for such cues. If they have any effect on us at all, they appear as feelings on which we may or may not act. Socrates both notes the cues and responds to them with intelligence. In so doing, he re-flects the discipline involved in being fully alive in the midst of one's circumstances and open to whatever the environment might be telling one.

We may not like the fact that our quality of life depends on the hard work of acutely attending to our environment; we might like even less that such acuity can still produce nothing in the way of the irrational good: we can do all the work involved in disciplin-ing ourselves to attend to what is and still find no divine energies blowing through our lives. The dynamic of the dialogue, though, suggests that the regular, daily positivity of being acutely engaged in the world inevitably produces the upsurges of divine energy that lift us to the highest human states and powerfully reinforce the great value of being alive. The *Phaedrus* reflects these dynamics in Socrates' life even as it argues for their fundamental importance in our own, even as it regularly reinforces the degree to which Socrates' life is dependent on the whiffs of divine breath that waft through the air on a daily basis.

Socrates insists that the good kind of madness, a product of divine release, is central to the quality of our lives. It is not an adjunct to our rationality or a recompense for the negative forms of irrationality, or even a way of combating the negative forces in our lives. Good forms of madness are what make life worth living; they are the organizing impulses at the center of our being that produce whatever value we find in life. We may only arrive at an understanding of those divine energies through the interplay of rational discourse and the effects of the bad forms of madness on our lives, but we come to see the ways in which our lives develop out of the energies that release us from ourselves and make us who we are at the same time. Reason is at best a handmaiden in this process, a means through which we determine the contexts that are most fitting for divine madness to appear in our lives.

|| Socrates offers additional arguments on behalf of the good forms of irrationality, though in the end his viewpoint is either intuitively recognized as true or found wanting. There are no rational arguments in favor of irrationality, even if there are other points to be made. After Socrates makes fun of himself as "Vain Man" by way of explaining the mistake he made in giving a speech out of self-interest, he offers the following recantation:

> That was a lie in which I said that the beloved ought to accept the non-lover and reject the lover, because the one is sane, and the other mad. For that might have been truly said if madness were simply an evil; but there is also a madness which is the special gift of heaven, and the source of the chiefest blessings among men. For prophecy is a madness, and the prophetess at Delphi and the priestesses of Dodona, when out of their senses have conferred great benefits on

Hellas, both in public and private life, but when in their senses few or none. And I might also tell you how the Sibyl and other persons, who have had the gift of prophecy, have told the future of many an one and guided them aright; but that is obvious and would be tedious. (60)

There is no doubt here of the centrality of irrationality in our life. It is characterized as "the special gift of heaven," and, not satisfied with such high praise, Socrates reinforces it by calling it "the source of the chiefest blessings among men." These are not arguments but declarations, and they assume we all know them to be true. The example at hand is prophecy, and Socrates speaks of the ways in which this form of divine madness has helped Athens in times of crisis. If it is true that "the prophetess at Delphi and the priestesses of Dodona, when out of their senses have conferred great benefits on Hellas, both in public and private life, but when in their senses few or none," everyone can see how important irrationality is for the maintenance of the state and the well-being of all. Just as clearly, Socrates distinguishes the different states of the prophetess and the priestesses, for when they are "in their senses" they have little to offer their fellow Athenians. They provide the guidelines for the future only when they are taken over by the irrational forces of the gods and are "out of their senses."

To Socrates, the great benefits bestowed on humans by divine madness are so self-evident he hardly feels the need to point them out. He declares: "And I might also tell you how the Sibyl and other persons, who have had the gift of prophecy, have told the future of many an one and guided them aright; but that is obvious and would be tedious" (60). Socrates assumes that everyone knows how important a prophet's guidance can be to individuals at crucial times in their lives, providing insight that is unavailable in any other manner. He could offer many such examples of the great power of this gift but chooses not to because the importance of divine madness "is obvious" and it "would be tedious" to recount situations in which this was apparent.

Socrates also offers an argument from origins on behalf of divine madness when he tells Phaedrus, "There would be more reason in appealing to the ancient inventors of names, who, if they had thought madness a disgrace or dishonor, would never have called prophecy, which is the noblest of arts, by the very same name . . . as madness, thus inseparably connecting them; but they must have thought that there was an inspired madness which was no disgrace; for the two words . . . are really the same, and the letter τ is only a modern and tasteless insertion" (60). Inasmuch as the words for *prophecy* and *madness* are virtually indistinguishable in the beginning, it follows that when names were first given to things, humans recognized that the two were closely allied. As Socrates demonstrates, madness is a larger category, of which prophecy is only a subset.

We are much less inclined to be convinced by arguments from origins, particularly when those origins have to do with the meanings of words. But we recognize that earlier meanings often provide a sense of the word we have lost, a viewpoint that shows us gaps in our way of thinking. Early Greece thought differently about the world than we do, and one of the chief reasons it continues to be so well studied is that its comprehensive and careful vision of reality presents life in ways that call into question many of our own views, even if it is also true that Plato inaugurated the rational orientation to things that led to our scientific studies of the world and our various forms of argumentation. At the center of their difference from us, though, we find this early Greek belief in the power and importance of irrationality, of divine madness, a force so strong that all of the chief vectors of the culture are in some shape or form organized around it.

Having established the centrality of divine madness to our lives, Socrates enumerates the various ways such madness manifests itself, though again, the later recapitulation of these distinctions is clearer and more succinct: "The divine madness was subdivided into four kinds, prophetic, initiatory, poetic, erotic, having four gods presiding over them; the first was the inspiration of Apollo, the second that of Dionysus, the third that of the Muses, the fourth that of Aphrodite and Eros. In the description of the last kind of madness, which was also the best, being a sort of figure of love, we mingled a tolerably credible and possibly true, though partly erring myth, which was also a hymn in honor of Eros, who is your lord and also mine, Phaedrus, and the guardian of fair children, and to him we sung the hymn in measured and solemn form" (79). True to his discriminating nature, Socrates distinguishes the various types of divine madness in order to better understand the ways in which our lives are moved by these most powerful forces. So, we are told, there are prophetic, initiatory, poetic, and erotic modes of divine madness, each presided over by a specific god. The very fact that the early Greeks had specific gods allocated to each of the good forms of irrationality attests to the care they devoted to these matters.

In the overall scheme of things, we can assume that most of our lives are taken up by "everyday" states of mind. Most of the time we are "in our right minds," or "in our senses." This means that we devote our attention to the sensory impressions and thoughts that come to us and evaluate them on the basis of one of the modes employed in everyday life to make sense of things. The most pertinent of these modes would be self-interest, for our primary orientation to the world is necessarily based on self-survival: we want to keep living, so we take in the relations of the world on the basis of what they can do to and for us. In addition, we have various modes of reasoning that help us sort things into categories. The rational modes contribute to our self-interested assessments of the world, as they help us discover what is in our interests once we have carefully and rationally distinguished what is going on at any given moment. But they can also be employed to produce disinterested forms of understanding that more or less purge self-interest from our sense of reality. This for Socrates is a great gift, and reason is much to be treasured because it allows us a disinterested viewpoint. Most of daily life can be accounted for in this way, as we tend to be occupied largely by these self-interested or rational states in various ways.

The early Greeks, though, lacked our sense of identity and the stability of selfhood. They invented a god, Proteus, to depict the labile ways in which our beings can be transformed by a variety of phenomena. Even in the everyday modes, we can organize our orientation to the world in purely sensuous ways, in accord with our feelings, on the basis of our thoughts about ourselves or the world, or in rational ways that attempt to distinguish the nature of things without regard for what those distinctions might mean to us. Each of these orientations is different from the others, and we pass into and out of them without realizing we are doing so. We assume there is a central force in our lives that governs the comings and goings of these various modes of being, whereas the early Greeks were more likely to see their natures in less centralized ways: sometimes they were oriented to things in this way, sometimes in that. Even from our more centered vision of things, though, we can note the ways in which our various states come and go, and we can also delineate the features of the states and the putative reasons why at any given moment one takes priority over the others.

Nevertheless, the comings and goings of our ordinary states usually pass without much notice because they occupy a similar field of intensity and affective character and are dominated by self-interested or rational perspectives. These states are not unified by a central self, but they are sufficiently related in tone and energy level as to constitute the sense of sameness in the background of our lives that passes for normality. Until recently most individuals would be inclined to subsume almost all of their behavior under these rubrics of everyday life. The emergence of more evangelical religious forms, like the earlier intrusion of some Eastern religious viewpoints, has broadened the affective range of some individuals' lives, but even with that expansion of psychic horizons, most people define themselves almost exclusively by the various everyday states that come and go without much thought on their part.

The early Greeks and Socrates offer a different understanding of the ways our lives work. They note the everyday modes and forms of life and go to great lengths to distinguish the processes at work in them, but they also recognize the many ways in which we occupy states where we are "not in our right mind," states that come and go and don't have the duration of our ordinary modes of being. But they are nevertheless insistently present, sent to us by the gods. We may not have control over them and cannot determine when they appear, but we are capable of devising ways of making ourselves available to them, and we can recognize when these irrational forces have temporarily taken over our lives. For the early Greeks the presence of these forces was often delineated in terms of the gods, just as Socrates establishes that the four good forms of divine madness are presided over by Apollo, Dionysus, the Muses, and Eros. This act of naming confirms the origin of these irrational energies and gives the Greeks a way of talking about their protean natures, a means through which to account for the manner in which Apollo or Eros could sweep one out of one's ordinary state and change one's life in an instant. The god simply appeared, and existence was transformed. Then the god departed, and one returned to one's ordinary life, though always altered by the force of the divine madness that had manifested itself.

As Socrates notes, there are forms of madness that are not divine, irrational states that are noxious and evil, but the good ones are presided over by the gods and transform our lives in specific, yet equally intense, ways. Thus, the prophetic form of divine madness that Apollo rules has the power to give an individual insight into the future, can overtake one's psyche in such a way as to give one knowledge of how the vectors in play in the present will unfold in the future. From our ordinary modes of understanding, this kind of insight is not possible. When taken over by Apollo, though, we can intuit something of what is to come; we can anticipate the direction in which the relationships in the present will move in the future. Depending on the context, Apollo's divine madness can provide highly specific and individual forms of insight, or the oracular forms can give direction to an entire social group.

Socrates insists on the great power of the prophetic and of divine madness in general when he declares that just as "prophecy is higher and more perfect than divination both in name and reality, in the same proportion as the ancients testify, is madness superior to a sane mind[,] for the one is only human, but the other of divine origin. Again, where plagues and mightiest woes have bred in a race, owing to some ancient wrath, there madness, lifting up her voice and flying to prayers and rites, has come to the rescue of those who are in need; and he who has part in this gift, and is truly possessed and duly out of his mind, is by the use of purifications and mysteries made whole and delivered from evil, future as well as present, and has a release from the calamity which afflicts him" (60). It is hard to miss the conviction that "madness is superior to a sane mind," just as it is impossible to ignore the argument that humans have often been saved from "plagues and mightiest woes" by an individual who, imbued with the gift of prophecy, "is truly possessed and duly out of his mind," who thereby makes "use of purifications and mysteries" to redress the evil of the time and overcome the "calamity" that has overwhelmed the community. There can be no more compelling, transformative forces in society than those that are produced by the prophetic mode in times of crisis.

If there are forms of divine madness that come from Apollo, there are also those that derive from Dionysus, what Socrates characterizes as the "initiatory" forms of irrationality. We might imagine these as the forms of ritual celebration that remain unconnected to any process of divination: the point of initiatory irrationality is not to know what the future will bring but rather to take up the forces of life in their most intense, sacred form, moving in the world as if among the gods. All ritual events partake of this kind of divine madness, whether Dionysian revels, ritual sacrifice, or mass celebrations of various sorts. In these states too we recognize we are not ourselves; we are out of our senses as we ordinarily understand them. It could be that the chief function of the initiatory form of irrationality is to reinforce group identity through what we think of today as mob psychology. These are states that produce the most violent and negative effects, as noted in the consequences of some of the Dionysian rituals—tearing the god apart—or in the kinds of mob violence that have always bedeviled communities. But they also provide the powerful ritual attachments that are essential to a people's collective vision of itself.

The poetic form of divine madness is distinguished from the other three in that it is the means whereby society's sense of itself is organized in a coherent and transmissible manner. In naming the world through the divine frenzy of the Muses, the poet reveals the world to us in the most basic and profound ways. The words evoke, pattern, and reflect the ways in which the relationships of the world unfold, and demonstrate the manner in which we are a part of those relationships. The poetic mode provides the history and theology of a people and can partake of the prophetic and initiatory modes as well, suggesting the path of the future and offering up ritual celebration that provides cohesiveness to a community. Its chief effects, though, are found in the patterned naming of the world, the manner in which it lays bare the lineaments of life and brings to attention the organized flows of energy out of which existence is constituted. The magical combination of energy and word, the force of truth inherent in language when it comes from the gods, is the domain the Muses inhabit.

Socrates informs us that this "third kind of madness, which is the possession of the Muses . . . enters into a delicate and virgin soul, and there inspiring frenzy, awakens lyric and other numbers; with these adorning the myriad actions of ancient heroes for the instruction of posterity" (60). If people today think the poetic sensibility is available to anyone with a gift for words or a desire to speak of heroes, Socrates insists that "he who, not being inspired and having no touch of madness in his soul, comes to the door and thinks that he will get into the temple by the help of art—he, I say, and his poetry are not admitted; the sane man is nowhere at all when he enters into rivalry with the madman" (60). Only those taken over by the madness of the Muses can produce the powerful words through which culture is established and celebrated.

Finally, the erotic forms of madness are well known, the bodily manifestation of the good irrationality of love. The focal point of the *Phaedrus* is love and the good it brings to human lives, so it is no surprise that Socrates has the most to say about it, or that he insists that this final form of madness "was also the best," the one that brought the most good to people. He declares that "the madness of love is the greatest of heaven's blessings, and the proof shall be one which the wise will receive, and the witling disbelieve" (61). Eros is superior to the others in part because it is available to almost anyone. There are relatively few individuals who are poets or prophets, but most humans are captivated by love at one time or another. Love is also the most compelling form of divine madness because it is so fully integrated into our being. The poetic, the initiatory, and the prophetic appear at irregular intervals and occupy small segments of life. Only love is capable of transforming the quality of everyday existence. Only love can bring most fully to life both body and soul, both the charm of one's own life and the splendor of humans in relation to one another. The other forms of good irrationality have links to the body, but none burnishes skin the way love does; none can fully charge the organism with the energies of life as Eros does.

Although Socrates doesn't spend as much time delineating the various aspects of the four modes of divine madness as I have here, his brief remarks give his interlocutor a good sense of the specific virtues of each form of the good irrational and contribute to his overall argument that the best aspects of life are subsumed under one or more of these forms of divine madness. They don't provide merely momentary pleasures or mindless diversions but rather offer the most profound and compelling sense of life we are capable of expressing. If the *Phaedrus* did nothing more than discriminate among these modes of irrationality and attest to their importance to everyone's life, it would have justified its cultural importance. If it did nothing more than celebrate the virtues of love and the ways in which it brings beauty to our lives, it would have done the same.

|| Socrates offers a hymn to love in the *Phaedrus,* and he expresses the virtues of the irrational at the same time. But he also manages to address the fundamental problem of dialogue, of rhetoric and its relationship to truth. Having begun on the wrong foot by offering a paean to the nonlover out of vanity, Socrates questions the nature of language and rhetoric and probes what distinguishes

a good speech from a bad one. Two principles emerge: "The first rule of good speaking [is] that the mind of the speaker should know the truth of what he is going to say" (73), whereas the second is "the mere knowledge of the truth will not give you the art of persuasion" (74). That one should know the truth of one's subject matter before one's speech might seem either obvious or beside the point, but people often speak of that which they do not know, and frequently they remain unaware of this. They don't carefully discern the parameters of their discourse, and they too easily assume they know what they are talking about. At the same time, many believe that speaking is entirely a matter of persuasion, and the truth of one's utterances is thought to be beside the point. As long as one can convince one's listeners, the speech will be effective regardless of its truth value.

Socrates takes a contrary view. He believes that a speech should be based on the truth even if it is designed to deceive its audience. His argument rests on the assumption that "there will be more chance of deception . . . when the difference [between the true and the false] . . . is small" (75). The smaller the differences between the deceptions of a speech and the truth it pretends to present, the more likely people are to believe it. If there were a large difference, it would be easily noted, and the speech would be discredited. "He . . . who would deceive others, and not be deceived," therefore, "must exactly know the real likenesses and differences of things" (75). Even the most deceitful speeches require the speaker to know the truth—the "real likenesses and differences of things"— in order to make the deception as slight as possible: "He who would be a master of the art must know the real nature of everything; or he will never know either how to contrive or how to escape the gradual departure from truth into the opposite of truth which is effected by the help of resemblances" (76).

At the same time, the truth is always insufficient in itself, "will not give you the art of persuasion" merely by being true. The art of a speech depends on carefully shaping one's words in accord with the truth—or with the intent to deceive—and organizing one's materials with care in order to produce the rhythmical unfolding of argument. Socrates never doubts that a speech requires artful composition, nor does he deny that the assessment of rhetorical devices is a crucial way of investigating the quality of a speech. He goes through Lysias's speech and points out its rhetorical weaknesses—too much repetition, a poor organizational scheme—and links these weaknesses to the fact that the speech is not based on truth. Most of the discussion of rhetoric presupposes the ability artfully to construct the organization and presentation of one's words. Socrates is more interested in the question of the truth or falsity of the speech than the means by which it convinces the audience of its probity.

The main problem with the art of rhetoric is that it can be used either to express the truth or to deceive. The difficulty is implicit in the definition of rhetoric Socrates proposes to Phaedrus: "Is not rhetoric, taken generally, a universal art of enchanting the mind by arguments; which is practised not only in courts and public assemblies, but in private houses also, having to do with all matters, great as well as small, good and bad alike, and is in all equally right, and equally to be esteemed—that is what you have heard?" (74). If rhetoric is the "art of enchanting the mind by arguments," the mind can as easily be enchanted by deceitful arguments as by truthful ones. Humans have endlessly sought ways to distinguish enchanting rhetoric that is deceitful from that which expresses the truth, but they have yet to come up with adequate means of separating the one from the other. Merely delineating the ways in which the speech produces enchantment articulates only the degree to which it moves people and not the degree to which it speaks the truth. This insoluble dilemma hovers on the edge of the *Phaedrus* from beginning to end, and although Socrates offers clear distinctions that help one learn more about the art of persuasion, it remains to be seen whether he is helpful in providing us the means of distinguishing true speech from deceit.

The best aspect of Socrates' inquiry into the nature of rhetoric is found in his ongoing discussion of the means through which good speeches are produced. The words of the rhetorician depend on "the faculty of division according to the natural ideas or members, not breaking any part as a bad carver might" (79). As noted, the speaker must first be able to discern the distinctions among things, and he or she must also be able to keep the various parts together rather than chopping them into disorganized bits that fail to reflect the whole. Knowing the differences in themselves is insufficient, even if one could argue that anyone who properly understood the differences on the basis of which his or her speech was produced would also know how best to organize them. If we assume there is a difference between the truth of distinctions and the art of presenting them, though, we can also assume that one might be adept at noting what distinguishes one thing from another without necessarily being able to put the various elements together in an artful way. One would need the truth of the distinctions and the aesthetic capacities of the artisan in order to present the distinctions in an enchanting manner.

A powerful rhetorician is thus both born and made: "The perfection of oratory is, or rather must be, like the perfection of all things, partly given by nature; but this is assisted by art, and if you have the natural power you will be famous as a rhetorician, if you only add knowledge and practice, and in either way you may fall short" (82–83). If one is born with natural gifts for oratory, one must still acquire a knowledge of the world, and one must develop one's skills through practice. As a result a speaker could "fall short" of the "perfection of oratory" because he or she hasn't mastered the distinctions of the world or the compositional practices of the rhetorician. As Socrates says, "All the higher arts require much discussion and lofty contemplation of nature; this is the source of sublimity and perfect comprehensive power. And this, as I conceive, was the quality which, in addition to his natural gifts, Pericles acquired from his happening to know Anaxagoras. He was imbued with the higher philosophy, and attained the knowledge of mind and matter, which was the favorite theme of Anaxagoras, and hence he drew what was applicable to his art" (83). Pericles is the consummate example of the gifted speaker because he learned from Anaxagoras the "higher philosophy" of the world, without which his speeches would have lacked sufficient substance. He "attained the knowledge of mind and matter" through his attention to Anaxagoras's words, and he took that wisdom and "drew what was applicable to his art." These remarks reveal two collateral elements to the creation of a fine orator: chance and the ability to change someone else's wisdom into one's own. If Pericles had never met Anaxagoras, he might well have become a gifted speaker, but he became the highest expression of the speaker's art only through his association with Anaxagoras. More pertinently, he didn't simply adopt Anaxagoras's words without modification. He modulated them through his own wisdom in order to transform them into his unique expression of the truth of the world.

The genius of Socrates' discussion of the power of persuasion is its simplicity, for in some respects great discourse is based on little more than being able to make careful distinctions and artfully organize them. Everything in the *Phaedrus* depends on these basic assumptions. Socrates adds only one additional requirement, as we see in his description of the ideal rhetorician: "If I find any man who is able to see unity and plurality in nature, him I follow, and walk in his step as if he were a god. And those who have this art, I have hitherto been in the habit of calling dialecticians; but God knows whether the name is right or not" (79–80). A fine rhetorical composition must reflect both the unity and the plurality of nature. It must give a sense of the whole of which we are a part, yet it can only properly do that through the careful distinctions it makes among the many things of which the world is composed. The greatest speakers—those worthy of the name of dialectician— express this unity and plurality. Socrates even goes so far as to say that if he were to find anyone with such powers, he would "walk in his step as if he were a god." Anyone who possessed this capacity would implicitly have the wisdom to know how the universe hangs together, even as it is divided among its countless fine distinctions, and would therefore almost be worthy of the title of god.

In equally lucid terms, Socrates establishes the ways in which an orator should proceed when considering how to put a speech together: "Ought we not to consider first whether that which we wish either to learn or to teach is simple or multiform, and if simple, then to inquire what power this has of acting or being acted upon by others, and if multiform, then to number the forms; and see first in the case of one of them, and then in the case of all of them, the several powers which they by nature have of doing or suffering" (83). Here we see Socrates' rational sorting machine at work, establishing the type of speech to be given—simple or multiform—and then determining the ways in which it will interact with those to whom it is given. If the speech is multiform in nature, each of the forms has to be considered separately for its effects, and their combined effect on the hearer must be considered as well. One needs to know beforehand what emotional appeals exist in the speech and the ways in which they will move the audience. Without understanding at least some of this beforehand, one will likely not produce great oratorical effects. At the same time, these considerations are preliminary to the divine wandering of the speech itself: one lays out the general parameters of the speech and then gives oneself up to the flow of words that is driven by the gods, as Socrates does in his evocation of the charioteer and the two horses. Calculation is important but secondary to the irrational flow of words it makes possible and loosely organizes.

The intelligence necessary to produce a good speech is thus a subtle combination of everything that goes into a persuasive mode of discourse: "Having arranged men and speeches, and their modes and affections in different classes, and fitted them into one another, he will point out the connection between them—he will show why one is naturally persuaded by a particular form of argument, and another not" (84). One must understand both humans and the specific effects of words before one can produce a fine piece of oratory, because the "modes and affections" of both speeches and humans need to be "fitted" to one another for the proper effects to be produced. The connection between the people and the speech depends entirely on the way "one is naturally persuaded by a particular form of argument, and another not."

Socrates' manner of speaking about the wisdom of a god—suggesting that it is a function of knowing the subtle differences to be found in all things—argues for a mode of knowledge based on relationships rather than objects. He does not suggest that one can discern the specific essence of all entities, only that one should learn how one thing differs from another. This relational form of knowledge presupposes that our understanding of one thing is connected to our knowledge of another and of everything else. The differences appear in weblike form rather than one thing standing out from another. As a result, the shades of difference among things can be gauged only in their links to other phenomena and can be useful manifestations of the truth only to the extent that those relations are made plain in the distinctions one makes.

The full burden of the wisdom a speaker must have is made completely clear in the summation Socrates offers of the orator's knowledge:

> Oratory is the art of enchanting the soul, and therefore he who would be an orator has to learn the differences of human souls— they are so many and of such a nature, and from them come the differences between man and man—he will then proceed to divide speeches into their different classes. Such and such persons, he will say, are affected by this or that kind of speech in this or that way, and he will tell you why; he must have a theoretical notion of them first, and then he must see them in action, and be able to follow them with all his senses about him, or he will never get beyond the precepts of his masters. But when he is able to say what persons are persuaded by what arguments, and recognize the individual about whom he used to theorize as actually present to him, and say to himself, "This is he and this is the sort of man who ought to have that argument applied to him in order to convince him of this";— when he has attained the knowledge of all this, and knows also when he should speak and when he should abstain from speaking, and when he should make use of pithy sayings, pathetic appeals, aggravated effects, and all the other figures of speech;—when, I say, he knows the times and seasons and all these things, then, and not till then, he is perfect and a consummate master of his art; but if he fail in any of these points, whether in speaking or teaching or writing them, and says that he speaks by rules of art, he who denies this has the better of him. (84–85)

Once more Socrates all but says that the orator must have perfect wisdom: he needs to know all the proper distinctions of his subject matter, he has to understand the various forms and modes of speeches and the manner in which they work together to provide the most persuasive account of those distinctions, and he must have an equally acute understanding of his audience. A full knowledge of the various nuances of the world will be ineffective if it is not modulated through the proper forms and modes of speech. Likewise, a full understanding of the world is insufficient when it is filtered through the proper forms and modes if it fails to consider the nature of the audience. The speaker has "to learn the differences of human souls" in order to know how best to appeal to each individual sensibility. As Socrates points out, "They are so many and of such a nature, and from them come the differences between man and man"; if one doesn't recognize these differences and the differences they produce in individual humans, there is no way for an orator to compose the speech properly.

The learning involved in discerning the differences among humans and the forms of speech that are suited to each kind is thus a long process. The speaker must "have a theoretical notion of them first, and then he must see them in action, and be able to follow them with all his senses about him." If he cannot do that, "he will never get beyond the precepts of his masters." One first obtains the precepts of eloquent oratory from one's teachers; one takes this theoretical knowledge and puts it into action, trying to discern the ways in which this form or mode works or fails to work with this group of people; one then attends "with all his senses about him" to the effects of the particular speeches in order to obtain the pragmatic understanding of the specific interaction of words with an audience that will be needed to become a gifted speaker. These strategies are in turn predicated on the irrational, yet hypothetically predictable, effects speeches have on people. It is not enough to figure out whether the audience understands one's words, for the goal is not understanding but persuasion. One must know how people feel about what one has said, which can only be established by noting body language.

In its most extreme form, persuasion depends on an awareness that everyone needs to be appealed to in different ways because everyone is oriented to the world in a unique manner. Of course no orator can begin to speak with a full knowledge of all the differences in the audience but rather must depend on a more general understanding of the various modes of human being. In theory, though, Socrates suggests that every individual has a specific point of entry through which he or she can be most powerfully moved by rhetoric. The ideal orator would know those fine distinctions and be able to appeal to them.

The strange, elusive, but fundamental matter at the heart of any persuasive moment is the manner in which the audience is moved, and all these millennia later we don't know much more about the power of words than Socrates did. We have terms like *body language,* and we have devices that can determine whether the pupils in the eyes of the audience are dilated or contracted, and galvanic skin monitors to sense whether the metabolic rates of the audience are increasing or decreasing. We still possess the same basic rhetorical strategies that were available to Socrates, so we can learn when best to "make use of pithy sayings, pathetic appeals, aggravated effects, and all the other figures of speech." We are also potentially capable of mastering the differences of the world and of individual human souls. But in the end our knowledge of these matters doesn't go beyond what Socrates has already established in the *Phaedrus.* At the core of Socrates' wisdom is the knowledge that the moving power of speech can no more be rationally encapsulated than its effects can be. If one has only technique, one will be applying crude strategies to unique situations, and the effects will be less than eloquent. If one has only art or strategy, one will never move people the way great orators do. The only way to affect an audience appropriately is to have a full understanding of the nuances of humans and the world as a whole, to comprehend the emotional effects of those nuances in specific linguistic contexts, and to allow the divine frenzy of the gods to shape one's words so they powerfully appeal to the audience on the basis of one's knowledge of its specificity.

Socrates ends up with the fundamental contradiction at the heart of the mastery of dialectic: one must understand the whole world, yet that understanding is nothing if one doesn't submit to the divine madness of the gods. At the same time, one cannot simply throw oneself into the hands of the gods without a comprehensive knowledge of reality. Our skeptical age may be wary of any term that has *divine* in it, but we remain impoverished in our understanding to the extent that we fail to provide a suitable replacement for the sacred implications of the divine. At the very least, the divine madness to which Socrates refers is not a form of self-centered discourse. As with arete, the goal of one's words is not to further one's own ends but to speak the truth: there is a non–self-centered objective at the heart of a speech driven by divine madness, and although such a mode can be faked, great speech still stems from a willingness to subordinate one's careful discriminations of the world and of language to the flow of words themselves.

In the twentieth century, Heidegger was given to saying that "language speaks man," his own way of talking about the divine madness at the heart of all poetic discourse. We have disregarded Heidegger's insight because we became overly confident of our understanding of language; like Lysias, we see discourse as a function of self-interest and crudely produced effects designed to "construct" an emotional appeal to an audience in order to persuade it of something that is always more in the interests of the speaker than the audience. The notion that language speaks man is no more a feature of our landscape than is the Socratic thought that great orators are overtaken by divine madness. But Socrates repeatedly insists that technique is not enough, that the art of speaking will always remain insufficient without a comprehensive knowledge of the world and without a willingness to accede to the irrational forces that produce powerful speech. Our ongoing disdain for the divine madness that moves through our lives and words engenders the same ugly effects ignorance has always displayed, and no one knows better than Socrates how poorly those like Lysias or Phaedrus understand the gift of oratory.

|| Given the discipline that is necessary to produce excellent discourse, Socrates can do several things, the most pertinent of which is to delineate carefully everything involved in powerful oratory. Much of the *Phaedrus* is devoted to this task, as we note in the discussion about divine madness, oratorical technique, and the understanding of the differences in the world and among people. *Phaedrus* employs several speeches of varying quality to make these points, specifically embodying the techniques in order to show how they work, even as Socrates regularly refers to the magical powers that move through his words as a result of the irrational forces to which he has submitted himself. Socrates thus produces the most comprehensive understanding of the power of words while showing how little can be known about the nature of persuasive discourse: inasmuch as divine madness is always at the center of great oratory, we concede from the outset that we cannot capture its essence, bottle it, and sell it on the street corner. It will always elude us except in the specific contexts in which it magically manifests itself thanks to the happy confluence of wisdom, understanding of the context, and willing submission to the flow of divine madness.

Socrates' delineation of the nature of oratory always circles back to one of the fundamental issues inherent in language: how to distinguish a speech committed to the truths of the world from one devoted to deceits or evasions. There are times when Socrates seems to distinguish between rhetoric and dialectic in ways that assume dialectic is discourse driven by truth whereas rhetoric is discourse driven by deceitful manipulation of language for the self-serving goals of the speaker. In the end, though, the most important—if distressing—fact is that the distinction between rhetoric and dialectic breaks down: there is no definitive way to distinguish between the two. Hence, it does no good to suggest that rhetoric deceives people while dialectic works with an audience to produce the truth. Rhetoric and dialectic become two aspects of the same human situation, even if each term emphasizes different elements in the dialogic context.

Put another way, we can say that both orator and audience gauge the truth value of a speech on the basis of irrational aspects of their being. Both might be driven by the divine madness that produces the greatest oratorical moments, but with or without those powers in play, speaker and audience measure the truth of utterances on the basis of intuitive and affective cues, both in the body language of the speaker and the audience and in the assessment of the patterns of distinction that emerge in the speech. The composite event of the speech depends on a careful calibration of these factors, yet none of them can be discerned by rational means. The speaker's words either seem to fit together as a whole or they don't, though rational consideration of the way the speech was organized and the figures of speech it used enter into one's assessment. The words either captivate or they don't, and after the speech the words either continue to move one or they start to ring hollow.

Here again Socrates' first speech is a good example because initially it had power over both Phaedrus and Socrates. Only as it came to an end did Socrates begin to think there was something wrong with it. We remember that as soon as his speech is finished, Socrates is eager to get away from it: "Leaving the tale to its fate, I will cross the river and make the best of my way home, lest a worse thing be inflicted upon me by you" (57). The language here implies that Socrates immediately has a bad feeling about what he has said; otherwise he wouldn't be concerned about whether a "worse thing" would be inflicted on him. He senses that the original context for the speech—Phaedrus's mistaken valuation of Lysias's words and the wager between Phaedrus and Socrates that Socrates could give a better oration—has polluted the speech from the beginning. Thus, he quickly disavows it. A careful audience would note Socrates' tacit revulsion and consider that stance before deciding on the truth value of the speech. But Socrates doesn't consciously seem to know how false his speech is until his daimonion appears when he is about to cross the river, suggesting that even the wisest of humans needs time and the utmost attention to judge the value of a speech.

If the truth value of a powerful speech can be properly gauged only in an ideal world where the audience has the wisdom of the gods, what are we to make of oratory in the real world where no such audience exists? Inasmuch as Socrates is committed to the pursuit of truth through the dialectic of discourse, he is hardly arguing for the end of oratory. He knows the dangers of every rhetorical context, but he also realizes that humans discern the truth through this most compelling form of divine madness. All speech takes place in highly specific, nonrepeatable contexts, and the true power of the dialectic manifests itself when speaker and audience engage in the subtlest of linguistic dances, allowing the flow of words to manifest the nuances of the universe through an appeal to the particular needs and inclinations of the audience. When such moments occur, divine madness has transmitted the truth of the world to both speaker and audience. The primary and the secondary effects of the speech are always assessed by intuition and affect, the elusive, irrational feelings that prompt our accord or disagreement with a speech. If both truth and falsity can be marked by the presence of powerful affects, we have no choice but to work diligently to enrich our sense of the intuitions and feelings that guide us. Wisdom inheres much more in these intuitions and feelings than in rational truths, which is why the Socratic mode is oriented to the irrationality at the heart of the world even as it employs whatever rational means are at its disposal to judge the value of the affects through which we make sense of our lives. In this way our soul, the charioteer, learns how to guide the good and the bad horses of our being and brings discipline and truth to them so that we may know the world and be in accord with it.

FOUR

BANISHING THE POETS

IF ONE approaches *The Republic* with the assumption that it reflects a Platonic change in orientation to Socrates, that the work
diminishes Socrates' interest in positive irrational states and places
reason above every other human orientation, one is struck by the
fact that Plato can't leave well enough alone. Having devoted large
portions of books 2 and 3 to his arguments for banishing poets
from the republic, Plato allows Socrates to proceed on his merry
way for another seven books, and then suddenly, just as the *Republic* is winding down, the repressed returns: Plato once again takes
up the attack against the poets. He has Socrates smugly assert at
the beginning of book 10: "Of the many excellences which I perceive in the order of our State, there is none which upon reflection pleases me better than the rule about poetry."[1] When Glaucon asks him what he is talking about, Socrates replies: "To the
rejection of imitative poetry, which certainly ought not to be
received; as I see far more clearly now that the parts of the soul
have been distinguished." Inasmuch as Glaucon still doesn't understand this shift in Socrates' thought, he asks yet again what Socrates means, and the reply is even more vehement: "Speaking in
cónfidence, for I should not like to have my words repeated to the
tragedians and the rest of the imitative tribe—but I do not mind
saying to you, that all poetical imitations are ruinous to the understanding of the hearers, and that the knowledge of their true
nature is the only antidote to them" (360, 361). Having banished
the poets, Socrates wants now to bury them, and the vehemence

with which he expresses himself is surprising: why not just let the poets die a slow death?

The only answer that makes any sense is that Socrates is obsessed by the conviction that the poets are a great threat to his republic. As a result, he must return to the attack as his meditations end to make sure he has done everything he can to strip poets of their prominent role in society. To be sure, the arguments in book 10 are somewhat different from the ones proffered earlier, but that is less important than the seemingly desperate need to undermine the credibility of the poets once more in the hope of irrevocably damaging their reputation. Why they should be more of a threat than other individuals—corrupt politicians, tyrants, or individuals who use their wealth to buy influence—remains a mystery, though if we assume the main issue is how best to educate young leaders so they will avoid the evils of tyranny and corruption, Socrates' fear makes some sense. Nevertheless, it is hard to avoid the feeling that Plato is undermining his own ideas through hypocrisy.

The most apparent form of double-dealing in Plato's attacks on the poets is his own competition with them for priority. He was not writing in a vacuum and so had to be aware that his own work jostled for attention in a cultural context that included the great poets. It is worth remembering how differently a writer such as Longinus considers Plato's relationship to the poets when he uses Plato as an example of the process of imitation through which writers become great. Longinus insists that Plato reflects those who are "inspired and succumb to the spell of the others' greatness," for it was "above all Plato, who from the great Homeric source drew to himself innumerable tributary streams."[2] Longinus insists that "there would not have been so fine a bloom of perfection on Plato's philosophical doctrines, and . . . he would not in many cases have found his way to poetical subject-matter and modes of expression unless he had with all his heart and mind struggled with Homer for the primacy, entering the lists like a young champion matched against the man whom all admire, and showing perhaps too much love of contention and breaking a lance with him as it were" (81). If Longinus can see that the writer Plato most imitated was Homer, the titanic struggle to kill off the father is readily on display in Plato's banishment of the poets. He wants to create a space for his own writing, and the best way to do that is to discredit those who came before him. So he argues that the work of the great poets is based on irrational distortions that can lead to chaos, in contrast to his more reasonable approach to civility. But the surprising virulence of Plato's return engagement with the poets in book 10 suggests that the source of the argument is as much irrational as it is rational: the poets must be banished if there is to be a place for Plato in the canon of great writers.

The problem inherent in Plato's attacks on the poets is a deep one, beginning with Longinus's insistence that Homer was Plato's primary imitative source. It is one thing to try to enhance one's legacy by discrediting one's forebears; it is another for a writer of putatively rational texts to deny and ignore the imitative—that is, irrational—sources of his own words. Plato can banish the poets only by ignoring his own imitative heritage, which can be seen in the way he bids farewell to Homer and the others, as if he is reluctant to send them on their way, knowing how much they meant to his own education. Even if we don't take the remarks too seriously, it is uncharacteristic of Socrates to begin his argument by saying he is "speaking in confidence, for I should not like to have my words repeated to the tragedians and the rest of the imitative tribe." Is he afraid of what they might say about his attempts to banish them? Probably not. The remark seems a bit of humor, a joshing way of edging up to the main argument. Jowett's expression "the rest of the imitative tribe" suggests as much. Still, if concern is expressed here, it could issue from Socrates' awareness of the unfairness of what he is doing. It indicates that he knows his attack on the reputation of the "tragedians"—he includes Homer in that group—will not be seen as either just or rational, acknowledging the weakness of his own arguments.

If Longinus's insistence that Homer was Plato's great imitative model isn't enough to remind us of this shift in Socratic perspective, Sir Philip Sidney makes it even clearer in his own attempt to justify Plato's attack with the full awareness that Plato was a consummate literary artist. As Sidney proclaims: "Truly, even Plato, whosoever well considereth shall find that in the body of his work, though the inside and strength were philosophy, the skin as it were and beauty depended most on poetry: for all standeth upon dialogues, wherein he feigneth many honest burgesses of Athens to speak of such matters, that, if they had been set on the rack, they would never have confessed them, besides his poetical describing the circumstances of their meetings, as the well ordering of a banquet, the delicacy of a walk, with interlacing mere tales, as Gyges' Ring, and others, which who knoweth not to be flowers of poetry did never walk into Apollo's garden."[3] Sidney quickly documents the fact that, however philosophical Plato's work might be, his means were literary, starting with the invention of the dialogue as a literary form, moving on to the way Plato "feigneth many honest burgesses of Athens to speak of such matters, that, if they had been set on the rack, they would never have confessed them," concluding with the various literary devices Plato uses, from metaphors and allegorical representations of the truth to the dramatic circumstances that are found in many dialogues as well. Plato can hardly be ignorant of these facts. He must know his own work is poetic, however much there are rational arguments within it. He must realize that his rationality depends on the irrational legacy of the word itself and the imitative processes through which one masters and is mastered by language.

At the very least, the *Republic* presents a view of the poets that is hard to reconcile with Socrates' earlier defenses of their divine dispensation. If Plato shifts away from any regard for the irrational states Socrates lauds in earlier dialogues, he provides no specific arguments to discredit either Socrates' views or his own employment of them in dialogues such as the *Ion,* the *Apology,* and *Phaedrus.* True, the *Republic* can be seen as an autonomous thought experiment that requires consistent thinking from beginning to end. From this angle, one assumes that the work is more concerned with following through on the premises inherent in the conception of an ideal community than it is in reconciling those premises with the irrationality at the center of human beings. One of the ways of noting the difference between this dialogue and the others is that there is little serious dialogue in the *Republic* in those sections dealing with the poets. Whereas Adeimantus is capable of giving Socrates an insistent sounding board in some places in the dialogue, neither Glaucon nor Adeimantus provide powerful arguments in favor of the poets. This is particularly noticeable in book 2, where Adeimantus is given to locutions that move the dialogue along without providing any serious insight. When Socrates opens his attack on poetic narrative, Adeimantus asks, "Which stories do you mean . . . and what fault do you find with them?" (72). As the argument proceeds, his contributions are too often simple restatements of what Socrates has already said: "Why, yes, . . . those stories are extremely objectionable" (73). When Adeimantus and Glaucon are called upon to speak, time and again they say little more than "Very good" and "Yes" and "That is my view." Socrates was a powerful interlocutor, so it is hard to find dialogues where he is properly matched with people of his own gifts. Still, there are some where the contest is fairly equal, as in his discussions with Protagorus in the eponymous dialogue. Even at the other extreme, in the *Ion,* for example, Ion is not a completely passive member of the discussion, though he is clearly not up to Socrates' level. The dialogue "feigns" its dialogic nature fairly well in spite of that fact. But Adeimantus and Glaucon don't provide a fitting defense of the poets in the *Republic,* perhaps reflecting Plato's own ambivalence about his attack on them.

These are troubling signs in the dialogue that indicate something is fundamentally wrong with the line of argument from the beginning. The final mark is once again the strange way in which the attack on the poets appears in books 2 and 3, then disappears almost completely until the very end when the argument about ideal, real, and fictive beds makes its appearance. Even if we acknowledge that writers of Plato's time didn't have our idea of form and unity, the placement of the arguments against the poets remains problematic from a formal perspective. They seem out of place, not properly suited to the contexts they occupy in the overall dialogue, even if the most important undertaking of the dialogue is the banishment of the poets. Plato is at odds with himself and with his mentor throughout the dialogue, and we might imagine that far from being concerned about whether the tragedians hear his arguments against the poets, he is hoping that Socrates isn't somewhere listening to what his great pupil has done with the Socratic legacy.

Although Plato's arguments against the poets are well known, fresh readings of the *Republic* reveal that the standard view of the poets' banishment is a distortion of the main line of thought. For whatever reason, the argument that sticks with people is the one that occurs in book 10, the delineation of ideal, real, and fictive beds. Plato banishes the poets, we think, because their images are twice removed from reality and hence distortions of the truths upon which our lives should be based. I have already suggested that this later argument seems tacked on, an eruption in the text that appears so Socrates has one more chance to condemn his literary kin. The arguments in books 2 and 3 are far more interesting, complicated, and pertinent than any talk of ideal, real, and fictive beds. Books 2 and 3 are more insistent that poets tell lies, pure and simple. It is not that they can't see clearly. They refuse to tell the truth. They must be banished because they have a legacy of deceit from which they can never escape.

Plato levels the gravest charges against the poets at the very beginning when Socrates explains to Adeimantus what is wrong with the poets' stories: "First of all, I said, there was that greatest of all lies, in high places, which the poet told about Uranus, and which was a bad lie too,—I mean what Hesiod says that Uranus did, and how Cronus retaliated on him. The doings of Cronus, and the sufferings which in turn his son inflicted upon him, even if they were true, ought certainly not to be lightly told to young and thoughtless persons; if possible, they had better be buried in silence. But if there is an absolute necessity for their mention, a chosen few might hear them in a mystery, and they should sacrifice not a common [Eleusinian] pig, but some huge and unprocurable victim; and then the number of the hearers will be very few indeed" (73). This passage is one of the most important and overdetermined statements in the history of Western thought. Under the guise of saving the future leaders of the republic from the instruction of the great poets, Socrates declares the poets to be liars, and not petty ones either. They have told "that greatest of all lies, in high places" about the origins of the gods that says horrible things about the gods' behavior. When Hesiod explains that Uranus feared his son and sought to kill him by burying him in the earth, and that Cronus in turn castrated Uranus and then suffered his own evil fate at the hands of Zeus, he depicts the bloody and violent origins of human civilization. There was no benign and peaceful beginning but rather a horrible, endless quest for priority, a fierce desire on the part of the older generation to suppress the young and an equally fierce desire on the part of the younger generation to overthrow the fathers.

One can readily understand why Socrates would want to bury this awful myth of origins, for it might give young people the wrong idea. If it leaves them assuming there has always been bloody contestation for priority in the world between father and son, and that the rivalries began with the original Titans, even before the Greek gods established their places, Hesiod's story implicitly authorizes their own desires to get out from under the power of the fathers and seems to legitimize behavior that is inimical to the republic. This is hardly the kind of story to be telling young people who are learning to take up their roles in society, and any reasonable person would agree that these kinds of tales should be kept from them. We might well give it an R on the movie-rating scale and suggest it is appropriate only for mature audiences.

Socrates, though, is not content to restrict dissemination of such stories. He wants them banished altogether, calling them lies, insisting that it "was a bad lie too," whatever that might mean. Perhaps Socrates is suggesting that the story is too outlandish to be believed, perhaps he means only that it was very bad to tell the lie so baldly and excessively. One way or the other, he denies the truth value of the story from the outset. It is not that Hesiod recounted a tale of origins that threatens the orderly upbringing of future leaders of the republic; he lied about the gods, pure and simple. Inasmuch as Socrates wants to banish the poets, he must do more than argue that their stories are dangerous, and what better way to intensify the charges against them than by calling them liars?

If the goal is to eliminate the poets from the polis, this would seem to be enough of an argument. But Socrates immediately begins to qualify his opening assertion by saying that "even if [the stories of the poets] were true, [they] ought certainly not to be lightly told to young and thoughtless persons." Having declared them lies, Socrates insists that their truth value is beside the point: they are dangerous regardless of whether they are true or not. But why even leave open the possibility of truth when one has just declared them to be lies? Wouldn't the argument be stronger if there were no doubt about their truth value? Socrates might think his case is stronger for admitting the irrelevance of the truth value of the tales, but then he shouldn't have begun his argument by declaring the poets liars. He should have insisted that their tales were dangerous because of the potential violence they could induce. He wouldn't have to malign the poets, and he wouldn't have to pass judgment on what the gods did and didn't do.

At the same time, the phrase "even if they were true" affords Socrates several options. It leaves open the possibility that he really believes the poets are telling the truth, that he is lying about their lies while covertly admitting that they told the truth. It is as though Socrates is telling two stories, one for the rabble and one for the cognoscenti: to the rabble he insists the poets lie, while to the cognoscenti he quietly acknowledges that he knows the poets are describing what really happened. It would make perfect sense for Socrates to argue in this duplicitous manner, for he would accomplish his objective of banishing the poets even as he left open his knowledge that the truth value of the poets' words is irrelevant. The average person is not capable of assimilating the complex notion that poets can tell the truth and are all the more dangerous because their statements are accurate; consequently, such people must be fed a story about poetic lies. Those whose minds can assimilate the full complexity of human experience will understand that truth value is irrelevant: the poets are a threat to the stability of the republic and therefore must be banished. At one level the statement compromises Socrates' honesty, but at another it reconfirms it. Nevertheless, one can't help but be troubled by the incompatible ways of reading Socrates' argument: their very instability shows how much Plato himself was a poet, how often his own statements reflected irrational rather than rational truths.

It is also striking how quickly Socrates enlarges the pool of those who are not capable of assimilating the poets' stories. His concerns about the future leaders grow to encompass "young and thought-less persons" in their entirety. And no sooner is the group expanded than it is enlarged further still, for if the stories should be "buried in silence," they must be so virulent that their toxicity places virtually everyone at risk. Here again Socrates' move is both understandable and distressing at the same time. The young haven't lived long enough to witness the abominations of which humanity is capable. Then, too, preadolescent individuals lack the necessary neural equipment to comprehend the full range of human behavior. Only when the complexities of their engagements with the world and their sexuality begin to manifest themselves do they start to understand their own potential strengths and weaknesses. So the young lack the capacity to understand Hesiod's story and should not be exposed to it until their development allows them to make sense of it.

Limited intellectual capacity is not found only in youth, though, which brings up the larger problem: it may well be that the future leaders should not hear the brutal truths about humanity in the early stages of their education, but there will still be problems with adults whose simplemindedness keeps them from making complex decisions of the sort that would allow them to acknowledge the gods' primal violence while recognizing that it is not in society's best interests for humans to act in this manner. It is too easy to conclude that if the gods do it, humans should be able to as well. Socrates may or may not be more interested in the problems inherent in educating the young as opposed to dealing with the educational incapacities of many adults, but in the long run the latter problem is at least as important as the former one, and it is as much with us today as it was 2,500 years ago. Regrettable though it is, there are many people who seem biologically incapable of taking in the overdetermined nature of experience, and it is not hard to see how this fundamental human problem plays itself out at every level of our society. If we did nothing more than look at four of the last five presidents of the United States, we would see how explicitly these basic human issues come into play. Both Jimmy Carter and Bill Clinton had supple minds that were fully capable of embracing the nuances of human behavior. Carter's mental dexterity didn't work well in a presidential context, while Clinton thrived in the midst of complexity and ambiguity, but their success is less important than the fact that they were elected in part because they were highly intelligent individuals who were capable of taking in the fullness of human experience.

In reaction to those capacities, both Ronald Reagan and the younger George Bush were voted into office because of their inability to assimilate experiences in ambiguous and complex ways. Reagan and Bush insisted that the world was straightforward, black-and-white. Some people were good and some were evil; some countries were good and some were evil. The president's job was to reward those who were good and to punish those who were evil in the best paternalistic fashion. Reagan was much more convincingly voted into office as a result of his nostrums than Bush was, but both operated on the same basis, and neither of them was capable of seeing the world in grays. The country's oscillation between presidents who evoke the full richness of the world and presidents who insist the world is a simple, clear place where decision making is easy seems not to be an accident. In Reagan's case, people were exhausted from the previous years' uncertainties and deliberately sought out his simplicity, perhaps regardless of whether his bromides were true. Bush too seems to have gotten as many votes as he did because his stark "moral clarity" was in contrast to the brilliant but deeply flawed motivations that governed Clinton: we don't like moral ambiguity and are often loath to admit it exists.

If one has the liberal bias, as I do, one can't help but think of the Reagans and the Bushes of the world as an expression of Socrates' point: there are a lot of "thoughtless" people who for one reason or another are incapable of addressing the mixed nature of their own experience. They want to see the world composed of good people and bad people, with nothing in between. They insist the world be construed in that manner, which also means they minimize their own unseemliness, lest they are forced to confess that all of us have the potential for violence and degradation. And so, Socrates' argument runs, if there are many individuals who cannot see how the gods' violence doesn't authorize our own, stories of such violence must be banished. There is no other solution in a world where many adults are no more able to admit their weaknesses than children are. Once again, though, even if this were so, one might think that Socrates could make the argument without so much duplicity.

The gravity of the situation Socrates depicts is reinforced by his insistence that these stories "had better be buried in silence." Mimicking Uranus's choice to bury his children and Cronus's to bury his by swallowing them, Socrates wants the tales of Hesiod and Homer not merely removed from circulation but completely cut off from human contact, hidden deep in the earth so no one can find them. In a few short sentences, Socrates has gone from saying that young people shouldn't be exposed to these "lies" to arguing that thoughtless people should be kept from hearing them to insisting that it would be best if no one at all heard them: let them forever be off-limits to humanity! These quick escalations suggest how grave the matter is; Socrates is willing to go to great lengths to get rid of these stories.

It is worth noting how much of Socrates' labors take place underground, as it were. The individual who wants to install reason as the central apparatus in human behavior devotes far more attention to emotional arguments than rational ones. It is not reasonable to say that the poets lie and then quickly declare that even if they didn't their remarks are dangerous. It is not rational to say that young people are the issue while quickly suggesting that adults are at least as much a problem as the young. The fact that Socrates refuses specifically to mention what Uranus, Cronus, and Zeus did suggests an emotional act of suppression: he doesn't want the lurid account of the gods to pass from his mouth, as though he would be polluted by specifying their bloody deeds. He will also be degraded if he mentions their desires, but that is part of the problem: Socrates is trying to deal with the irrational unseemliness of the species in rational ways, but his arguments are motivated by emotion, by the suppression of it in those cases where he withholds statements, and by the tacit evocation of emotion when he exaggerates the dangers of the poets by going so far as to say that their words "had better be buried in silence."

The need for caution is linked to the grave fears all of us have about the potential for violence to overwhelm our lives. Socrates' concern is legitimate. And having taken us to the brink of fear by exclaiming that the great poems should be buried deeply in the earth, Socrates goes one step further by suggesting that "if there is an absolute necessity for their mention, a chosen few might hear them in a mystery." If we were worried before, we should be even more concerned after we see how far Socrates wants to go. The suggestion that there might be "an absolute necessity for their mention" conjures even more horrifying possibilities: what on earth could make it absolutely necessary for these tales to be told? One can assume that only equally lurid and destructive behavior would produce such a compulsion. If Socrates goes so far as to imagine a situation in which these primal acts of violence need to be mentioned, and if he further suggests that the only way to deal with it is through a "mystery," we have to assume he is speaking about the absolute failure of reason. The implicit argument would be that when every reasonable attempt to deal with the primal violence inherent in us fails, when the primal violence threatens society no matter what we do, the only choice we have is to resurrect the original stories of such violence in a ritual context that exposes those in the midst of that sacred mystery and purges them of the primal tendencies in the same act. That is what ritual is for:

exposure to pollution, purgation, immersion into the sacred madness at the center of the species, elimination of the furies inherent in the sacred by containing them in a highly controlled setting.

As Socrates' insistence that "the number of the hearers will be very few indeed" suggests, the ritual containment of violence and evil is best left to the high priests. They absorb the toxins of human violence in order to keep them from spreading, and the rituals through which they soak up human pollution address threatening situations that reason cannot contain. As before, one can't help but be frightened by the scenario Socrates suggests, because his main argument is that we need to learn how to be rational people in a rational society. At the same time, he is wise enough to recognize that there will be occasions when nothing is capable of overcoming the primal violence other than its mimetic counterpart, the rituals governed by high priests. We can infer from these remarks that Socrates too is frightened by the full potential of the species and has therefore wisely laid out various strategies to contain it.

The larger point inherent in this discussion is that Socrates is induced to tell a lurid tale in order to get rid of the lurid tales at the beginning of human culture. The *Republic* is devoted to imposing a rational regime on the world where everything is in its place and everything is clear. But in this small paragraph Socrates quickly abandons reason and moves his audience through a series of irrational stratagems that are highly effective precisely because they are irrational, that is, poetic. Socrates tries to damp down primal fears of violence by arguing that the stories which speak to those fears should be buried, even as his own oblique remarks have the opposite effect: they suggest monsters are hovering just beyond our consciousness that will come forth no matter how reasonable we are. Reason is thus overcome by emotion, logic gives way to religious ritual, and Socrates defeats his own arguments by escalating the potential violence that we will have to undertake to put down the primal violence that never disappears. How could such remarks have been the foundation for an ideal republic? How could they have been so instrumental in introducing humans to more than two millennia of the dream of reason? How could Western civilization have been built out of such a flawed, faulty, compromised structure?

|| When one reads books 2 and 3 of the *Republic* after visiting the trial of Socrates in the *Apology,* one is struck by the fact that Socrates was accused of introducing new gods into the Athenian world and of disregarding the local deities. However much these accusations concern questions such as his reliance on his daimonion, and however much they are trumped-up charges designed to destroy Socrates' reputation, one can't help but see hubris in play from the beginning of the *Republic.* We have already noted that Socrates seeks to banish stories of the gods that might be true just because they are harmful. But if the gods created the world, who is Socrates to banish knowledge of their capacities? Isn't he attempting to usurp their powers by burying stories of their cruelty?

If we had any doubt about Socrates' hubris and heresy in the *Republic,* it is quickly dispelled when we see the arguments that follow the opening attack on the poets. Socrates declares that "if we mean our future guardians to regard the habit of quarreling among themselves as of all things the basest, [no word should] be said to them of the wars in heaven, and of the plots and fightings of the gods against one another, for they are not true" (73–74). As will be the case in the rest of his assertions in book 2, Socrates doesn't provide a subtle argument to explain why the gods have traditionally been portrayed at war with one another, plotting and contending for priority among themselves. He simply says that such stories are "not true." Homer, Hesiod, and the other poets who have provided the foundational myths of Greece are lying, intentionally or otherwise. As with the original argument against the poets, Socrates' main intent is clear: he doesn't want future leaders to see warring and contention between the gods because such disorder will give them the wrong idea about how the republic should be governed. As with the earlier argument, Socrates' concern is legitimate. But one doesn't deny the nature of the gods so definitively without risking charges of impiety. It is conceivable that the poets have either been lying for centuries or have misunderstood the nature of the gods, in which case Socrates' assertions might be worthy. But to deny the gods' nature as it has come down through history is to deny the gods. No matter how much the good of society is behind that rejection, it is always risky to undermine the gods' power, even if only by hiding the negative aspects of their being.

After the first act of denial, Socrates proceeds more boldly still, inducing Adeimantus to agree that "few are the goods of human life, and many are the evils, and the good is to be attributed to God alone; of the evils the causes are to be sought elsewhere, and not in him" (75). In spite of the fact that the Greek gods have been the source of both evil and good—reflected in the wars among themselves that Socrates has already buried—Socrates simply ignores this fact. The responsibility for evil in the world has always been a deep problem for society, just as it has created difficulties for every theology: if the gods are the source of evil, why should they be worthy of devotion? Socrates' remarks make it clear that, in his estimation, there is far more evil in life than good, and if the gods are responsible for it and indifferent to its presence, belief in the gods should fall away. From this angle one might think the Christian God is an improvement over the Greek ones because He is thought to be the repository of the good only—Satan is the source of evil. But the Greek gods are more comfortably matched with our own capacities. They mirror our weaknesses better, demonstrating that the evil in our heritage is as essential as the good, however much we might wish it otherwise, however much a good society would be far more likely if evil weren't an intrinsic part of both the gods and the human race.

Socrates' goal in the *Republic* is to separate the Greek gods from the evil that is attached to them, whether in warring against themselves or intruding in selfish ways in human affairs, from rapes of young women to arbitrary interventions in wars when it suits their play. If Socrates can create an environment where the gods are the repository of good alone, he can also imagine a polis that is organized around the good, one that will be capable of eradicating the evil that has so far clung to every human who has been born. To state things so baldly, though, is to contend with the gods, something Socrates feels he cannot risk. So he attacks them indirectly by trying to eradicate a large portion of their natures: they will henceforth be the site only of the good, and anyone who says otherwise will be banished. Yet again we are reminded of the harshness involved in Socrates' edict that the poets must go. He is sweeping out more than just the poets; he is denying a fundamental part of human nature, and of the gods' nature as well.

It follows that "we must not listen to Homer or to any other poet who is guilty of the folly of saying that two casks 'Lie at the threshold of Zeus, full of lots, one of good, the other of evil lots'" (75). The intent behind this shift in theology is not only to purge the gods of evil so we can imagine ourselves similarly cleansed. It is also designed to create an ethos that is not based on randomness or chance. It is bad enough that the gods are evil. It is even worse that they are indifferent to our fate. It is still worse that our fates are completely arbitrary and unrelated to any efforts we might undertake on our own behalf or any other principle that would help us govern our lives and make the good more prevalent in society. An arbitrary world is one in which there are no reasons for anything, and it is impossible to imagine an orderly society of people who are capable of governing themselves if the universe as a whole is seen to be random. So Socrates thinks, and therefore he must bring order to the gods' world even if they have been indifferent to it themselves.

Socrates is nothing if not systematic, so once he has severed the link between evil and the gods and argued that they are only the source of the good, he moves on to another troubling aspect of their nature, their ability to take on any form they want. They are, after all, the gods, so surely they should be able to become whatever they want to be. But no, Socrates insists, this is a mistaken way of thinking of them: "Shall I ask you whether God is a magician, and of a nature to appear insidiously now in one shape, and now in another?" (77). At this point, one cannot help but be impressed by the manner in which Socrates has thought his arguments through, for he intends no simple airbrush job on the gods, brightening them up by denying their attachments to evil. He is equally offended by the fact that they are protean in nature. Philosophically, the argument is that inasmuch as they are already completed Being, they would not need to take on other shapes. The poets must once again be mistaken in asserting that the gods regularly assumed alternate guises. Never mind that there are many episodes where gods like Zeus become swans, or Athena becomes Mentor. Never mind that the Greeks were wise enough to invent Proteus in order to conjure the shape-shifting nature of the universe. For Socrates, different principles take priority. He argues that "everything which is good, whether made by art or nature, or both, is least liable to suffer change from without" (78). Given that, the gods must be one thing rather than many. Socrates further inquires, "Well, but can you imagine that God will be willing to lie, whether in word or deed, or to put forth a phantom of himself?" (79). When the presumed answer is no, it follows that no god would want to deceive anyone by becoming a "phantom of himself" or adopting a disguise for any reason.

Socrates has thus further contained the nature of the gods, and it doesn't take long before we begin to see how thoroughly he is dictating to the gods what they shall be in the future. They may have enjoyed being protean in nature. After all, shape shifting is playful, engaging in a variety of ways, and if the gods did it for no other reason than their own sport, it would have kept them from being bored. But the playful is the enemy of the good because it lacks seriousness, rational order, and predictability: there is no telling how things will play out. Socrates therefore must domesticate the gods. Otherwise, the prospects for the republic will be weakened by the human tendency toward playfulness, the desire to throw things into the air and see what the result is.

It may well be that the shape shifting of the gods is too playful, amoral, and purposeless for Socrates to countenance it, but we must wonder if there are other motivations inherent in his decision to eradicate their protean nature. At the very least he operates on the same principle that was involved in separating the gods from evil: above all, Socrates seeks moral clarity. Everything must appear as it is: if humans can't know for certain what a thing is, they can't know how to value it either, to calibrate it as good or evil, to place it in the center of society or to cast it out to the periphery. Socrates devotes considerable attention to the protean nature of the gods because no moral clarity is possible unless one can imagine a world in which humans perceive a stable reality and are capable of acting on that basis. If the gods change form, so can humans, and so can everything else. And if everything can change form, the possibility of locating the principles of order in the universe fades into the distance.

Once more I want to emphasize how thoroughly Socrates has usurped the role of the gods by patiently dictating the conditions on which he will continue to allow there to be talk of them in his republic. No greater scene of hubris exists in Greek literature. It competes with all the spectacular scenes in other literary forms, as when, for example, the Chorus in *Oedipus Rex* makes it clear to the gods that the Thebans will no longer believe in them if they don't punish Oedipus for his pride, taking upon themselves the imperative to get rid of Oedipus as though they were the messengers of the gods.[4] But the great poets of the past had the humility to let the gods be who they were. They simply depicted them as fully as they could, reflecting the received wisdom of the culture and passing it on. Socrates is far more aggressive. As with the sternest of gods, he disposes of the world in categories that suit him without concern for anyone or anything. If the gods are going to remain, they will have to measure up to Socrates' reasonable ideas, and so too must humans. The dream of reason manifests itself as the most unrelenting of forms and the most unreal; it insists on things being other than they are and then seeks to set everything straight on the basis of those principles.

It is not an accident that Socrates is at his least playful in the *Republic*. The much-heralded ironic tendencies so readily on display in many of the other dialogues are virtually absent. Irony itself is, after all, a shape-shifting principle, saying one thing, meaning another, leaving meaning to hover somewhere between what one has said and what one seems to be saying. There can be no such irony in the ideal society. Nor can humans simply play with things. Yet even in the *Republic* there is at least one putatively playful moment when Socrates asserts in the middle of an argument that he doesn't know where the dialogue is going: "I really do not know as yet, but whither the argument may blow, thither we go" (95). This remark gets to the heart of the playfulness inherent in Socrates' dialectical scheme of things, for dialogue presupposes an ongoing play among ideas whose end is never in sight. This is to say nothing for the more banal notions inherent in playfulness. Socrates has various kinds of fun when he plays in the dialogues, amusing himself even as he relishes the seriousness of getting to the bottom of things.

|| Once Socrates has straightened out the gods, he has achieved his primary goal. The rest is window dressing, but it is important enough for Socrates to go to some lengths so we can see what follows from his earlier arguments. Most pertinently, if the gods have been simplified and corrected, it follows that humans must likewise adhere to a new standard. They have been created in the gods' image, which was a problem when the gods were evil, protean, and dissolute, but now that the gods are only good and only one thing, humans can brush up their own image. So Socrates sets out to mend us as well. Somewhat surprisingly, the first issue he takes on is the warrior code, attempting to root out that which would undermine the soldier: "And can he be fearless of death, or will he choose death in battle rather than defeat and slavery, who believes the world below to be real and terrible?" (82). To be sure, every state must have a fearless fighting class that is willing to risk everything in defense of the polis. Still, Socrates sees the need to bolster the confidence of the soldiers so much that he wants to eliminate any mention of those awful underworld places like Styx that might make individuals fear for their lives. Rather than allowing warriors the potential knowledge that the world below is both "real and terrible," Socrates banishes this awareness.

In our own day we might assume that knowledge of the fearsome prospects of the underworld is built into humans, either lodged in their unconscious or framed by their daily fears about what might happen to them. At the same time, we have done everything we can to create a society in which people remain largely oblivious of their potential fate after death. In some respects contemporary America is the quintessential Socratic paradise, for the overwhelming majority of people believe in God and heaven, yet fewer and fewer of them believe in either hell or the devil. Perhaps we have been more Socratic than we imagined, at least in this respect. We have certainly worked hard to eliminate thoughts of unpleasant prospects as much as we can, and this is surely at the top of the agenda for the republic.

Getting rid of any mention of awful underworld experiences is just another act of censorship that blocks awareness of human possibilities, but what follows is an attempt at behavior modification: "And shall we proceed to get rid of the weepings and wailings of famous men?" (84). We remember the scenes in the *Iliad* and the *Odyssey* where famous warriors weep and wail. Odysseus himself is one of the best wailers, lamenting his fate at every turn, consumed by self-pity every time something goes wrong. He is equally given to crying without restraint and feels no embarrassment at doing so. Socrates is opposed to such behavior and can consequently be seen as the originator of the macho man, who has come in for so much criticism in our own time. Homer has no trouble portraying his protagonist as a hero with a wide array of affects, but we came to believe that men aren't supposed to show emotion, that a stoic front is best.

Up to this point we might think Socrates is working hard to make the warrior's job as easy as possible by presenting him with an image of a comic-book hero, never questioning his duty, never showing anything but courage, never allowing emotion to enter into his mission. However problematic this is as a way of shaping lives, it makes sense if one believes that soldiers need to be fearless and that society must breed them to become so. Socrates' next step, though, veers from that track, for he insists that "persons of worth, even if only mortal men, must not be represented as overcome by laughter, and still less must such a representation of the gods be allowed" (86). First we note that Socrates is performing mop-up operations here: he forgot to mention in his earlier remarks about the gods that henceforth they can never laugh. He takes care of that omission at the same time he tells us worthy individuals are above laughter. The phrase "overcome by laughter" leaves room for humor in their lives and suggests that the main issue, as always, is avoiding situations in which the individual loses control of his feelings. Laughter in moderation might be possible, but no uncontrollable laughter, no unseemly hysteria that goes on for any length of time and makes one vulnerable.

This great caution about any state that would keep one from maintaining a sober, rational front is most striking, for the relentlessness of Socrates' attempt to reduce human beings to a narrow range of behavior and emotional response becomes increasingly unpleasant. It is bad enough that he feels the need to dictate what human behavior should be like. It is far worse that he is compelled to turn individuals into near automatons of the state who behave only in ways their leaders think are appropriate. Well before Socrates takes away the prospect of being overcome by laughter, the reader should be chilled by his willingness to strip humans of so much of their heritage.

These passages demonstrate the lengths to which Socrates will go to make his state a safe and secure place. If he had confined himself to the elimination of "false" representations of the gods that were designed to give humans a nobler idea of how they should live, we might think his intentions were good. Few of us are proud of our emotional outbursts, particularly when it comes to states such as anger, and most of us would prefer to be less fearful, even as we are shamed by our maledictions. From this angle, the improvements Socrates proposes are ones that in the best of cases we should choose to undertake ourselves. The species might be less interesting if evil were diminished and fear put at bay, but Socrates is right that it would also be more orderly. Most humans would probably make the trade-off.

When he gets to the point of stripping virtually all intense emotional contexts from the human domain, though, Socrates has demonstrated that his real enemy is human affect of any kind. For his state to be successful, humans must be little more than Swift's Houyhnhnms, emotionless creatures whose responses are always measured out in reasonable tones, no serious inflections in the voice, no rising or falling tenor, no emotional uplift or downdraft at any time. Thus, Socrates shows us how far he is willing to go to sacrifice human characteristics for the preservation of order even as he demonstrates what happens when people begin to imagine ways of improving the species. They start out with obvious factors, eliminating fear and sorrow, and end up with sweeping proposals that get rid of many of the crucial characteristics of the species. The incremental approach to the improvement of the species always manages to find one more "negative" characteristic without which we would be better off. When we consider the prospects for cloning that are already on the horizon, we might take Socrates as a cautionary tale for our desires to straighten the species out: after one begins such an endeavor, it is difficult to know where it will end up.

Once he is finished stripping human life of most of its emotional tenor, Socrates turns to more predictable terrain, insisting, "In the next place, we must not let them be receivers of gifts or lovers of money" (89). This is a dual-edged imperative that speaks both to the tendency to give bribes to people in high places and to the reasons why bribes are so frequently present in the power structure: because many if not most humans are "lovers of money." As long as people prize money above everything else, there will be "gifts," bribes offered for preferment. Socrates finds this situation problematic for a whole variety of reasons. First, we must remember his own spotlessness. He admires himself because of his poverty and because he is unwilling to take money for instructing people. In the *Apology*, he flaunts the fact that he has managed to live seventy years without making any money, however strange it appears to his fellow Athenians that he should have worked so little to secure comforts for his old age. Socrates believes that money is the root of all evil and has done everything to uphold that belief. For that, we can only salute him.

At the same time, the love of money and the use of bribes to gain preferment are long-standing weaknesses of human beings. Socrates is right that greed and bribes lead to the corruption of the state and undermine individuals' confidence in their own futures. Bribes disrupt the orderly and rational disposition of fates in a social context, thereby overturning an idea of fair play that is essential to any society that hopes to minimize unrest. People need to believe that their labors can affect their future in positive ways or they lose faith in the social structure and withhold their energies. This too is readily apparent in any society where the tendencies toward greed and bribery have gotten so out of hand that people refuse to give their best efforts.

Likewise, every society seems to need to devote considerable resources to maintaining the often artificial distinction between those who labor honestly and those who have succumbed to the corruption of bribes and greed. One can have no doubt, for example, that George Bush is completely convinced of his own probity in his business affairs before he became president. That his energy company was in effect bought for him has dropped out of his image of who he is and what he has done; that he ran the energy company into the ground and had to be bought out in suspicious circumstances, in effect being handed a million dollars he didn't earn, also seems to be construed in completely different ways by Mr. Bush. That he then got rich while owning the baseball team he bought with the money he was at least metaphorically "bribed" with is likewise beyond the measure of comprehension for Bush. In his mind, he is a hard-working entrepreneur whose labors resulted in wealth and the presidency with no interventions, no greed, and no bribery. If his opponents go too far to the other extreme to paint this picture, it still shows how thoroughly an individual can work to deny his own relative lack of rectitude.

It is worth noting that there are useful distinctions between the Socratic proposals that are designed to eliminate characteristics of the species that many would find essential and proposals that reflect age-old concerns, as in the case of greed. As always, the lines are not perfectly clear, for throughout much of the nineties in the

United States greed was indeed thought to be good. Many saw it as the primary engine of productivity and therefore the only way to achieve a higher standard of living. We know that greed got so much out of hand that, as in the twenties, it seemed almost everyone devoted considerable time to imagining his or her way to riches. Just as the shoeshine boy in the twenties who offered stock tips to the wealthy was a sign of greed gone wild, so the day traders of the nineties and the ordinary folk who would come home at night and check on the progress of their 401(k) plans reflected that we had all more or less decided that greed was good, that there was an easy way to riches, and that it was only a matter of time before we would achieve a society in which people labored more or less effortlessly to obtain a high standard of living. The current mania for buying houses suggests that the only recent change is a shift in the means through which easy wealth is produced.

Socrates' remarks about greed show that in many ways he understands the weaknesses of the species. He inveighs against rape as well (90), an even more unseemly violation of the social order that has highly destructive effects. Socrates is devoted to drawing borders that everyone can see so that things are clear-cut, and no border is more important than the one that allows each of us to maintain the integrity of our bodies. We need to be able to dispose of our relations with the world in ways that are appropriate, and that means that our bodies should not be usurped for other people's needs, most especially when it comes to sexual inclinations and rape.

|| If we concede that anything that promotes the potential for disorder must be banned, we can be comfortable with Socrates' pronouncements. We then come to see how much his arguments finally end up with a more pertinent principle: "We shall have to say that about men poets and story-tellers are guilty of making the gravest misstatements when they tell us that wicked men are often happy, and the good miserable; and that injustice is profitable when undetected, but that justice is a man's own loss and another's gain—these things we shall forbid them to utter, and command

them to sing and say the opposite" (91). Socrates has already dealt with a wide variety of corrosive elements in social existence that have induced countless wars and insurrections. Most of them in one way or another address Nietzsche's great foe, *ressentiment*. Those elements of existence that cause resentment in humans are the most toxic facts of social life; they lead to discontent, to bitterness, and to the desire for revenge, each of which threatens the social order. This is why Socrates is so intent on straightening out human nature: if it loses its emotional volatility, and if the causes of resentment are removed, one can imagine a harmonious community at peace with itself.

For this reason, Socrates insists that the "gravest misstatements" of the poets concern some of the most corrosive aspects of life, chiefly those that convince individuals that wicked men can be happy and good people can be miserable. Most cultures have invented a rule of fair play that suggests good behavior produces a good life and bad behavior leads to unhappiness. Humans have a hard time accepting the fact that they can be good and still have a miserable life. Even harder to digest is the prospect that some evil person will prosper from his evil and thoroughly enjoy his life. It shouldn't matter whether someone else is unjustifiably happy or not; the only thing that should concern us is our own well-being. But we are social creatures, and as a result we measure our happiness in relation to our perception of other people's lives: if they seem to be getting more out of life than we think they deserve, or if they are getting more than we are, resentment rears its head and undermines our existence.

All societies depend on the labors of their citizens, yet work is difficult to undertake. However much we seem to live in a world of workaholics today, most people throughout history probably would have preferred not to work or to work less. If society is to harness the energies of the individual, it must convince people that there is a meaningful ratio between work and life satisfaction. It must persuade them they will get what they have coming to them. If they think otherwise, they might become malingerers. Inasmuch as most of us tend to measure what is right and fitting without serious regard for our own tiny sins, we are inclined to think we are entitled to a bit more of the world's riches than we are. We weigh the scale in our favor and then measure how well our efforts pay off in fitting gratifications. When they don't, we are resentful.

The problem is that too often it seems there is not enough correlation between our labors and our rewards. At best, life can feel like playing the odds in a casino: the house always finds a way to win, but—at least in the old days—it gave the players enough money back along the way to induce them to think they could break even. Humans need that prospect, but the hope is made problematic because each of us is literally the only spot on the planet that measures its gains and losses on the basis of our own perspective. Other humans are doing the same thing, not worrying too much about whether their friends and neighbors have a level playing field. This makes perfect sense because each of us is the only person to inhabit our particular space and time and therefore the only one who can calibrate the relations of that location. But this perspectival limitation can lead people to expect more from life than is appropriate.

Inasmuch as our individual perspectives legitimately induce us to measure the world from our relations within it, it becomes all the more difficult for us to bear perceived unfairnesses, both the unmerited misfortune that comes our way and the unmerited fortune of our neighbors. It is impossible to become an adult without having run into at least one person whom one is convinced is both highly successful and evil. This rankles the average individual so much that he or she must work hard to find ways of overcoming the burden of resentment. If an overly rich person is known to have gotten his wealth by illegitimate means and still manages to be a prominent member of the community who lives in the best house, dines at the best restaurants, and always seems to be enjoying life to the fullest, most people strive to convince themselves that these are illusions, that eventually the person will get his comeuppance. One of the most frequently repeated nostrums of the Bible is that the meek shall inherit the earth, that it is difficult, if not impossible, for the wealthy to get into heaven.

These words exist for the same reason Socrates calls the poets liars because they suggest that evil people can be happy: we believe evil people can have wonderful lives but can't bear the thought. Therefore, any reasonable society has to conjure a world in which just deserts are the means through which behavior is gauged: in the end, if not now, one gets what one deserves. Society might have to invent another world after this one to provide that rectification, but justice must be served if social cohesion is going to have a chance.

If we realize how committed Socrates is in these two books of the *Republic* to rooting out the fundamental causes of resentment in humans, we can see why more than two millennia later Nietzsche would insist that the most grievous sin of our species is resentment. Socrates sought to eliminate it by lying to the citizens of his ideal society. In contrast, Nietzsche recognizes the impossibility of censorship and understands that the chief bar to our development is the rancor that is seated at the center of almost everything we do. Hence, Nietzsche's Zarathustra asserts without equivocation: "For *that man be delivered from revenge,* that is for me the bridge to the highest hope, and a rainbow after long storms."[5] Nietzsche's ideal society is predicated on the same level of awareness as Socrates', which is no accident, since the wise are likely to perceive the same virtues and limitations in the species over time. The main difference is that Socrates believes that corporate lying about the facts of life is the best we can do, suggesting the impossibility of eliminating the spirit of revenge. In theory, over several generations the corporate lies might minimize our species' tendency toward rancor, but, taken as a whole, the *Republic* suggests otherwise. The fact that Socrates tries to bury the truths about the Titans even as he suggests there will be times when there is an "absolute necessity for their mention" implies that the act of censorship will not eliminate the desire for revenge. It will simply produce a world where we strive (futilely) to deny our own feelings.

It is no accident that the thinker most devoted to overturning the Platonic legacy of reason—Nietzsche—would also declare it to be the greatest of swindles. It is also no accident that Heidegger in turn would characterize reason as "the most stiff-necked adversary of thought."[6] Among other things, reason can find no way of eliminating the gravest of human problems, our inclination to undermine the quality of our lives through rancor over perceived unfairnesses in life. If the best it can do with this problem is bury it and banish the poets, it has failed from the beginning. This is Nietzsche's argument,[7] and his deliberate breakdown of the border between poetry and philosophy is one of the ways he attempts to overcome the Platonic legacy of lies on which the dream of reason is built. That is why it is so important for Nietzsche to have Zarathustra say: "For *that man be delivered from revenge, that is for me the bridge to the highest hope, and a rainbow after long storms.*" Nietzsche sums up the human dilemma at least as well as Plato does, first by assuming along with him that resentment must be eradicated if humans are to find a way of living decently with one another. Second, in contrast to Plato, Nietzsche acknowledges that no human device—including reason—has eliminated it (though Plato suggests as much with his secret mystery and ritual sacrifice). Third, Nietzsche recognizes the need for hope to move beyond resentment. And fourth, reflecting the same contradictoriness we find in Plato, Nietzsche insists that humans must abjure resentment even as the phrase "that man be delivered" implies a deus ex machina to accomplish the task: we must get rid of our resentment yet seem incapable of doing so on our own.

At the same time, in contrast to Plato, Nietzsche insists that humans must confront their fundamental *ressentiment* rather than running from it. He doesn't want leaders to lie to people about it, he doesn't want to leave the impression that it is not intrinsic to the human situation, and he doesn't want to invent a god to save us. Nietzsche declares the great difficulty in overcoming resentment and acknowledges that his highest hope has so far been beyond human capacity. But he wants to conceive of a species that can confront and overcome this provocation toward resentment rather than imagining a community based on lies and censorship. His overman is the human who has moved past resentment through self-overcoming rather than self-denial. Whether this prospect bears any weight remains to be seen, but it is a salutary contrast to the rational approach toward resentment.

‖ Plato understands the nature of narrative and the nature of forms, so he is not content merely to remove the stories that speak of the potential threats inherent in human nature. He wants to remove the formal problems as well. If he has difficulty imagining gods that adopt more than their original shape, he is similarly upset by writers who take on the narrative voice of their characters. Thus, "when the poet speaks in the person of another, may we not say that he assimilates his style to that of the person who, as he informs you, is going to speak?" (93). This tendency toward narrative assimilation troubles Plato for two reasons. First, Socrates insists that "we will not allow those for whom we profess a care and of whom we say that they ought to be good men, to imitate a woman, whether young or old, quarreling with her husband, or striving and vaunting against the gods in conceit of her happiness, or when she is in affliction, or sorrow, or weeping; and certainly not one who is in sickness, love, or labour" (96). The imitation of human types allows the depictions of actions that are unseemly and threatening; as a result there is no reason they should be depicted at all, particularly in the guise of the character him- or herself. To do so is to give credibility to situations that are unhealthy and dangerous. "Neither must they represent slaves, male or female, performing the offices of slaves" (96), Socrates asserts, claiming that such individuals can only present unworthy models to the citizens of the republic.

The more troubling inclination is to have the narrative voice switch around like Proteus and his many guises. If humans must strive to be only one thing, it does no good to have writers adopting different voices. Doing so suggests the multiplicity of human inclinations rather than their singularity, conjuring once again the danger of people who are uncanny, unpredictable, irrational in any number of ways. Humans must be consistent in their actions and thoughts because each of us must be convinced of our unity and our singularity in order to create the individual responsibility that is necessary for an orderly society. Such a system cannot have a narrative model in which the narrator becomes one thing and then another. That is the worst of human inclinations as far as Plato is concerned (notwithstanding the fact that Plato's dialogues mimic such a form themselves), so Socrates dispenses with any complex forms of narration.

Not satisfied with eliminating the multiplicity of voices inherent in every human, Socrates strips the narrative of its variety as well, those elements that are hidden deeper in the composition: harmony and rhythm. Given the constraints already imposed on writers, it is not surprising that Socrates proposes further restrictions: "And you would agree with me in saying that one [style] is simple and has but slight changes; and if the harmony and rhythm are also chosen for their simplicity, the result is that the speaker, if he speaks correctly, is always pretty much the same in style, and he will keep within the limits of a single harmony (for the changes are not great), and in like manner he will make use of nearly the same rhythm?" (98). Inasmuch as a simple, noncontradictory whole is the goal of Socratic narrative, it follows that the rhythms and harmonies should be simple as well. If they contrast with the main narrative, they leave the impression that humans can be at odds with themselves or can be more than one thing. Good style suggests the narrative is one thing, the characters are straightforward and unified, and the rhythms and harmonies are of accord.

As with voice, there is both a banal and a subtle argument about the nature of harmony and rhythm in the *Republic*. The lesser claim suggests that harmonies are specifically tied to certain human traits and should be eliminated for that reason. Thus, Socrates says he needs to get rid of the harmonies linked to "lamentations and strains of sorrow" (100) and the "drinking harmonies" (101) as well. In contrast, he wants to keep the warlike harmonies (101) because they foster the proper attitude in the soldier. The deeper argument is that the more complex the rhythm and harmony, the more likely there will be confusion, evoking a complex version of human nature, one that violates the law of noncontradiction. Such struggles—even when they are displayed with beautiful harmonies—are a threat, and perhaps a larger threat than the narrative dangers because they work unconsciously. It is easy to see that the struggle among the Titans raises serious questions about the human obsession with priority. It is more difficult to discern the ways in which various harmonies and rhythms contribute to similar notions and engender inclinations toward unseemly irrational actions. People don't necessarily recognize that rhythms induce particular states and that harmony inclines people to be disruptive or unsettled.

In the end, Socrates declares that "such a style is unsuitable to our State, in which human nature is not twofold or manifold, for one man plays one part only" (99). Everything comes back to the need to present humans as simple, unified creatures whose inclinations are not at odds with one another. Even worse, these patterns are said to be essential because they reinforce the viewpoint that individuals are fated to take up only one role in society: the cobbler will be a cobbler, the warrior a warrior, the painter a painter. These are the roles into which various humans will fit, and in an orderly society people will not have ideas about playing more than one part. Once they begin to imagine other roles, they introduce uncertainty.

From our distance, these ideas seem incredibly naive—after all, we in the United States have adopted the opposite view. Any society that insists its citizens will have many different jobs over the course of a lifetime and will constantly have to be retooling and mastering new skills has turned Plato on his head. Rather than accepting the limitations that came with the idea that most humans were only good at one or two things, we insist that people are protean and should adapt to their flexible natures. If Plato envisions a society where every human knows his or her place and occupies that slot with contentment, we imagine the equivalent of the character in the movie *Groundhog Day* who, when he finally accepts that he will be living the same day over and over again forever, masters an entire range of human skills: he becomes a gifted pianist, a consummate sculptor, a man with perfect medical technique, and a wise interlocutor, knowing just what each human being needs when he or she needs it. The only thing that limits humans is time.

Our insistence on the plasticity of the species is as absurd as Plato's argument that we should all accept our singular nature. Likewise, it is clear that, like Plato, we have adopted a view of the species that suits the cultural imperatives of our day. The "creative destruction" of capitalism has grown so insistent that we are now supposed to imagine societies that thrive best by being in constant ferment. Plato's views of society seem sterile and stagnant from our vantage point, and there is no doubt that the rigid imposition of ideas of human character on the members of the republic is stultifying in the extreme. But our social machinations are at least as restrictive in their own way and at least as contrived as Plato's.

In effect, Plato wants to create a society in which every human is contented with his or her limited lot. This may promote stability in a social system, but it does so at the expense of the humans who compose it: they are stripped of their variousness, they are lied to constantly, and they are rigidly encouraged to think of themselves in only one way. Even today vestiges of this model exist in contemporary societies. We continue to think of ourselves as essentially unified creatures in spite of the fact that a moment's thought reveals our multifarious natures and our self-contradictory behavior. There is no way to reconcile our desire for love, our commitment to reason, and our basic bodily impulses, everything from our sexual desire to the necessities imposed on us by various bodily functions. We may be constituted by these elements, but there is no way to make sense of them or to work them into a simple, unified vision of who we are. But like Plato, we feel more comfortable imagining ourselves as one person with an identity that permeates everything we do, so we continue to believe that that is what we are.

Socrates insists that everything in society and in our narratives must follow the same simple rules. When he gets to his discussion on rhythm, then, it is no surprise that his remarks are virtually identical to the ones we witnessed in his critique of narrative, voice, and harmony: "Next in order to harmonies, rhythms will naturally follow, and they should be subject to the same rules, for we ought not to seek out complex systems of metre, or metres of every kind, but rather to discover what rhythms are the expressions of a courageous and harmonious life; and when we have found them, we shall adapt the foot and the melody to words having a like spirit, not the words to the foot and melody" (102, 3). Socrates assumes there are specific rhythms that express "a courageous and harmonious life," and this is a bit surprising. We might rather think there are a variety of rhythms suited to various purposes, beginning with the degree to which they express a light or a heavy tone. That there would be rhythms devoted to courage is going a bit far, but the important point is that Socrates doesn't want complex rhythms to come between listeners and the views expressed in poems. The meter should be kept simple, and it should correspond to the sense of what is taking place. Lest there be some who assume rhythm is the most important aspect of poetry, Socrates declares that "we shall adapt the foot and the melody to words having a like spirit, not the words to the foot and melody." Poets often assume rhythm takes priority over meaning, and Socrates wants to avoid this notion at all costs. It suggests that the emotional undertow of words is more significant than their meaning, and if their affective capacities were given the primary role in the poem, meaning could too easily be lost.

Socrates is subtle enough to recognize that there are varying kinds of simplicity, so he carefully distinguishes the rhythms he is asking for from the lesser expressions of the same idea: "Then beauty of style and harmony and grace and good rhythm depend on simplicity,—I mean the true simplicity of a rightly and nobly ordered mind and character, not that other simplicity which is only an euphemism for folly" (104). Simple rhythms can be found in various linguistic forms—nursery rhymes, for example—that are hardly up to the task of conveying important moments of courage and determination. The simple but graceful expression of the nature of things is far superior to these lesser forms, and Socrates doesn't want to advocate the equivalent of pablum.

Books 2 and 3 of the *Republic* have completely revised traditional ideas of poetry even as Socrates speaks out of both sides of his mouth. He has argued that the poets ought to be banished because the lies/truths they tell are too dangerous for the well-being of the polis even as he carefully describes the poetic terrain he would allow in the republic, suggesting that a heavily controlled and censored poet working for the good of the city might be acceptable. By so rigidly restricting what poets can and cannot say, Socrates shows how afraid he is of the freedom of their tongues, acknowledging that poets are dangerous because they say what comes to them, what the gods give them through inspiration. Even so, divine inspiration never enters the discussion. In the *Ion,* Socrates repeatedly points out that poets are not in their right minds when they compose their verses, but there is no such talk in the *Republic.* There couldn't be, for it would make clear how hopeless Socrates' regulatory efforts are. If they aren't even in their right minds when they utter their lines, how could poets begin to have control over their discourse? Heavy editing after the fact couldn't cover a kind of expressiveness that is preconscious or inhuman in various ways. As a result, Socrates assumes a model of the poet that doesn't apply to any reality he acknowledges in other dialogues that deal with the nature of poetry. He comes close to reducing poets to rational, calculating liars who carefully consider the messages they want to disseminate in their poems before they recite them for the first time.

|| The major transformation in Socrates' view of what animates poets—the movement away from divine inspiration toward careful calculation of message and content—is most pertinent all those pages later when Socrates finally returns to verse in book 10. At that point he takes up the issue of ideal, real, and poetic beds so he can declare the poets' words thrice removed from the genuine article. This shift in tactics is important, yet the argument of the beds depends on the kind of Socratic questioning that always appears a bit strange to modern eyes. It requires us to take seriously the question of where the poet gets his knowledge about various

human occupations and stations, and otherworldly ones as well. How could the poet know the manner in which the gods behave? How could he have a proper understanding of the knowledge generals possess? Or cobblers? Or anyone else with a meaningful role in society? We are far less troubled by these questions than Socrates is. Few of us would go to a poet to learn how generals command, and we don't worry too much about the versions of generals or factory workers we find in our narratives. For Socrates, though, the accuracy of such portrayals is crucial because it presents the putative fundamental truths of the way humans occupy their stations in society. If the roles are wrong, there will be mistakes in the way people take up their place in the scheme of things.

Socrates concludes that the poets work on the basis of illusion rather than truth:

> And so, when we hear persons saying that the tragedians, and Homer, who is at their head, know all the arts and all things human, virtue as well as vice, and divine things too, for that the good poet cannot compose well unless he knows his subject, and that he who has not this knowledge can never be a poet, we ought to consider whether here also there may not be a similar illusion. Perhaps they may have come across imitators and been deceived by them; they may not have remembered when they saw their works that these were but imitations thrice removed from the truth, and could easily be made without any knowledge of the truth, because they are appearances only and not realities? Or, after all, they may be in the right, and poets do really know the things about which they seem to the many to speak so well? (366)

The poetic bed is deeply flawed because it is so far removed from the true essence of the bed. Inasmuch as poets are imitators, there is no inherent connection between what they describe and the real thing: their words can present images that "could easily be made without any knowledge of the truth" and so should be considered deeply suspicious. They are "appearances only and not realities" and should therefore be discredited. This passage ends by suggesting that perhaps the poets really do know what they are talking about, but the burden of the argument in book 10 is that they couldn't possibly speak the truth because they are incapable of mastering all the human roles and therefore have to present the various possibilities without sufficient knowledge. We remember that this indirectly came up in the *Ion* when Socrates argued that the poet's knowledge had to be divinely inspired because there was no way he could know what a general or any of the other people he represented in his poems did without having lived such roles himself. Therefore, the gods must give him this knowledge.

In book 10, though, there is a conflation of arguments that is designed to undermine the credibility of the poet once and for all: his imitative nature is linked to the fact that he doesn't know enough about human situations to present them accurately. The conclusion is that poets present appearances rather than realities and thus put the truth at risk. However much all the arguments against the poets get at serious problems inherent in our linguistic representation of existence, they are also less subtle than the ones that are found in the *Ion* because they seem intent on ignoring the fact that imaginative space differs from reality yet is a function of it. Socrates overcomes this gap in the *Ion* by declaring the poets' words to be divinely inspired. In the *Republic* he assumes poems are constructed in a rational manner, concluding that poets can only present appearances rather than realities.

From a calculating point of view, this argument makes sense because it relies on a simple misunderstanding of the nature of poetry. It argues that poets ought to be valued on the basis of how well they present the truths of warriors or generals or leaders and then finds them lacking when it becomes clear that poets know little about such lives. But this is logic chopping in spite of the fact that there are grave considerations about the fictive nature of poetic artifice that are genuinely in play in the dialogue. Even if we go beyond the portraits of people taking up various roles and speak of human capacities instead, asking whether the poet could know all the states he represents—the full range of happiness, sadness, grief, and woe to which people are inevitably exposed—the argument remains specious because each of us measures the truth of poetic representations on the basis of our personal knowledge of them. Few of us are docile enough to assume that the poet must have everything right because he or she is a poet.

The remarks in books 2 and 3 are far more interesting because they are alert to the threat that poets present to the city. Imitation is an essential and yet dangerous phenomenon, one that is still not properly understood. People today tend to go to one extreme or the other, like Socrates, assuming either that humans model their behavior on imitative processes that are based on reduplicating the images of individuals they deem worthy of emulation or that we learn how best to express ourselves in nonmimetic ways. We still have the reductive idea of imitation that was in play before the Romantic era undermined it, and we have the simplistic nostrums about individuality that have taken over since the Romantics changed our view of ourselves. There is little in that rocky middle place that recognizes the highly mimetic nature of the species even as it acknowledges the degree to which each of us freely expresses our individuality. Writers such as René Girard have attempted to get a better handle on our imitative inclinations, but the century in which ideas of human nature opened up was quickly replaced by yet another era that is committed to the notion that human beings are simple imitative creatures.[8] The movement away from Romantic truth toward cultural criticism has swung from a non-mimetic notion of our behavior to one that simplifies the ways in which we pick up things from our context. The superficial truths in this idea—we do absorb ideas of race, class, and gender from our local environment—overwhelm the more complex question of how we are mimetic creatures. They also thoroughly ignore the question of why we have spent so many millennia willfully misunderstanding the ways in which we are imitative from the ground up.

That is why someone like Girard is so much closer to the Socrates we find in books 2 and 3 of the *Republic:* both Girard and Socrates realize the volatility of our imitative capacities and seek to sniff out their dynamics. Socrates is quick to banish the poets because of the dangerous irrationality inherent in any mimetic display, whereas Girard is intent on getting to the bottom of the various ways our behavior is constantly mimetic in the hopes of understanding how we are shaped by these impulses. But we can assume that Socrates' hasty abandonment of the poets is based on an acute understanding of mimesis because he understands it well enough to be frightened by it. We can likewise assume that Socrates knows more than he is saying, perhaps being fearful of exposing the kinds of mimetic madness that take over human beings every day. The most fundamental mystery of the species is its mimetic nature, yet because it exists prior to any control we might exert over it, and because history provides us with countless instances where individual and collective mimesis have gotten out of hand, we run from the subject as quickly as Socrates buries the lies/truths about the gods.

Between appearance and reality lies mimesis. That is what Socrates declares throughout the *Republic*, though he is not very clear about what this might mean. What role does mimesis play in the evolution of reality, and how is it related to the truth or falsity of the visions of existence we have? The best that can be said is that the desire to banish the poets reflects the seriousness with which the mimetic capacities of the species are taken. But the understanding of our imitative nature is moved forward only indirectly, by the misrepresentations Plato establishes, as the ideal, real, and poetic beds make clear. This argument speaks to the curious issue inherent in all artifice: how can it be fictive and yet true at the same time? Plato doesn't resolve this endlessly bedeviling question any more than those who follow after him, but at least he takes it seriously. The *Republic* concerns itself from beginning to end with the question of how best to live, and with the question of whether the best life is fabricated out of truths, lies, or something in between. It can't answer these questions any more than it can establish the nature of justice. But it can keep the questions open rather than assuming a series of simplistic answers to the enduring enigmas of our lives.

One of the ways of getting at the fundamental problems Plato raises in the *Republic* is to ask why he develops such a reductive idea of poetic artifice in the dialogue. He assumes that poems exist to mean rather than be, and this shift in orientation is not taken as seriously as it should be. In one respect the Platonic insistence that poems must be in control of their meanings and fully aware of their implications is a reflection of the tremendous changes in thought that come about once reason takes priority. Surely Homer was not concerned about the kind of meaning that dominates Plato's thought. That is one way of speaking of the difference inherent in their respective works. Plato seeks to institute a radical shift in poetic form, one that straightens out the narrative so it fits comfortably with the ideological views of the leaders of the polis and also one that promulgates specific thematic viewpoints about what it means to be human. Homer presents life experience in a narrative stream, and along the way he tells stories that could be construed as parables about human nature. The goal is not instruction in any way Plato would imagine.

Some might consider this difference in terms of entertainment versus education, and no doubt Homer meant to entertain more than Plato did. But that is less the issue than the degree to which the authors encourage the narrative of reality to make rational sense. In the *Odyssey,* the world fits together in its own way, but it fails to cohere in any reasonable manner. Much of the action is given meaning of a sort by the narrative stratagem of Athena's support of Odysseus, for example, but Athena disappears for long stretches of the poem. To use the biblical metaphor, the hairs on Odysseus's head are not numbered. He is left to his own devices except when otherworldly forces such as Poseidon intervene. Homer is not intent on creating narrative coherence in this way any more than he wants each moment of Odysseus's life to fit into a highly wrought pattern.

Plato is a meaning monger. He wants the stories to say specific things in didactic ways so that people can learn something about the nature of their lives while reading him. Without this learning process, the literary purpose is defeated. Plato takes time to delight his audience with his literary craft, but he comes down hard on Horace's instructive side of the equation, transforming Western civilization into a prescriptive machine: poems must produce meaning through their narratives, whatever their character, or they must be banned. Even though literature will oscillate between meaning and the pleasures of narrative over the centuries, it will never be the same once this standard—an idealized notion of abstractive reason—is imposed on it. For better and worse, meaning takes on a greater and greater role in what literature becomes.

The cultural critics are the Platonists of our day because they insist that every text must speak the same message about race, class, or gender. They declare that literature's first prerogative is to convey a didactic message, to instruct its readers in how to be better human beings. Like Plato, they have a highly specific idea of the instructional value of texts. They insist that the ethical import of literature be trained to the necessities of the moment and then define those necessities in terms of sociological categories that are putatively designed to eliminate inequities in the social system— this in spite of the fact that much of Western literature is at best secondarily concerned with such problems. The cultural critics' grid is even more rigid than Plato's because they are even more desperate to make meaning where none was intended. Whether this works to the best advantage of society (and literature) remains to be seen, but it is certainly striking to see seemingly left-wing critics so thoroughly exceeding the didactic strictures of a right-wing prescriptivist like Plato.

Nevertheless, both Plato's right-wing extremism and today's left-wing expression of the same didactic excesses address the gravest threats to society. Both rightly believe that human violence and irrationality always remain antagonists of the peaceful organization of individuals in a community, even as they realize the essentially relational nature of community. The weakness inherent in both proposals for reform is that they never work because they are contrary to human behavior. Plato can banish the godlike and human characteristics that give the wrong impression of how to act, but the behavior will continue, and people will be resentful for being dealt with arbitrarily. Cultural critics can insist that literature continue to measure up to their prescriptive ideas of it, but their abstract grid is at least as unreal as Plato's and will be resisted for the same reason. It may not be a good thing that both Plato and the cultural critics are doomed to fail, for it is conceivable that they are humanity's best chance for a decent society. But deliberately lying to people and obsessively trying to shape their character always fail in the end because these actions ignore the irrational flow of life at the center of the species.

The alternative to the Platonic grid is to allow for a play of things, to acknowledge the ways in which life imposes its own devices on humans regardless of their wishes. The Nietzschean perspective involves accepting the full range of human behavior, not trying to escape our revulsion against who we are by imposing resentful schemes on behavior but rather working through our capacities to overcome resentment about that which cannot be changed. To be sure, current thinking assumes there is no such thing as human nature, arguing instead for the completely constructed view of the individual. But that is what is at issue: the prescriptivists assume that human nature is what it is only because of bad models: history has made us what we are, and we can change ourselves by redefining our ideal images. To a certain extent, this makes sense: people can change some aspects of their behavior, and they can learn how to regard their lives in new ways. But human biology still has to be addressed, and it resists facile notions of change that are imposed on it from the outside.

Nietzsche's model urges us to begin by accepting our violent and irrational natures, by celebrating their capacities even as we recognize their dangers. More important, Nietzsche insists we must learn how to accept that we are stuck in time and always will be. That is why his signal ethical pronouncement is *amor fati:* we must learn to embrace our fates in every respect and concede that nothing in them can be changed.[9] Only by accepting the irrevocability of our past can we begin to imagine changes in our orientation that will be salutary to the lives of everyone. Nietzsche proposes this difficult imperative fully aware of what he fights against, as best represented by Plato and Christianity, each of which suggests the impossibility of such an acceptance. He knows the odds against *amor fati:* humans will probably continue to resist their natures no matter what happens or what prescriptive views are imposed on them. The terrible double bind is the opposite of Plato's: we must fully accept who we are in order to become a better species, whereas Plato proposes that we must deny who we are if we are to improve ourselves. There is no choosing between these viewpoints, because they emerge from deep-seated attitudes that evolve from our actions. Yet each perspective imagines a radically different idea of humanity.

|| There is one other element of the Platonic legacy we must deal with before we leave the *Republic,* and that is the rigidity of Plato's human ideal. He wants to straighten the species out. We have seen how he stripped his models of gods and humans of anything extraneous or potentially problematic: the gods cannot be associated with evil, they cannot assume various forms, they must be only one thing; the same also applies to humans, in addition to which they need to learn to bury their fear of death, eliminate their self-pity, escape from their tendency toward laughter, and so on. Plato assumes that the goal of our species is to create a perfectly straightforward, rational creature. He wants to breed out of humans any of the irrational diversity of character that is on display in the races, genders, and cultures of the world. The cultural critics too want us all to live under a highly "rational," predictable grid of human behavior that should in theory produce an entirely good individual in an entirely pleasant social world. However much these dreams of reason seem at odds with the species, there will always be individuals who think this is the best way to proceed into our future.

Rigid attempts to improve the species through prescriptive grids, though, always run up against the same obstacles, and they present the same problems we find in our farming practices: Would the world and the species be better off if we produced a monocultural view of humans (we are already moving toward such an "ideal" in any case as a result of the virulent spread of "global capitalism")? We know that the greatest risk of agricultural monocultures is that they make the food supply vulnerable to shifts in the wind: one particular virus or fungus can ruin an entire crop. If farmers plant a variety of corn or wheat seeds, any particular pest can harm only part of the yield. Having witnessed the devastation that can be wrought by monocultures as far back as the great potato blight in Ireland, we learned to maintain heterogeneous plant stocks to avoid this problem. At the same time our crops have become more and more monocultural because modern farming techniques require the same kind of seed to work their magic: the pesticides and fertilizers are targeted for a narrow range of seeds. In spite of our best knowledge, we are increasingly vulnerable to a particular blight should one come along that is capable of destroying everything that is planted.

In the cultural field, one might assume that ideas of diversity would also dominate the growth and development of the species. Here, too, though, we seem to be moving more and more toward monoculture as defined by the practices of capitalism. These processes might have been partially slowed by the Muslim rebellion against Western culture, but it is hard to believe that the flow of capitalist ideas is anything more than temporarily thwarted, and ongoing developments in countries like China and India are far more likely to reflect the future. Capital has a life of its own, and "it" seems intent on taking over the entire globe. Needless to say, when all areas of the world are equally driven by the mania toward acquisition and accumulation, all will be committed to laying waste to the resources of the planet, which, by some accounts, are already pressed to the limit. This would make the species far more susceptible to shifts in nature, everything from a potentially horrific fallout from global warming to a simple lack of arable land. We put ourselves at great risk by inducing everyone to follow our model, yet we seem intent on doing so nonetheless.

Ever since communities developed, there have been individuals who assume the best path for humanity is an insistent imposition of a reductive viewpoint on one and all: snuffing out differences leads, we are told, to a more orderly arrangement of our relations with one another. Plato reminds us of this inclination toward the end of the *Republic* when Socrates sums up his stand against the poets:

> Therefore, Glaucon, I said, whenever you meet with any of the eulogists of Homer declaring that he has been the educator of Hellas, and that he is profitable for education and for the ordering of human things, and that you should take him up again and again and get to know him and regulate your whole life according to him, we may love and honour those who say these things—they are excellent people, as far as their lights extend; and we are ready to acknowledge that Homer is the greatest of poets and first of tragedy writers; but we must remain firm in our conviction that hymns to the gods and praises of famous men are the only poetry which ought to be admitted into our State. For if you go beyond this and allow the honeyed muse to enter, either in epic or lyric verse, not law and the reason of mankind, which by common consent have ever been deemed best, but pleasure and pain will be the rulers in our State. (378)

Heterogeneity and the full measure of the human past may be energizing in some respects, and the creative impulses of the species may depend on them, but given the choice, leaders always opt for a narrower scheme in which only their vision is allowed to disseminate itself. In spite of a radically different perspective in other dialogues, Socrates remains convinced here that "hymns to the gods and praises of famous men are the only poetry which ought to be admitted into our State."

The millennia since Socrates' attempt to straighten out the species would attest to the opposite need. They show that most people always already have more than enough of an inclination to see the world in binary terms. Instead, they need to be urged to take up the full complexity of their being, to embrace the highly mixed and heterogeneous elements of which they are composed. Education in this view would not banish the poets for telling the truth or for lying. It would celebrate them for their multiplicity of viewpoints. It would embrace them because they are willing to speculate about the nature of our lives so that new angles on experience are opened up. It would concede that however dangerous it is to remind people of the full burden of being human, it is even more dangerous to act as though the world is a simple place where people are either good or bad, where everything can be known and expressed in straightforward terms, and where people can be measured by the nostrums of those who think each of us should have an identity that chains us rigidly to the everyday world we inhabit. Only when we begin to side with the other Socrates, the one who is always open to the embrace of the irrational—whether through the divine wandering at the center of his dialogic journeys, the other forms of divagation he participates in, or the voice of his daimonion as it proscribes choices for him—will we properly appreciate the variousness of individuals and the species. Socrates' life was a rich and exemplary feast because he knew best when to heed his rational or his irrational inclinations, and the only way to learn how to discern the usefulness of these capacities is to be exposed to their full burden and to be encouraged to assume the difficult task of sorting out the knowledge and wisdom that accrue to each of us when we take up our place in the universe.

CONCLUSION
THE MULTIPLICITY OF VOICES

THE IMAGE OF Socrates most worth considering is that of a man in the full play of his various capacities, reveling in the exercise of all of them. As I have said from the beginning, my goal has never been to diminish Socrates' commitment to reason and to its fundamental importance in our lives. That commitment is regularly on display in the dialogues, and the rational strategies Socrates employs to pursue the nature of things become essential to the history of Western civilization and to the world as a whole, mixed though that history has been. Reason is a powerful instrument that receives its most eloquent expression in Socrates' use of it.

What we have lost sight of is the degree to which unreason is even more central to our lives, essential to our well-being and connected to the processes of reason that provide us with a perspective on the various irrational ways through which our lives unfold. We haven't adequately charted the manner in which reason and unreason contribute to one another, but we know there is a dialectical relationship between them as much as there is between us and those with whom we have discourse. Socrates' commitments to the unreasoning aspects of life provide us with a fitting model of the virtues and limitations of these irrational modes of being even as they suggest an idea of human character that is more attuned to our full nature than the narrow, analytical conception of identity we have thought should be our guide.

The simplest point to make about our irrationality is that it is both our greatest danger and our greatest prospect for joy. Plato understood how volatile our irrational capacities can be and was thoroughly aware of the risks inherent in unreason both for ourselves and for our communities. This is most evident in the *Republic,* where anyone who is likely to induce potential discord through irrationality is banished. I would choose to keep the poets, but I would do so in the full knowledge that they always present a risk in their evocations of human capacities. We see more than enough evidence of this every day: to be irrational is potentially to be susceptible to violent swings of passion that can be highly destructive. In the most extreme irrational states, we are not in our right minds, and those states can have devastating effects. We are a dangerous animal and need to remember that.

I would add that whereas this aspect of our irrational capacities is a major concern for humans, it also makes us interesting. However much we refuse to admit it, awareness of an element of danger in our lives makes for a richer existence than if we were capable only of good and benign things. Our capacities for violence make it possible for us to react in extreme circumstances to those who would do us harm. There is also something in us that likes to rub up against the threshold between violence and civility every now and then, if only so we remember the difference between the two. I don't mean to encourage violence, for there is always already too much of it. But the prospect of the appearance of irrational danger is a crucial aspect of our attention that keeps us focused on ideas of order when we wouldn't have to bother if irrationality were purely a good thing. Plato was right to want to banish the poets for these reasons, but perhaps it is nonetheless better to believe that societies need that form of irrationality, beginning with its use as a measure for the passage beyond decorum and decency.

The negatives inherent in irrational states are hardly confined to violence against the people and things of the world, though. The passion of love can produce great negativity for an individual, first if the love is directed at the wrong object, second if the ardor underlying the love is too irrational. Yet again, there is a border beyond which passion becomes desperate obsession, at which point the irrational state becomes harmful to all involved. To say as much, though, is to recognize that all human states are dangerous if they are pushed to an extreme. Individuals who are too rational face similar difficulties, and the extremes of reason can also become a form of passionate obsession. An extremely rational person approaches another border of inhumanity in his or her machine-like determination to banish everything from life that doesn't parse in logical ways. There are no human states that can't be pushed too far, so we shouldn't hold it against our various irrationalities that they can go to extremes. Socrates' commitment to the fitting proportions of a life measured in terms of arete is a more appropriate way of dealing with the potential dangers inherent in the species.

As Socrates makes clear in the *Phaedrus,* love is the best form of irrationality because it brings the most pleasure to life. Few of us have the capacity to divine the future or to prophesy, and few are able to be poets. These forms of irrationality are available to individuals in a variety of ways, but the average person has much more to do with love. It is the affect that brings a shine to people's lives. A person without love or the prospect of it is devoid of the most powerful communal attachment to the world of which humans are capable. This is more difficult to discern in our day when there is so much emphasis on individual achievement, career structures, and life goals. People seem to be stuck between two clichés. We know that work alone does not produce the best of lives, yet it is often more under our control than love, which forces us to take another's needs as seriously as our own. So we may feel the desire for love but prefer the control that is available at work.

Nevertheless, love brings riches to life, adds a charm to existence that is not available in any other way. The enticements are mostly irrational in nature, but some of them have rational off-shoots as well. It makes good sense to be involved in other people's lives so they will reciprocate that interest. It is rational to want to be loved, to seek out some form of recognition in one's life. It is reasonable to think that a shared life eases some of the burdens of existence and makes other tasks easier. Likewise, many if not most humans find it easier to deal with their own mortality in the face of a love that has endured for a long time. If society as a whole values love and stable relationships, it can reinforce the value of being in love, doing everything from producing a tax structure that favors marriage to creating social structures that induce one to think stable relationships are better for individuals and society as a whole. There is always a calculating element to human actions, and it is as much at work in love as it is in less emotional contexts.

The powerful value of love is reflected in the irrational feelings it produces, in the hormonal flows it engenders in the brain, and also in the longer life that comes from the distribution of those flows throughout the body. Precisely because it is irrational, the effects love has on our lives cannot be adequately accounted for any more than we can explain why bodies cry out to be hugged and touched or why sexual activity produces intense pleasure. Hugging, touching, and sex are also parts of love, even if they are separable from it. But love is the most complete human state because it is capable of producing the most powerful pleasures in all aspects of our existence, from the bodily and sexual to the emotional and intellectual. Reasoning can produce bodily reactions, but it doesn't embrace all of the satisfactions that are found in love.

Likewise, both reason and love can induce optimism in an individual and hope for the future, another essential ingredient in a healthy life. But the optimism and hope of love are richer, once again because they are written into all aspects of one's being and are bodily experiences as much as mental or spiritual ones. No other human state is so capable of embracing everything we are and of orienting all aspects of our being toward the future with hope and cheer. This alone accounts for its great power, both as an idea and in fact, however much our experiences never measure up to that ideal. The physiology, the psychology, and the spirituality of love can in themselves make life worth living even as they make it gratifying from day to day. No other rational or irrational state can make that claim, which is why the first honors always go to love and love alone.

There are other forms of irrationality that add to our lives, even if the most powerful ones—Socrates' list of prophecy, divination, and poetry—aren't often available to us. That love is more or less possible while these other irrational states tend not to be a part of most people's lives is worth inquiring into: why should we be capable of love but seldom able to partake of the powers in the other irrational states? In some respects one would assume these are questions of the neural networks in our brains and the complex relations that are worked out within them. We know, for example, that each of us is born and develops with certain innate biases built into the brain, an inclination toward analytic thought, say, or a relatively greater ability to intuit the emotional nature of our surroundings. We assume in turn that almost all of us are capable of nurturing various capacities so we become adept at the lesser inclinations in our brains and quite capable in the use of our strengths. Someone who has significant mathematical ability but minimal emotional links to the world can be taught to be more aware of the affective valence of experiences just as someone with great intuitive acuity can usually become fairly good at various analytical activities. There will be limits to how far the lesser capacities can be extended, but they can be developed.

The irrational features of human being that Socrates links to prophecy, divination, and poetry are found within the limbic system of the brain. Even if this is so, though, someone who is adept at reading other people's emotions isn't necessarily going to be a master of poetic discourse. Nor would such an individual invariably be able to discern the parameters of the future in the emotional nexus of the moment. These irrational strengths of the species may well be a function of the limbic system, but the complexity of that system suggests there are various combinations of neural activity that produce powerful versions of one or the other of the irrational aspects of our being. We don't at present know how to break these matters down with clarity, though there is no reason why we shouldn't be able to in the near future.

Even assuming relative acuity in the various forms of irrationality, we still need to know why there aren't more people who are capable of making better use of their irrational capacities, or who even know they possess them. A good part of this stems from the fact that the Western world has never greatly prized the affective aspects of humans, except in the cases of prophets and great poets. Even then the figures are often met with indifference or scorn. This is not surprising in a culture that has long favored analysis over intuition, but it needs to be redressed. For if there are few prophets and poets, there are many more individuals who could make better use of such capacities if they were encouraged to note and develop them. Their ignorance of the value of these abilities leads to their neglect and diminishes the opportunities within the community for people who are gifted in this way to explore their strengths and make use of them.

Within the range of human capacity, there are some who are inclined toward the extreme end of one side of the spectrum or the other. Those who take the measure of the far end of analytical inclination are the mathematical (and musical) geniuses who produce the great insights in their area of endeavor. Those who are most powerfully attuned to the world in irrational ways provide the poetic, prophetic, and divinatory insights that most closely hug us to the emotional core of our lives. In the middle of the spectrum we find the great mass of people who are more or less attuned to their analytical capacities, more or less capable of intuitively grasping the gist of their environment with complexity. This middle segment can be encouraged to assimilate the world more acutely, even as it can be prodded to pay more attention to the nature of things in general. To the extent that individuals do so, they will profit more from their irrational and rational capacities and will thereby lead fuller lives.

The problem in our day is that human capacities quickly get reduced to economic quotients. If the irrational aspects of the species have gotten slightly more attention lately, it is largely because we have learned they have great economic value. Thus, one finds books such as Daniel Goleman's *Emotional Intelligence* that are quickly linked to various moneymaking and productivity schemes.[1] Instead of seeing such works as testament to the fact that we have paid too little attention to the affective aspects of our lives, we use them to increase our chances of financial success. Or we employ them to explain why people with very high analytical IQs are often much less successful than they might otherwise be. We develop road shows to train executives to be more attuned to their emotional intelligence in order to become better managers and therefore be more successful in the workplace. There is nothing wrong with these stratagems beyond the fact that they greatly reduce the import of such ideas: much if not most of the world comes to us in affective ways, and those who are most acutely aware of the affects through which they discern the cues in their environment will lead richer, better lives. This simple gist always gets lost in the tendency toward hucksterism in our culture. Still, the tremendous value of our irrational capacities has become more and more apparent in recent years, suggesting that it is time for us to reappraise what Socrates has to say about the great value of those aspects of our being.

‖ When considering the multifarious nature of our lives and the overdetermined complexity to which Socrates regularly calls attention by example and through argument, one always comes back to the fact that Socrates was possessed of a daimonion to which he ceded significant mental territory. When the daimonion suggested he shouldn't do something, he abided by that imperative without question. It was an essential form of guidance in his life he never ceased to acknowledge. I have already discussed how such a voice is related to various kinds of inner imperatives to which we respond. If I have argued throughout that the great value of Socrates' life is the way in which it encourages us to revise and expand our ideas of the multiple and irreconcilable ways we orient ourselves to the world, much of the power of that argument is found in the nature of the daimonion, in part because we seem not to have just one voice but several, perhaps many. If we had nothing more than these voices swirling through our heads and bodies, we would be multiple rather than unified, overdetermined rather than self-contained in our identities.

My favorite contemporary poet, Czeslaw Milosz, has done the best job of articulating this sense of the multifariousness of the voices to which we attend in his famous poem *"Ars Poetica?"* In speaking of his own rich, yet terrible poetic fate, Milosz asks,

> What reasonable man would like to be a city of demons,
> who behave as if they were at home, speak in many tongues,
> and who, not satisfied with stealing his lips or hand,
> work at changing his destiny for their convenience?[2]

Although Milosz refers here to a particular human being—himself—and to a specific kind of human being—a poet derived from the Romantic tradition of poetic inspiration—all of us are cities of demons. We possess many voices that "speak in many tongues" and work hard to change our destinies "for their convenience." It may be that we have long trained ourselves not to think of existence in this way, so much so that when others speak about hearing voices, we suspect some form of mental derangement or mistaken interpretation of experience. If Odysseus hears Athena in his head, that is one thing: he comes to us from ancient days, and we might imagine Homer practicing some form of poetic license. If a fundamentalist Christian speaks about the ways in which God talks to her, we write that off as the delusionary creation of a hungry mind. If Son of Sam says he hears voices in his head that induce him to kill, we know we are witnessing one of the most pathological forms of human consciousness. In this way we dismiss all forms of multiplicity, leaving, perhaps, a small space for the voice in our heads that quietly suggests various choices to us. Yet we can see that the better part of Socrates' work was not devoted to banishing the irrational elements of human being but rather carefully distinguishing between the irrational forms that provide us with the best life has to offer and those that are destructive. If we work within this distinction, we must return to the most apparent site of irrationality, the manifold voices we hear every day.

When we think about the various demons that inhabit us—keeping in mind that from a Miloszian perspective demons are neither necessarily good nor evil—we can easily tote up a variety of tongues that speak to us. Given its fundamental importance, I would begin with the Socratic daimonion. As the sharer or apportioner of our fate, this element of our being provides the crucial bridge that always exists between who we are at the moment and what we are about to become. As the leading edge of our being, the daimonion is the relational point of our existence that produces and is produced by our interactions with the world. It is of us without being us, the site through which the universe expresses itself as us and the manner in which the universe extends itself in time. It is the means through which we aesthetically calibrate the rhythms of existence that provide our ethical sense of what is fitting and appropriate for our lives at any given moment. And it is as much a response to the way the air hits our skin as it is a manifestation of our constant, subconscious attention to all the antennae we employ to take in the cues of the world. The daimonion is our most important guide every day of our lives, even if most of us are seldom aware of its tutelary presence.

There are other voices, though, beginning with the most obviously derivative: over time we acquire the voice of authority, usually a parent, often the father, a voice that Freud would characterize as the superego, always there to tell us what we should do. Then there are the voices of loved ones and friends—alive and dead—that speak to us in various ways without provocation throughout life. We can call on them, but they are just as likely to appear on their own. Next there are the social voices that speak to us about the relational world of the community, everyone from our friends and peer groups to the commercials and movies we see on television and the other media that saturate our lives. These take up space in our consciousness, sometimes in pertinent ways, sometimes not, as, for example, with jingles one finds popping up in one's head for no good reason.

These various personal and individual relations are not merely metaphorical voices; they literally take up space in our minds, tacitly and overtly shaping our sense of the world, the choices we make, and the determinations we establish about who we are and what our priorities should be. If we had only these acquired voices in our head, we would have more than enough "demons," good and bad, to chaffer at us constantly in one way or another about our behavior. That they don't sing in unison goes without saying, which is a good part of what makes us multiplicities. Like Milosz, we always have to contend with the "city of demons" in our head and sort out the traffic among them. They "speak in many tongues," and they all have designs on us; they won't be satisfied until they change our "destiny for their convenience." These powerful voices can alter the course of our lives in a second, for good or ill, which is all the more reason to be aware of their presence and to strive to develop ways of attending to them without letting them overwhelm us.

In addition to the voices we accumulate as we move through life, there are ones that are at least partially built into our biological machinery. The so-called voice of reason, for example, is a kind of halfway house between biology and society: the inclination for its strategies is built into the mechanisms of the species, yet without training it is not likely to be adequately developed. If one lives in a society that cultivates reason, over time it becomes an insistent presence. It is always there at some level of one's deliberations, helping to determine the rationality of one's choices, always ready to point out the degree to which they correspond to the dictates of reason or need to be corrected. This voice too can intersect and yet be in conflict with other voices in one's head. It may be that reason and parental authority come together at points, depending on the animating principles of the parental authority we absorb when we are young. The voice of authority is always larger than reason because it is composed of things that aren't reasonable as well, but it can reinforce reason in a variety of ways if it has been a priority in the home life of an individual. Likewise for the other voices: when they intersect the terrain of other claims on our attention, they can be reinforced or undercut depending on the degree to which they accord with or differ from the most insistent declarations.

A composite voice of the sort I am speaking of would be something like the call of our self-discipline, which talks to us in a variety of ways, sometimes quite noticeably, as when it carefully guides us through a process (we literally talk to ourselves, saying, "Don't turn that screw any tighter," "Avoid that hole in the road," "You must get up even if you don't want to"), less noticeably when we go through the routines we establish in order to accomplish our goals. We don't necessarily talk to ourselves throughout the day as we work, though we may do so ("You need to finish this section of the essay before you can move on to the next part of your day," "You should think about calling so-and-so before the day is out"). These forms of self-discipline guide us, provide focus for our energy, and contribute to the quality of attention we bring to various aspects of our lives by reinforcing the need to be acutely involved in this and to avoid wasting time on that.

The voice of self-discipline comes from the imperatives of biology even as it is modulated through various mediated contexts like the discipline of the home or the structure imposed on us by our school and work lives. In each of us the voice of self-discipline is the call of internal or external imperatives depending on the degree to which our lives are oriented toward responding to others or heeding our bodily inclinations. The more we insist on doing things our own way, the more likely it will be that our self-discipline is an organic product of our being. The more we attune our relations to other people, the more likely it will be that our self-discipline is a product of the superego that informs us of the appropriate social mechanisms to which we should accommodate ourselves.

Self-discipline is also a voice that relates to Socrates' daimonion, which is a guiding or shaping voice that pulls us into the future through its admonitions and subtle—and not-so-subtle—hints about what we should be doing and how we should be doing it. We all possess a tacit telemetry that guides us through life. Inasmuch as we have a heritage based on the subject/object dichotomy, we imagine ourselves as individuals who make self-aware choices about life as we withdraw from the immediate context in order to consider what to do. In fact, though, more often than not our choices are induced from the daimonion in our heads, or at least can be. As Socrates' repeated references to the daimonion suggest, one can always go against what the guiding voice tells one to do, but the better life derives from attending to the things it points out.

The voice of the daimonion is related to what we characterize as intuition, though, again, I would argue that the two have distinct functions. Intuition is an affective voice that induces us to perceive the choices we should make in a given context. It shares space with the daimonion, which also induces fitting decisions. But intuition is the immediate affective response we have to the situations of our lives, so it is more than a guiding voice that helps shape our behavior. It is also the voice that alerts us to the subtle cues of our environment in order to allow us to discern the nature of things. It produces the most basic form of awareness we have and thereby helps orient us to the experience at hand. It informs us of the cues emanating from friends and strangers, from animals and other phenomena in our immediate situation. The vast repository of our knowledge about the world is composed much more of this tacit, intuitive knowledge than of the things we self-consciously take in and try to remember. That is why intuition is both the quietest and most insistent voice in our heads, the one we are least likely to note and yet the one that always alerts us to our context, pointing out uncertainties and inducing us to move in this or that direction in accord with its imperatives.

Intuition is in turn related to and dependent on the voice of the body, the longest-lasting, ever-present call in our lives. This voice is first and foremost the general hum of our being, the frequency our organism emits at any given moment, our most profound and basic orientation to the world, that which determines the quality of our day. We almost always know how our body feels about the situation in which it finds itself thanks to the hum of the organism. When things are going well, when the body is healthy, its frequency cues us to our good fortune and well-being. When things are awry or the body is sick, the hum produces a different frequency that alerts us to the dangers inherent in our situation. This is equivalent to the rhythm of the universe, both derived from it and akin to it in that few of us are aware of its constant presence. Even if we try to sense the hum of our body, we often fail to discern it. It is something that can be felt with careful attention, but usually it is notable only by its absence: we immediately recognize when the body is not in accord with its environment. These are things we tacitly know and sometimes feel, but they require the utmost attention, the subtlest assessments of our being.

The hum of the body is a voice that calls out to us (and to others), and it is related to the basic rhythms of the body as well. It might be that the rhythms of the body are not a voice so much as the ur-structure upon which the hum of the body is based, out of which, in turn, the other bodily voices emanate. But the rhythms of our organism might just as well be thought of as the voice through which we speak to the universe while it speaks back to us. Like the hum that derives from them, they are the most personal way we relate to the world and the most insistent marker of our well-being. When we are in rhythm, our body hums well, and the rest of our voices speak to us with clarity and insight, even if not as a unified whole that sings the same song. When we are out of rhythm, the voices of our being are much less likely to be consonant with one another. Again, I want to emphasize that our orientation to the world through the multiple voices that inhabit and define us leads to no unity or identity of being. We are multiple, and even when our voices combine in pleasing ways and harmonize in a variety of circumstances, they are never one, except, perhaps, at the most exceptional of moments, those ecstatic states when we are so wholly who we are that we cease to be anything at all. The rest of the time we are multiplicities who strive to attend to and govern the various demons that inhabit us. Still, when the rhythms of the body work in consonance with the world, the hum of the body and the other voices to which we attend are capable of producing the life we all seek.

The voices of the body also include more obvious phenomena, the ones we usually characterize in terms of urges, desires, and bodily imperatives. Everything from the proverbial "call of nature" to the itch that needs to be scratched are distinct voices, though again we often don't consciously pay much attention to them. We listen when our body tells us it is exhausted, and we know when we are hungry, both bodily statements that we ordinarily think of as cues rather than voices. But they are distinct voices with messages that are specific to their own imperatives. They are the song of everyday life we pay least attention to yet are most dependent on. It is far better to have bodies that constantly talk to us, leaving our conscious attention free to focus on other things. As with the other bodily activities, these voices depend on the hum of the organism and work to sustain it. When the voices aren't answered, the hum gets disrupted, and we don't speak to the world in the right frequency anymore.

There are still more voices that warrant discussion. Dreams are certainly voices of the body, though we don't know exactly what they are trying to tell us. It may be that their chatter is nothing more than a "processing" device through which the brain rearranges its neural chemistry every day so that a new order prevails in the face of the experiences we've just gone through. Although I don't believe that dreams have specific messages for us, there is little doubt that their content and arrangement say certain things to us, whatever they might be. Dreams of fantasy or anxiety reflect various needs or they wouldn't take up our brainwaves during sleep periods. They could be indirect means of telling us what specific pathways were opened up during the day, reminding us of patterns we haven't paid attention to for some time, or calling our attention to modes of organization in our behavior we don't ordinarily notice. Even if they are nothing more than strange neural firing patterns that meld the new with the old in our brains, they still remind us of the necessity of this activity by alerting us to the fact that much of our behavior takes place below the surface, without any intervention or awareness on our part. There may be other such voices of which we are currently unaware. Even without any others, though, it is clear that we speak to ourselves in a multiplicity of ways and get constant feedback from those voices as we negotiate our place in the world.

|| If one assumes that humans have many voices that speak to them every day, one has to wonder why people haven't been inclined to think of their behavior in this way or even to take it seriously when it comes up. Milosz himself seems embarrassed to admit that he is a city of demons, as though that makes him grotesque. Then too we are reminded that Socrates' daimonion seemed to be as unusual in his own time as it would be in ours. If the Athenians went so far as to accuse him of establishing new gods because he listened to his daimonic voice, we can assume they didn't organize themselves around a similar call to duty. This might be because they chose not to heed their daimonion, whereas Socrates had always been extremely attentive to his. Or it could be that most people don't really possess a Socratic daimonion and don't have multiple voices speaking to them all the time. Perhaps this is an illusion or a false metaphorical imposition.

It may also be, as Plutarch argued, that most of us don't notice the daimonic voice or any of the others because they can't be heard over the din of the world. More than ever we strive to avoid quiet, resist solitude, prefer the embrace of the crowd. As long as the voices of the community fill our minds, we won't be able to hear our own less insistent voices, whether we think of the daimonion that guides us through life or the other voices that burble up from our being. Perhaps in quieter times people were more likely to hear these voices and recognize them for what they were. Perhaps too we have not wanted to hear them because they are considerable taskmasters: they take over our fate for their own purposes rather than leaving us to other devices. We prefer the freedom that comes from inattention to the cues of our organism.

We might also assume that we don't register the call of our various voices because we have constructed a world with no space for them. The scheme of identity and unity—a tacit and not-so-tacit imperative imposed on us by the cultural constraints of Western civilization—constantly suggests we should be one thing rather than many. As a result we seldom note the strange shifts in the quality and tenor of our consciousness, its vapors and pockets of acuity, its moments of intensity and its lapses: consciousness too easily becomes nothing more than a kind of backstory to our lives to which we pay little heed and of whose qualitative values we have no sense. If our consciousness seems to be a unified flow that testifies to our identity, it follows that we will think of our being in this consistent, coherent way. The more we do so, the more we filter out the multitude of voices that inhabit us or the range of conscious states we move into and out of every day.

We might assume that the constraints we have placed on consciousness and the interpretations of our behavior go back to Plato's banishment of the poets: we deny that we have voices and are multiple because the idea seems dangerous, unduly risky, too pliant, protean, and uncertain. So we choose to bury the notion that we are various and decide that we shall be one thing and one thing only. This is Plato's image of god, in contrast to the history of his own people and in violation of the most basic premises of human being. For 2,500 years we have striven to be one thing, to turn the multiple voices of our being into a smooth stream of singular cadence that speaks always of us, only us, that self-identical creature known to all for his or her unique stance in the world. This is how we have imagined things, and so that is what we think we have become, in spite of the fact that we remain various, in spite of the fact that there are many voices in our heads and bodies that speak with different imperatives, emotional valences, and levels of approbation or disapprobation.

We remember that one of the gravest threats that comes from accepting our multiplicity is that human behavior becomes problematic and frightening at both ends of the spectrum. If one extreme is the person who has only one voice, who only sees the world from a narrow perspective, presenting an image of humanity that is monomaniacally unreal, at the other end is the individual whose voices are so detached that he or she doesn't recognize them as his or her own. So-called multiple personality disorder is a fearful prospect, greater even than the monomaniac who compulsively strives always to be only one thing. When the voices become detached from our being, they are potentially dangerous to all. We can often temporarily override the voices we attend to, from the one that tells us we need to urinate to the one that insists we should wake up early tomorrow morning. But when the voices detach themselves from the tissue of our body, we have lost control of them. It is not an accident that this is one of the most frightening forms of madness, and perhaps it has been best for us to bury our multiplicity in order to hide from it.

If we accept that most of us are constituted by and capable of modulating the various voices that are always speaking to us, though, we recognize that the fear of multiple personalities is no more rational than would be the fear of a lapse into a comatose state: these situations are always possible but highly unlikely. But such awareness requires a perspective—including a knowledge of and a willing responsibility toward those unseemly voices that produce so much of the evil in the world—that we have chosen not to embrace. Like Plato, we decided not to take the step into full maturity that is required of one who accepts the potential inherent in his voices.

In the end, Milosz provides the perfect description of the human situation even as he lays out the poet's role in presenting it to us:

The purpose of poetry is to remind us
how difficult it is to remain just one person,
for our house is open, there are no keys in the doors,
and invisible guests come in and out at will. (31)

The good and the bad of being a multiplicity is found in the fact that we learn over time "how difficult it is to remain just one person." We may be cities of demons whose multiple presences "come in and out at will," but we still need to maintain the dignity inherent in being just one individual, a person of composite voices rather than multiple individuals with no coherence to them. But the coherence Milosz envisions is as much an act of determination as it is a function of our being. We must always strive to be one person in spite of the difficulties in doing so. We must work to articulate the ongoing relationship within our variousness rather than lapsing on one side or the other. For there are two easy victories: falling back into the sense that we are only one person, or embracing the multiplicity without coherence that abjures any attempt to be a complete human being with a recognizable footprint that can be traced over time. This doesn't mean that we "construct" the coherence that keeps us perfectly in between the false security of identity and the hopeless abandon of multiplicity without coherence, but it suggests that serious labor is required every day to maintain that balance.

The virtue of being always only who we are is that "our house is open" and we are therefore capable of taking in new experiences and profiting from them. The limitation is that because "there are no keys in the doors," we are also more susceptible to intrusions that could be harmful to us. We must work harder to sort out those voices that belong from those that are artificial intrusions. The genius of Milosz's lines is found in the declaration, "The purpose of poetry is to remind us / how difficult it is to remain just one person." It is not just that it is hard to continue to be who we are, that it requires a lifetime's labor. It is also that we forget how hard we must work each day to continue to be the person with multiple voices that we are. Inasmuch as the efforts we devote to this task accumulate over time as we learn how to control the various elements of our being, we lose sight of how much of our energy goes to maintaining ourselves. Every day we can decide not to hold on to the integrity of our multiplicity. And yet every day we get up without realizing it and go about the business of continuing to be who we are without much regard for the efforts that are involved in doing so.

Plato banishes the poets for the same reason that Milosz insists we depend on them for basic sustenance: both call attention to the difficulty, the danger, and the great reward inherent in being as wholly human as we can be. Plato assumes that humans aren't up to the task. Milosz believes that we have no choice but to accept the burdens of being who we are, striving always to maintain the balance that preserves our integrity. Plato believes that the world must be built on a tissue of lies and repression, whereas Milosz insists that our labors are worthy in themselves and only need to be acknowledged every day so we can properly appreciate the efforts we undertake to continue to be who we are.

Plato may have used Socrates to bolster the Platonic vision of the ideal human community, but Socrates would seem to be more of Milosz's camp, an individual who was sublimely suited to explore his variousness, to celebrate it, to value it above the more typical priorities like wealth and power, and to insist through example that we are all capable of being who we are and taking up the richness of the world. Socrates asks no more of himself than that, and he demands no more of us than the same: a full embrace of our capacities, rational and irrational, bodily, mental, and spiritual.

Socrates has captivated our imagination for so long because he assumes we can bear these burdens and relish them, in contrast to Plato, who believes we are not capable of maintaining dignity in the face of our multiplicity. And even though we have a long history of following Plato's lead and assuming a brittle form of identity in order to avoid the challenges of being human, we have always had Socrates there to encourage us to live within the larger capacities inherent in us. We likewise have regularly produced writers of Milosz's stature who remind us of this great task even as they urge us to take it up more diligently than we have, insisting that it is past time for us to embrace the city of demons, the multiple voices, the variousness of our existence. Whether we answer that call or retreat to Plato's cave for more of the shadowy life to which we are accustomed remains to be seen, but the alternative is always in front of us, beckoning with the full risks and possibilities inherent in who we are.

NOTES

INTRODUCTION

1. Emerson, "The American Scholar," in *Emerson: Essays and Poems,* 66.

ONE: THE HOLY

1. Plato, in *Critical Theory since Plato,* 12. Subsequent quotations from this dialogue are from this translation and will be noted parenthetically with page numbers in the text.
2. See Poulet, *The Metamorphoses of the Circle.*
3. See Auerbach, *Mimesis,* 3–24.
4. See "The Idea of Order at Key West," in *Wallace Stevens: The Collected Poems,* 128.
5. See Damasio, *Descartes' Error.*
6. Of course, Whitman himself recognized that the equivalent of a divinity spoke through him in his poetry.
7. See, for example, LeDoux, *The Emotional Brain;* Hobson, *The Chemistry of Conscious States;* Damasio, *Descartes' Error.*

TWO: ON THE SIGN OF SOCRATES

1. Plato, *Apology,* in *The Republic and Other Works by Plato.* Subsequent quotations from this dialogue are from this translation and will be noted parenthetically with page numbers in the text.
2. Sophocles, *Oedipus the King,* 239: "What god, / what dark power leapt beyond all bounds, / beyond belief, to crush your wretched life?"
3. Plutarch, "On the Sign of Socrates," *Moralia,* 451. Subsequent quotations from this work are from this translation and will be noted parenthetically with page numbers in the text.
4. Xenophon, *Socrates' Defence,* in *Conversations of Socrates,* 43. Subsequent quotations from this work are from this translation and will be noted parenthetically with page numbers in the text.

THREE: DIVINE MADNESS

1. Plato, *Symposium and Phaedrus,* 58. Subsequent quotations from the *Phaedrus* will be from this translation and will be noted parenthetically with page numbers in the text.

FOUR: BANISHING THE POETS

1. Plato, *The Republic,* 360. Subsequent quotations from this dialogue are from this translation and will be noted parenthetically with page numbers in the text.
2. Longinus, *Longinus on the Sublime,* 81.
3. Sidney, *A Defense of Poetry,* 19, 20.
4. See *Oedipus the King,* 209, 210.
5. Nietzsche, *Thus Spoke Zarathustra,* in *The Portable Nietzsche,* 211.
6. Heidegger, "The Word of Nietzsche," in *The Question Concerning Technology,* 112.
7. See Heidegger's masterful discussion of the centrality of resentment to Nietzsche's thought in *What Is Called Thinking?;* see also my *The Question of Value.*
8. See Girard, *Violence and the Sacred.*
9. Nietzsche, *Ecce Homo,* 258.

CONCLUSION

1. Goleman, *Emotional Intelligence;* see Goleman, *Working with Emotional Intelligence.*
2. Milosz, *"Ars Poetica?"* in *New and Collected Poems,* 30.

WORKS CONSULTED

Adkins, Arthur W. H. *Merit and Responsibility: A Study in Greek Values.* Oxford: Clarendon Press, 1960.

——. *From the Many to the One: A Study of Personality and Views of Human Nature in the Context of Ancient Greek Society, Values, and Beliefs.* Ithaca, NY: Cornell University Press, 1970.

Adkins, A. W. H., Joan Kalk Lawrence, and Craig K. Ihara, eds. *Human Virtue and Human Excellence.* New York: Peter Lang, 1991.

Allen, R. E. *Socrates and Legal Obligation.* Minneapolis: University of Minnesota Press, 1980.

Arieti, James A. *Interpreting Plato: The Dialogues as Drama.* Savage, MD: Rowman and Littlefield, 1991.

Armstrong, A. H. *An Introduction to Ancient Philosophy.* Boston: Beacon Press, 1959.

Auerbach, Eric. *Mimesis.* Trans. Willard R. Trask. Princeton, NJ: Princeton University Press, 1953.

Benson, Hugh H., ed. *Essays on the Philosophy of Socrates.* London: Oxford University Press, 1992.

Brickhouse, Thomas C., and Nicholas D. Smith, eds. *Socrates on Trial.* Princeton, NJ: Princeton University Press, 1989.

Burger, Ronna L. *Plato's "Phaedrus": A Defense of a Philosophic Art of Writing.* Birmingham: University of Alabama Press, 1980.

Calcidius. *Calcidius on Demons (Commentarius Ch. 127–136).* Trans. J. Den Boeft. Leiden: E. J. Brill, 1977.

Calder, William M., III, Bernhard Huss, Marc Mastrangelo, R. Scott Smith, and Stephen M. Trzaskoma. *The Unknown Socrates.* Wauconda, IL: Bolchazy Carducci Publishers, 2002.

Caldwell, Richard. *The Origin of the Gods: A Psychoanalytic Study of Greek Theogonic Myth.* New York: Oxford University Press, 1989.

Cohen, S. Marc, Patricia Curd, and C. D. C. Reeve, eds. *Readings in Ancient Greek Philosophy: From Thales to Aristotle*. Indianapolis, IN: Hackett, 1995.

Cooper, Lane. *Plato on the Trial and Death of Socrates*. Ithaca, NY: Cornell University Press, 1941.

Damasio, Antonio R. *Descartes' Error: Emotion, Reason, and the Human Brain*. New York: G. P. Putnam's Sons, 1994.

———. *The Feeling of What Happens: Body and Emotion in the Making of Consciousness*. New York: Harbrace, 1999.

Dannhauser, Werner. *Nietzsche's View of Socrates*. Ithaca, NY: Cornell University Press, 1974.

De Romilly, Jacqueline. *The Great Sophists in Periclean Athens*. Oxford: Clarendon Press, 1992.

Detienne, Marcel. *The Masters of Truth in Archaic Greece*. Trans. Janet Lloyd. New York: Zone Books, 1996.

Dodds, E. R. *The Greeks and the Irrational*. Berkeley: University of California Press, 1951.

Emerson, Ralph Waldo. "The American Scholar." In *Emerson: Essays and Poems*. New York: Library of America, 1996.

Euben, J. Peter, ed. *Greek Tragedy and Political Theory*. Berkeley: University of California Press, 1986.

Figes, Eva. *Tragedy and Social Evolution*. New York: Persea Books, 1976.

Freeman, Kathleen. *Ancilla to the Pre-Socratic Philosophers*. Cambridge, MA: Harvard University Press, 1957.

Garland, Robert. *The Greek Way of Death*. Ithaca, NY: Cornell University Press, 1985.

Girard, René. *Violence and the Sacred*. Trans. Patrick Gregory. Baltimore: Johns Hopkins University Press, 1977.

Goleman, Daniel. *Emotional Intelligence: Why It Can Matter More Than IQ*. New York: Bantam, 1995.

———. *Working With Emotional Intelligence*. New York: Bantam, 1998.

Griswold, Charles L., Jr. *Self-Knowledge in Plato's "Phaedrus."* New Haven, CT: Yale University Press, 1986.

Gulley, Norman. *The Philosophy of Socrates*. London: Macmillan, 1968.

Hadot, Pierre. *Philosophy as a Way of Life*. Ed. Arnold I. Davidson. Trans. Michael Chase. Oxford: Blackwell, 1995.

———. *What Is Ancient Philosophy?* Trans. Michael Chase. Cambridge, MA: Harvard University Press, 2002.

Hans, James. *The Origins of the Gods*. Albany: SUNY Press, 1991.

———. *The Play of the World*. Amherst: University of Massachusetts Press, 1981.

———. *The Site of Our Lives: The Self and the Subject from Emerson to Foucault*. Albany: SUNY Press, 1995.

———. *The Sovereignty of Taste.* Urbana: University of Illinois Press, 2002.

———. *The Question of Value: Thinking through Nietzsche, Heidegger, and Freud.* Carbondale: Southern Illinois University Press, 1989.

Havelock, Eric. *Preface to Plato.* Cambridge, MA: Belknap Press, 1963.

———. *The Muse Learns to Write: Reflections on Orality and Literacy from Antiquity to the Present.* New Haven, CT: Yale University Press, 1988.

Heidegger, Martin. *Being and Time.* Trans. John Macquarrie and Edward Robinson. New York: Harper, 1962.

———. *Early Greek Thinking.* Trans. David Farrell Krell and Frank A. Capuzzi. New York: Harper, 1975.

———. *On the Way to Language.* Trans. Peter D. Hertz. New York: Harper, 1971.

———. *Poetry, Language, Thought.* Trans. Albert Hofstadter. New York: Harper, 1971.

———. *The Question Concerning Technology and Other Essays.* Trans. William Lovitt. New York: Harper, 1977.

———. *What Is Called Thinking?* Trans. Fred D. Wieck and J. Glenn Gray. New York: Harper, 1968.

Hobson, J. Allen. *The Chemistry of Conscious States.* Boston: Little, Brown, 1994.

Jaeger, Werner. *Paideia: the Ideals of Greek Culture.* Trans. Gilbert Highet. New York: Oxford University Press, 1945.

Irwin, T. H. *Plato's Ethics.* London: Oxford University Press, 1995.

Jaynes, Julian. *The Origin of Consciousness in the Breakdown of the Bicameral Mind.* Boston: Houghton Mifflin Company, 1976.

Kereny, C. *The Gods of the Greeks.* London: Thames and Hudson, 1951.

Kerferd, George. *The Sophistic Movement.* Cambridge: Cambridge University Press, 1981.

LeDoux, Joseph. *The Emotional Brain: The Mysterious Underpinnings of Emotional Life.* New York: Simon and Shuster, 1996.

———. *Synaptic Self: How Our Brains Become Who We Are.* New York: Viking, 2002.

Longinus. *Longinus on the Sublime.* Trans. W. Rhys Roberts. Cambridge: Cambridge University Press, 1935.

Maximus of Tyre. *The Philosophical Orations.* Trans. M. B. Trapp. Oxford: Clarendon Press, 1997.

McKirahan, Richard D., Jr. *Philosophy before Socrates.* Indianapolis: Hackett, 1994.

Milosz, Czeslaw. *New and Collected Poems (1931–2001).* New York: HarperCollins, 2001.

Nehamas, Alexander. *The Art of Living: Socratic Reflections from Plato to Foucault.* Berkeley: University of California Press, 1998.

Nietzsche, Friedrich. *Thus Spoke Zarathustra*. In *The Portable Nietzsche*. Trans. Walter Kaufmann. New York: Viking Press, 1968.

———. *Ecce Homo*. Trans. Walter Kaufmann. New York: Vintage Books, 1967.

Plato. *Ion*. In *Critical Theory since Plato*. Rev. ed. Ed. Hazard Adams. New York: Harbrace, 1992.

———. *Symposium and Phaedrus*. Trans. Benjamin Jowett. New York: Dover Publications, 1993.

———. *The Dialogues of Plato*. Trans. Benjamin Jowett. Oxford: Oxford University Press, 1953.

———. *The Republic*. Trans. Benjamin Jowett. New York: Vintage Books, 1991.

———. *The Republic and Other Works*. Trans. Benjamin Jowett. New York: Anchor Books, 1973.

Plutarch. *Moralia, Volume VII*. Trans. Phillip H. DeLacy and Benedict Einarson. Cambridge, MA: Harvard University Press, 1959.

Poulet, Georges. *The Metamorphoses of the Circle*. Trans. Carley Dawson and Elliott Coleman. Baltimore: Johns Hopkins University Press, 1966.

Prier, Raymond Adolph. *Thauma Idesthai: The Phenomenology of Sight and Appearance in Archaic Greek*. Tallahassee: Florida State University Press, 1989.

Reeve, C. D. C. *Socrates in the "Apology."* Indianapolis, IN: Hackett, 1989.

———, ed. and trans. *The Trials of Socrates: Six Classic Texts*. Indianapolis, IN: Hackett, 2002.

Rist, J. M. *Stoic Philosophy*. Cambridge: Cambridge University Press, 1969.

Rohde, Erwin. *Psyche: The Cult of Souls and Belief in Immortality among the Ancient Greeks*. Trans. W. B. Hillis. Chicago: Ares Publishers, 1987.

Rudebusch, George. *Socrates, Pleasure, and Value*. London: Oxford University Press, 1999.

Rutherford, R. B. *The Art of Plato: Ten Essays in Platonic Interpretation*. Cambridge, MA: Harvard University Press, 1995.

Seeskin, Kenneth. *Dialogue and Discovery: A Study in Socratic Method*. Albany: SUNY Press, 1987.

Sidney, Sir Philip. *A Defense of Poetry*. Ed. J. A. Van Dorsten. Oxford: Oxford University Press, 1966.

Snell, Bruno. *The Discovery of the Mind in Greek Philosophy and Literature*. Trans. T. G. Rosenmeyer. New York: Dover, 1982.

Sophocles. *Oedipus the King*. Trans. Robert Fagles. New York: Penguin, 1982.

Sprague, Rosamond Kent, ed. *The Older Sophists*. Indianapolis, IN: Hackett, 2001.

Stevens, Wallace. *Wallace Stevens: The Collected Poems.* New York: Random House, 1982.

Stone, I. F. *The Trial of Socrates.* Boston: Beacon Press, 1988.

Vernant, Jean-Pierre. *Myth and Society in Ancient Greece.* Trans. Janet Lloyd. New York: Zone Books, 1988.

———. *Myth and Tragedy in Ancient Greece.* Trans. Janet Lloyd. New York: Zone Books, 1988.

Versenyi, Laszlo. *Socratic Humanism.* New Haven, CT: Yale University Press, 1963.

Vlastos, Gregory. *Socrates: Ironist and Moral Philosopher.* Ithaca, NY: Cornell University Press, 1991.

———. *Studies in Greek Philosophy, Volume I: The Presocratics.* Princeton, NJ: Princeton University Press, 1993.

———. *Studies in Greek Philosophy, Volume II: Socrates, Plato, and Their Tradition.* Princeton, NJ: Princeton University Press, 1995.

Wheelwright, Philip, ed. *The Presocratics.* New York: Odyssey Press, 1966.

Xenophon. *Conversations of Socrates.* Trans. Hugh Tredennick and Robin Waterfield. London: Penguin Books, 1990.

INDEX

acuity, and evaluation of discourse, 120, 191, 201
Adeimantus, 146, 147, 156; and Glaucon, as weak interlocutors, 146
Aeschylus, 203
aesthetic decisions, 195; how best to live, 104; and intuition, 195
affective/intuitive nature, 47, 48
agora, 85, 194
agricultural monocultures, 183
amor fati, 182
Anacreon, 109
analysis, 39, 95, 190, 192–94, 202, 203
Anaxagoras, 132, 133
Anytus, 66
Aphrodite, 117, 123
Apollo, 123, 126, 127; garden of, 145; and prophetic madness, 126
Apology, The, 22, 51, 55, 56, 66, 77, 83, 145, 155, 163, 200
arete, 46, 57–64, 70, 72, 73, 76, 79, 90–95, 97, 98, 138, 189, 190; and daimonic voice, 97; as difficult to practice, 60; as excellence, 57; as harmony, 57; as matter of disposition, 64; as non-self-centered mode, 58; as not self-interested, 59; and pleasure, 60; and teaching, 61; as unteachable, 61; as virtue, 57
Arginusae, 67

"Ars Poetica," 194
art, 22, 25–28, 30, 33, 39, 40, 43, 100, 128, 130–33, 135, 137, 138, 158
Athena, 99, 100, 158, 180, 194; as Mentor, 158
Athenians, the, 33, 51–53, 56–60, 63, 65–69, 72, 74, 80, 85–90, 93, 94, 98, 122, 163, 198, 201; and daimonic intimations, 89; and the examined life, 90; and Socrates' daimonion, 201
atonement, 102, 103
attack against the poets, 142
attention, 23, 34, 46, 49, 56, 57, 72, 75, 100, 103, 105, 112, 120, 124, 128, 133, 140, 143, 152, 159, 188, 189, 192, 193, 195–97, 199, 200, 204
Auerbach, Eric, 35
authority, 82, 86, 195, 196

Bacchic maidens, 28, 49
banishing the poets, 142
baseball, 164
battle of Arginusae, 67
beautiful, the, 22, 23, 27, 28, 30, 31, 113, 172
beauty, 104, 108, 129, 145, 174; of style, 174
beds, Plato's three types of, 146, 147, 175, 179

friendship, 44
fundamentalist Christianity, 194
furies, 37, 154

gadfly: Socrates as, 22, 74, 75, 79, 197–99; versus senator, 75
galvanic skin sensor, 137
genuine dialogue, and non-self-centered viewpoint, 106; as dialectic, 114
Girard, René, 178; and human volatility, 178
Glaucon, 142, 146, 185; as weak interlocutor, 146
global capitalism, 183; and monoculture, 184
god, 27, 28, 30, 31, 34, 36, 37, 39, 40, 42, 46, 48, 52–56, 74, 81, 82, 86–88, 94, 99, 114, 117, 119, 124, 126, 127, 133, 134, 156–58, 161, 169, 194, 202; as playful and amoral, 158; stripped of Protean abilities, 158; and transformation of life, 126
gods, the, and good irrationality, 117
Goleman, Daniel, 192
good, the, 57; as aesthetic standard, 57
good forms of madness, and worthwhile life, 121
good irrational forces, 120
good speech, and faculty of division, 131
Greek gods, versus Christian God, 156
Greeks, the, 36, 59, 80, 84, 87, 123, 131, 148, 156, 159; culture of, rhapsodes in, 36
Groundhog Day, 172
Gyges' Ring, 145

harmony and harmonies, 38, 49, 57, 88, 104, 171, 172, 174; and rhythm, 171

heaven, 99, 121, 122, 129, 155, 161, 167
Heidegger, Martin, 54, 138, 168, 169; and "language speaks man," 138
Hellas, 122, 185
Heraclea, 26
Hesiod, 39, 43, 147, 148, 150, 152, 155; and myth of origins, 148
Hobson, J. Allen, 47
holiness, 32, 113
holy, the, 21, 30, 32, 37, 39–41, 49, 112–14, 194
Homer, 22–27, 30, 39, 40, 42–44, 46, 99, 100, 143, 144, 152, 155, 157, 161, 176, 180, 185, 194; and fluid psyche, 35; as greatest of poets, 185; and Hesiod, and foundational myths of Greece, 155; as Plato's imitative source, 144
Homeric viewpoint, the, 35, 44, 46, 143
hope, 79, 85, 91, 104, 119, 143, 167–69, 190
Horace, and instructive poetry, 180
Houyhnhnms, 115, 163
hubris, 155, 159
humanity, 33, 40, 64, 78, 90, 150, 152, 183, 184, 202
human variousness, and dialogue form, 205
hymns: to the gods, 185; to love, in Phaedrus, 129

Ibycus, 102
id, ego, and superego, dialogue among, 204
images, 36, 147, 176, 178, 182
imagination, 34, 38, 201, 205
imitation, 143, 170, 178; and René Girard, 178
imperatives of biology, and daimonion, 197
impersonality, 31, 37–39
incommensurability, 70, 80, 88, 92, 100

oratory, 132, 134–36, 138, 139, 141;
   and enchantment of the soul, 135
ordinary ways of men, respite from,
   118
origins, myths of, 122, 123, 148
otherworldliness, 176, 180, 194
overdetermined states, 147, 151, 192,
   193, 202, 204, 205
overdetermined humans, and Nietzsche, 182
overman, 169

painter, the, 172
patterning of mind, 202
patterns, 41, 82, 118, 140, 172, 200,
   201, 202
peace, 50, 166
Penelope, 36
perfect wisdom, and orator, 136
perfection of oratory, 132
Pericles, 132, 133
peril, 197, 198
peroration, 103, 107, 119
persuasion, 26, 94, 130, 131, 133, 136,
   137
Phaedrus, The, 101–3, 105–9, 111–17,
   119–22, 124, 128, 129, 131, 133,
   137–40, 145, 189; as hymn to love,
   129
Phaedrus, 102, 106, 114, 116; miscon-
   strues rhetoric, 106
phenomenology, 24
pheremonic interactions, 118
piety, 22, 52, 103, 194
pity, 53, 98, 161, 183
plasticity, 173
Plato, 21, 22, 31, 48, 49, 51, 57, 73,
   95–98, 100, 102, 115, 123, 142–45,
   147, 150, 157, 169–73, 179–84, 187,
   188, 203–5; and banishment of
   poets, 49, 144; and brittle form of
   identity, 205; as competitor of
   poets, 143; as first novelist, 21;
   legacy of reason of, and Nietz-

sche, 168; as meaning monger,
   180; rigid human ideal of, and the
   Republic, 183; on our volatile
   capacities, 187
Platonic dialogue, 101, 203
Platonic emphasis on reason, 204
Platonism, and cultural critics, 181
play, 33, 35, 38, 44–46, 56, 76, 86, 88,
   94, 107, 109, 115, 118, 126, 140,
   151, 155, 156, 158, 160, 164, 166,
   177–79, 182, 187, 201–7
playfulness, 103, 158–60, 193
pleasure, 54, 60–63, 96, 108, 185, 189,
   190, 191; and arete, 60, 61; of discourse, and irrational viewpoint,
   108
Plutarch, 88, 89, 95, 99, 100, 201; and
   daimonic voice, 201; and daimonion, 89; —, as divine, 100; On the
   Sign of Socrates, 88; and Socrates'
   daimonion, 95; on Socrates'
   daimonion, 99
poetic bed, 176
poetic forms of madness, and Muses,
   128
poetic state, 38; and impersonality, 38
poetry, 23, 25–32, 34–36, 40–43, 46–
   49, 128, 142, 145, 169, 174, 175,
   177, 185, 191, 203, 204; democratized, 42; divinely inspired, 25;
   impersonality of, 31; and inspiration, 26; and intuition, 48; not
   human, 30; versus newspapers, 41;
   and transport, 34; as work of God,
   30
poets, 22, 23, 25–28, 30–32, 37, 39–
   43, 46, 48–50, 129, 142–50, 152,
   153, 155, 157–59, 165, 166, 168,
   169, 174–79, 185, 188, 189, 192,
   195, 202, 204; and divine possession, 40; and divine power, 39; and
   ecstasy, 29; and the holy, 32, 40;
   and imitative nature, 177; as
   inspired, 27; as lacking reason, 32;

poets (*continued*)
  as liars or truthtellers, 149, 168; as
    mouthpiece of the gods, 32; as
    oracles and holy prophets, 40; as
    threat to Republic, 143; saying
    wicked men are happy, 165
politics, 67–72, 74, 77, 80, 92
possession, 28, 36, 37, 40–42, 48, 49,
    88, 128, 194; of the Muses, 128
Poulet, Georges, 24
power, pursuit of, 62
prayers, 119, 127
prescriptive viewpoints, 91, 92, 181,
    183
prescriptivism, and cultural critics,
    181
pride, 86, 87, 100, 114, 159
priestesses, 52, 54; of Dodona, 121,
    122
prophecy, 40, 121–23, 126, 127, 189,
    191; and madness, origins of
    words, 123
prophetess at Delphi, 122
prophetic madness, and Apollo, 126
prophets, 30, 39, 40, 49, 129, 192, 195
Protagoras, 73, 146
Proteus, 124, 158, 170; as symbol of
    labile psyche, 124
Prytanes, 67
psyche, 35, 36, 39, 40, 45, 126, 196
"purifications and mysteries," 127
Pythian Priestess, 51

quality of life, and attention to
    environment, 120

rage, 38, 115
rational perspectives, 125
ravishing effects, and irrational
    viewpoint, 108
Reagan, Ronald, 151, 152
reason, 21, 22, 29–35, 38–40, 43, 44,
    52, 54, 55, 58, 63, 64, 70, 74, 80, 85,
    87, 94–98, 101, 105, 107–9, 116,

  121, 122, 124, 142, 147, 152–54,
    158, 159, 166, 168–71, 173, 180–83,
    185, 187, 189–91, 195, 196, 202–4;
    as handmaiden to irrational, 121;
    and impersonality, 38; and Plato,
    95; as supreme virtue, 39
rebellion, 60, 184
recognition, 56, 189
reductive poetics, and Plato, 179
relational status of humans, 194, 135,
    181, 195
religious viewpoint, 37, 45, 84, 125,
    154, 194
religious mystics, 194
Renaissance, the, 44
Republic, The, 29, 31, 32, 49, 51, 142,
    143, 145–48, 150, 154–56, 158–61,
    168, 170, 171, 173, 175, 177–79,
    183, 185, 188, 205; and banishment
    of irrationality, 188; book 2, and
    attack on poets, 147; book 10, 147;
    —, shift of tactics against poets,
    175; on harmony and rhythm,
    171, 182; and lies, 168; and mono-
    culture, 185; and Nietzsche, 169;
    and rational poetry, 177; and
    resentment, 79, 166–70; and revi-
    sion of poetry, 175
respect, 22, 32, 65, 81, 89, 100, 115,
    117, 161, 180, 182, 190, 194
revenge, 166, 168, 169; and delivery
    from, Nietzsche, 168
rhapsode, 22–30, 33, 37, 40, 42, 43;
    and desire to be envied, 22; and
    divine inspiration, 26; and divine
    possession, 42; and divinity, 27;
    and ecstasy, 29; and inspiration, 27;
    and intuitive powers, 46; and
    magnetic attraction, 27; and
    power of music and meter, 28;
    and transport, 23
rhetoric, 66, 94, 103, 104, 106, 108,
    109, 111, 114, 116, 119, 129, 131,
    137, 139; and art of enchanting the

mind, 131; and body language, 137; and discerning differences, 136; and Lysias's speech, 131; unity and plurality in nature, 133; versus dialectic, 139

rhythm, 21, 31, 41, 111, 171, 173, 174, 198, 199, 201

right-wing extremism, and Plato, 181

ritual, 53, 119, 127, 128, 153, 154, 169; containment of violence, 154

Romantics, the, 43, 178, 194

rules of good speaking, 130

sacred, the, 42, 49, 52, 70, 112, 113, 120, 127, 138, 153, 154, 178

sacrifice, 127, 147, 163, 169

Sappho, 109

Satan, 156

self-contradictory behavior, 173

self-interested assessments, 124

senator, 67, 68, 75, 77; versus gadfly, 75

Sermon on the Mount, the, as sacred site, 113

sexuality, 34, 60, 165, 173, 190

Shakespeare, William, 43–45

shape shifting, 158, 159

sharer, daimonion as, 82, 195

Shelley, Percy Bysshe, 40; and unacknowledged legislators of the world, 40

Sibyl, the, 122

Sidney, Sir Philip, on Plato and poets, 144, 145

signs, 40, 55, 81, 100, 105, 107, 146, 194

sin, 104, 168

sincerity, 69, 76, 104, 192, 193, 203

slavery, 160, 170

Socrates, 21–37, 39–41, 43, 46, 48–61, 63, 65–91, 93–34, 136–50, 152–66, 168, 170–79, 185–87, 189, 191, 193, 201, 205; accusations against, 56;

aesthetic standard, 58; affective links to the world, 46; affective relation to words, 111; and the affective world, 46; against rape, 165; and *arete,* 58; as avoiding politics, 68, 72; as banishing laughter, 161; benefits of divine madness, on, 122; as celebrator of poetic energies, 50; and charge of impiety, 80; and commitment to *arete,* 93; and daimonion, 55, 80, 193, 194, 197; and defense of poetry, 49; devotion of, to god, 52; and dialogic forms, 78; discourse of, and flow of words, 111; and disinterested inquiry, 107; and divination, 94; on divine powers, 48; as diviner, 102; and divine wandering, 196; doing god's work, 54; as exemplary model, 201; fear of, 65; as gadfly, 79, 189, 198; and the greatest good, 79; on harmony of composition, 171; and heresy, 155; and hubris, 86, 155; and ignorance, 192, 195; and insincere discourse, 114; and intuition, 195, 72; and intuitive awareness, 98; as intuitive master, 196; and intuitive promptings, 103; and the irrational, 186, 187; irrationality of, and ancient sages, 109; —, as impulsive response, 110; —, full bosom as judgment, 109; on limitations of poetic language, 32; on making the state safe, 162; as master of reason, 21, 39, 196; and moderation, 58; moral habits of, and daimonion, 91; and need for atonement, 103; and needs of the city, 197; and non-self-centered viewpoint, 104; as object of envy, 66; opposition to status quo, 85; and overdetermined behavior, 192; and piety, 22, 52; and prayers to